Proust

Gide

Mauriac

Three Studies in Modern French Literature

Studies in Modern European Literature and Thought

ERICH HELLER, *General Editor*

Marcel Proust
BY J. M. COCKING

André Gide
BY ENID STARKIE

François Mauriac
BY MARTIN JARRETT-KERR

Three Studies in Modern French Literature

New Haven: Yale University Press

PROUST: First published 1956
GIDE: First published 1954
MAURIAC: First published 1954

Three titles issued under one cover as a
Yale Paperbound September 1960

Printed by the Colonial Press Inc., Clinton, Mass., U.S.A.

Marcel Proust

EXPERIMENTS

A la recherche du temps perdu is at once the story of
how its hero Marcel came to know his vocation as a
novelist and the novel which he wrote as a result. The
novel is Proust's; the vocation is a fictional transposition of Proust's. The recent publication of *Jean Santeuil*
and *Contre Sainte-Beuve* has provided new evidence
of the reality of Proust's vocation; the chapters which
follow attempt to sketch that reality, interpret the fiction and explore some of the ways in which they are
related.

In 1896 Proust published *Les Plaisirs et les jours,* a
collection of short stories, essays and poems, with music
by Reynaldo Hahn, illustrations by Madeleine Lemaire
and a preface by Anatole France, which was dismissed
by most of Proust's friends, and is still dismissed by his
critics—apart from its interest as a document on the
development of Proust's mind and method—as the work
of a dilettante exploiting the more precious tastes of his
time. When *A la recherche* began to take its present
shape, either in Proust's mind or on paper, is not precisely known. It was assumed, until recently, that he set
to work on it seriously between 1904 and 1906, and that
between 1896 and the conception of *A la recherche* he
did little in the way of writing but translate and comment on Ruskin and fill a number of notebooks with
ideas and scraps of conversation for future use.

When André Maurois was preparing his *A la recherche de Marcel Proust,* published in 1949, he was allowed access to these notebooks by Proust's niece, Mme Mante-Proust. He found there early versions of episodes later rewritten for *A la recherche,* and passages apparently intended for a novel written in the third person of which Swann was the hero. Some of these passages concerned events later to be narrated, still in the third person, in *Un amour de Swann*; others were to be transferred from Swann to Marcel and take their place in the self-narrative of *A l'ombre des jeunes filles en fleurs.*

After Maurois had published his book, a research student, Bernard de Fallois, consulted him and was introduced by him to Mme Mante-Proust, who put at his disposal not only those remaining exercise-books which Maurois had not stayed to decipher but some boxes of papers hitherto unexplored since Proust's death. There were found a great quantity of loose sheets of paper, in some cases torn. Fallois put them together to make a kind of novel, and named it *Jean Santeuil* after the principal character, who is obviously the precursor of the Marcel of *A la recherche*—gifted, sensitive and obsessed with the past like him, but unsuccessful, like Swann. Towards the end of 1951 some short passages of this work were published in periodicals, and the whole was issued in three large volumes in 1952. Two years later Fallois presented a further group of hitherto unpublished manuscripts under the title *Contre Sainte-Beuve.* Some of these passages are directly concerned with Sainte-Beuve's critical method; others, though indirectly connected, lead away from Sainte-Beuve to Proust's own affective life, or to the lives of fictional creations like the Guermantes.

The exact dates when Proust began and abandoned

4

these works—the early 'novel' and the study of Sainte-Beuve—are still unknown. But *Jean Santeuil* no doubt bridges the gap between *Les Plaisirs* and the Ruskin translations, and *Contre Sainte-Beuve* appears to have been written in 1908 and 1909, at a time when Proust had already started on his second attempt at a long novel and was uncertain whether his energies were to find expression in a novel or something else. *Les Plaisirs* and *Jean Santeuil* are both feeble compared with *A la recherche*. *Contre Sainte-Beuve* is still the work of an explorer rather than a discoverer. But all these works mutually reflect light which can be caught and concentrated back on to the last. The Proust who wrote the first two was a fundamentally unhappy and frustrated man, and his unhappiness was in some ways very like Baudelaire's, in which Proust himself sensed a close affinity with his own. We may put this down to inherited temperament, as both Baudelaire and Proust were inclined to do, or we may believe with the Existentialists that they chose their suffering. Or we may think that the reality was too complicated to suffer any explanation as simple as either, and complex enough to include something of both. The fact remains that Baudelaire spoke of a 'feeling of loneliness from childhood, the feeling of an eternally lonely destiny', and that Proust, too, felt cut off both by his exaltations and his abasements from the people among whom he lived. Both found their satisfactions and sympathies in works of art; both felt, when they had created their own, that they were showing the reader, who was blind but willing, truths, some of them unwelcome, which it would profit his soul to see. All this partly because the two men were naturally alike, but partly also because Proust, having felt the likeness, was anxious to do, in his own way, as well as Baudelaire had done.

5

Proust felt not only something of Baudelaire's loneliness, but his sexual obsession and sexual guilt; aggravated, in his case, by the guilt of perversion—though he appears to have convinced himself that Baudelaire, too, was a homosexual. But if Baudelaire could shift some of the responsibility for his moral weakness on to his mother as well as his inherited temperament, Proust never used his mother as a scapegoat. He added another guilt, the suffering his moral spinelessness inflicted on the people who cared for him most; and a terrible fear of what the knowledge of his secret life might add to it.

Like Baudelaire, too, Proust knew moments of escape from responsibility and remorse into a sense of freedom and perfect happiness, felt sometimes in connection with books or music, but also—a most un-Baudelairean sentiment which Proust later found it hard to reconcile with his own philosophy of art—before natural beauty. From the joy of these experiences grew his conviction that he was himself a natural artist.

But he could not easily find a way to actualize in words his sense of artistic 'vision', even to particularize the sense into something specific for his own mind to grasp, something other than a vague if positive elation. His duty seemed to lie in the direction of self-exploration and critical scrutiny of the work of other writers; the discovery of what he had in himself to express, the pursuit in accomplished works of clues as to what to look for and what means might be used to express it. But—as far as his 'vision' was concerned—frustration; and, added to frustration, another guilt—snobbery; and another temptation—that of an all-too-easy social success which, he felt, wasted the time he should have spent in self-scrutiny and atrophied the sensitive inner self at which the scrutiny was directed.

Nor were the consequent strains constantly set in the

same pattern, the pulls in the same direction. Proust seems to have been torn between lucidity about his own predicament and the desire to rationalize away the unbearable sense of guilt, torn also between guilt and resentment that fear of remorse should set itself between him and his own kind of sensual paradise: guilt and remorse when he gave way to temptation, resentment and regret when he resisted the temptation of opportunity, frustration when he had no opportunity save in imagination. The perversion itself he ascribed to inherited physiological causes; but he seems to have realized that his illness was, to some extent, a withdrawal from responsibility. He saw how far his weaknesses were the condition of his sensibility, and also how they endangered the will to put his gifts to creative purpose. Yet perhaps some compromise was possible. Perhaps the drama of moral guilt could itself be made into literature. Proust, who always looked high for his models, may have once thought of himself seriously, as he later did half ironically, as another Phèdre; at the age of twenty he wrote the name of Phèdre as his favourite heroine, but, on second thoughts, characteristically substituted Bérénice. Social ambition, too, though it seemed to him to be the enemy of his *real* vocation—the expression of his vision—might yield a harvest; perhaps the observation of people and manners, however far removed from those subjective states which seemed to be the essence of the kind of supernatural experience with which the greatest art should be concerned, could be turned to good, if perhaps comparatively humble, literary account.

But Proust's urge to confess, and to make literary capital out of confession, was held in check by a need for discretion as much personal as aesthetic. There were things Proust wanted to explain, aspects of his intimate struggle which even those closest to him had not been able to understand, of which the understanding must mean from the outside world less condemnation and regret, a more unreserved concession of sympathy. But there were also things which these same people must never suspect.

In *Les Plaisirs et les jours*, confession is transposed into the third person and recounted of fictional characters, the most important of them women; it is limited, and eked out with the experiments of a writer who still has his originality to discover, whose determination to write often forces him to inflate slight conceptions, whose pursuit of originality often gives rise to strained preciosity or flippant ebullience. Yet to the retrospective eye, beneath the camouflage and the superficial cultivation of contemporary literary fashions, Proust's obsessions appear—in *La Mort de Baldassare Silvande, Violante ou la mondanité, La Confession d'une jeune fille, La Fin de la jalousie*: death, and the need to come to terms with it; to learn not to fear it, but also not to desire it as a release from destiny unfulfilled, from the task of discovering in himself the god disguised as a fool which Emerson, in a passage quoted by Proust as an epigraph, had called the soul; sexual temptation and remorse, and the decline, with habit, of both remorse and pleasure; illness and its effect on the mind, turning it in upon its own most intimate life from which health, activity and the pursuit of social pleasures may turn it away; the corrosive effect of these social pleasures on the soul itself, which ought rather to be cultivated in music, meditation, solitude, charity and natural beauty; the crowding in, at moments of discouragement and self-disgust, of poignantly contrasting memories of childhood and maternal cherishing; the contrast between the innocence of the mother-centered childhood Eden

8

and the world in which the serpent (here, in *Violante* and *La Confession,* the part is played, for the heroines into whom Proust has transposed himself, by a young cousin) has hissed its promise of sensual pleasures, never again to be done without but always treacherous, unsatisfying and corrupt; the strength and suddenness of impulse, the weakness of will; the constant procrastination of the effort towards the salvation of settled and calm work; the flight from solitary temptation into the distractions of society and the consequent redoubling of the difficulty of choosing solitary contemplation and the life of the soul; and, over all, the complex of hypocrisies which is felt to be not a part of the true self, with which the true and, somehow, always inviolable self is overlaid.

The stories of *Les Plaisirs,* in so many respects cautionary tales, and tributes to a wisdom their author accepted but could not act on, show also a keen awareness of and interest in the ecstasies of the flesh. Anatole France's reference, in his preface, to a depraved Bernardin de Saint-Pierre and an ingenuous Petronius is to the point, though it could be applied more pointedly to certain passages of *A la recherche*—for in that novel Proust has managed more than once to recount events proper to Petronius with an amorality which is not unlike Bernardin de Saint-Pierre's assumption that the passion he is narrating is natural, innocent, and likely to delight the reader's heart. The encounter between Charlus and Jupien, at the beginning of *Sodome et Gomorrhe,* is grotesque; but into this grotesque passion which leaps up in two middle-aged men Proust has transposed some of the poetry which, for Musset, attended *le lit joyeux de deux jeunes époux.* The Petronius in Proust became steadily less ingenuous. When, like Baudelaire, he had shed moral responsibility and

9

guilt in his writing, the result was often, from a literary point of view, happy; the appearance of an all-pervading humour is one sign of the change of attitude. But complacent nastiness was liberated as well as poetry, indecent slapstick as well as comedy. And, when Proust was creating a world in which the hypocrisy which weighed on him was made universal, he universalized also the assumption that every adolescent and adult, when social constraint can be sloughed off, naturally slips away to gratify his appetite for furtive and mostly artificial sexual pleasure.

Les Plaisirs tells us not only something of what Proust needed to write out of his system but something of his exploration of means. Later he was to discard the kind of confession he is using here, the narrative of temptation, sin and remorse which is his own moral drama transposed into the third person but otherwise close to life. Already he is concerned with other aspects of self-expression: with style, for instance, in its traditional sense—the manner of handling words considered as independent of matter, those constants of a literary mind which appear as characteristics whatever the business on which it is engaged. Like Robert Louis Stevenson, another writer with a burden of experience to be thrown off and an experience of delight to be expressed, but a sporadic and too easily derivative imagination, Proust was learning to 'play the sedulous ape', scrutinizing and feeling his way into other literary skins with a success to which the excellence of his pastiche bears witness.

Proust is also concerned with that crude form of catharsis arrived at through cynicism and a withering contempt for the figures to be met with in the social life which inspired such mixed feelings in him. What we miss, in *Un dîner en ville*, is the humour of *A la recherche* and the willingness to concede that the snobbish and ambitious figures at this dinner-party exhibit anything but the contemptible features of human life. The style is neat but too intentionally corrosive. Yet the effectiveness of this contempt and the neatness of its expression depend on that faculty for separating out the strands of a mood or a state of mind which, developed and matured, produces, in the reader of *A la recherche,* the conviction that Proust's account of mental flux is (within the limits of the kind of mental flux with which it deals) both analytically precise and comprehensive, lucid without sacrifice of shades.

Serious and typical as are the preoccupations which underlie the writing of *Les Plaisirs et les jours,* to move from these finished but fragmentary exercises to the shapeless mass of *Jean Santeuil* is to enter the workshop where the real labour is going ahead. This book is a collection of personal impressions and experiences, of ideas about literature, love and social ambition, of vignettes, caricatures and social situations; all unrelated except that they are felt, thought, observed by Jean Santeuil. This 'novel' has no design, no shape and no climax. To account for its inconclusiveness, perhaps, as well as to satisfy the instinct to put distance between confession and himself, Proust attributes the writing of it to the novelist C. C. dies without leaving a manuscript, but his work is published by the narrator of the prologue and his friend who, when they had met C. on holiday in Brittany, had been given a copy of the work as it then stood.

But C. and Jean Santeuil are as intimately related as the Swann and Marcel of the later book. Jean, it is pointed out has some of C.'s faults, more good qualities, like sensibility and kindness, and much poorer health. But at this stage it is Jean Santeuil who has suffered most and shown much talent for no particular art, while C. is the successful novelist; later Swann is to be the failure and Marcel is to be gloriously successful.

C. writes in Brittany, and the people he meets there come into his books. But the things and people he writes about (we are told in the prologue) are only the pretexts for the working of his visionary power. The most trivial events can awaken his imagination and liberate his sense of poetry, can become 'these moments of deep illumination when the spirit penetrates to the heart of all things and lights them as the sun can light the depths of the sea'. This idea of artistic vision piercing to the infinite soul of things reminds us of Emerson and Beaudelaire; and, just as Baudelaire considered in parallel the ecstasies of imaginative vision and drugs, Proust writes that C.'s joy is one which other men 'seek in poisons only to expiate in suffering'.

C., in fact, has in his make-up more of the typical poet than of the typical novelist. He has, he says, no power of invention; the people he writes about and the situations they find themselves in are those he has come across in his own life. But the narrator, musing on this, is sceptical of its absolute truth. Did C. *really* know all the characters he wrote about? How far did he change the reality of his life to make his books? What are 'the secret relations, the necessary metamorphoses which exist between the writer and his work, reality and art, or rather . . . between the appearances of life and the reality itself which permanently underlies life and which art reveals'? Proust is writing here as a would-be Symbolist who has not yet discovered the Way.

And, in the novel itself, Jean Santeuil is presented as a 'subjective idealist'; but he has not yet thoroughly learned the symbolist lesson that, as an apprehension of the 'real', art is more direct and 'truer' than philosophy. Marcel's heroes and spiritual guides are to be the artists Bergotte, Elstir, Vinteuil; Jean Santeuil's hero is his philosophy master, M. Beulier—as Proust's, at the age of twenty, was M. Darlu, who had taught him philosophy at the Lycée Condorcet. Traves, the novelist Jean meets in the story, is a visionary like C. himself; but he does not know it. His overt philosophy is materialistic; M. Beulier could have taught him, as he had taught Jean, that science leads to blind scepticism, that the self is absolute, that God exists. For God, whose absence in *A la recherche* Mauriac has deplored, is named in Jean Santeuil as the sanction of the beauty which is also truth; it was later that Proust exercised his intelligence to the utmost to do without the sanction while keeping the value of the experience.

Here God, as, later, beauty, is revealed only in subjective vision; the outside world (so the theory implies) has no interest except as providing occasions for this. Proust is exhibiting the kind of spiritual onanism which Hegel thundered against, and which so many self-styled Hegelians among the Symbolists, who did not grasp the difference between Hegel and Fichte, exhibited; and he takes it upon himself to correct Stendhal's view of love, to transpose it into his own terms. For, according to Proust, Stendhal is an artist in spite of his philosophy, which like Traves's, is 'materialistic'. Stendhal attaches value to relations between the self and the outside world, and, consequently, to the outside world; this, according to Proust, is a mistake. Of the two brands of romantic Idealism, that which is paralleled by the objective Idealism of Hegel and that which is paralleled by the subjective Idealism of Fichte; of the two kinds of romantic eroticism, that which seeks to express itself in fertility and action, and that which seeks a narcissistic self-possession—Stendhal stands for the first and Proust for the second. Here is the very root of Proust's conception of love, which is to play so great a part in *A la recherche*; and some will judge it to be a piece of sophistry based on a pathologically limited experience. For Stendhal, writes Proust, 'what gives us a love of solitude and a thousand thoughts, what makes nature comprehensible and eloquent . . . is love. We cannot go so far. Love is indeed like poetry in that it frees us from other people, plunges us into solitude and makes us feel the charm of nature. But it is a queer phase of life, this constraint of poetry which debars an individual from every individual concern, this unity of nature reduced to a dual individuality. An individual, however remarkable—and in love the other individual is usually anything but remarkable—has no right to limit our inner life in this way.' There is no relation, Proust affirms, between this 'other' and our own inner life. For Proust the Platonic hermaphrodite has become a Narcissus who projects his own image on to a stranger. The sophistry is the more persuasive in that it contains an observable truth; no doubt the romantic lover projects, but not on to a blank screen. And what he projects is itself not necessarily as narcissistically self-contained as Proust would have us think. Imagination can collaborate with, as well as merely 'use', instinct, at the point of integrity which Proust and his like deny. It is a pity that Proust, with his penetration, and his own kind of integrity, which is intellectual rather than moral, had not a greater range of experience to account for.

If his theory of love, in *Jean Santeuil*, is settling into a form which could shape a number of separate love stories, Proust is obviously having difficulty in applying his transcendental aesthetic to his own case, in putting the theory into practice. C., we are given to assume, does not write about his experiences of divine illumination but about the experiences which are the occasions of the illumination; and the visionary quality is conveyed by the manner of his recounting. But Proust, strong in his philosophical conviction, has an essentially didactic side to him; he longs to get straight to the point, to demonstrate the transcendence, to talk about the visionary moments as such, to explain how they are linked to the rest of his experience—for instance, as we have just seen, to love. And, when he concentrates on the centre of it all, the visionary moments themselves, there is nothing much to talk about. He can only state, in 'elevated' style, that such moments are known to the artist; they seem to be like the similar moments referred to, but not in essence recaptured, in *A la recherche*—the obscure message of the Martinville spires, for instance, and the Balbec trees. Instead of writing poems, like Baudelaire, or novels, like Traves, which *are* the transcendent experiences, Proust can only talk *about* them, and about a life spent in the attempt to discover how to write a novel like Traves's—like Stendhal's—but, perhaps, more purely expressive of the beauty which is also truth. But the sense of beauty, of rising out of the mortal state, does not seem to have arisen often, for Proust, out of the spectacle of human life; rather out of a pattern like the steeples, a glimpse of nature like the trees, and, principally and most vividly, out of the peculiarly abrupt and clear memories to which sensations could stimulate his mind.

The cult of memory, and the connection between memory and the experience of transcendence, of plenitude and freedom, are already firmly established in *Jean Santeuil*. The pleasure of remembering is connected with the pleasure of reading, and carries with it the idea of vocation, of an impulse and even a duty to write.

Comparison of the two novels leaves no doubt that Proust's mind was persistently occupied with the problem of explaining a felt correspondence between reading books and remembering his own past, and explaining what, for him, was the peculiar and unlifelike pleasure of both.

There were hints to be found in the literature of the nineteenth century in which he was steeped—the literature which Jean reveres as the revelation of 'mysterious truth' and puts far above the previous century beloved of Traves, who, in this respect also, is like Stendhal. Proust himself mentions, in *Le Temps retrouvé*, instances of affective memory released by sensation in Chateaubriand, Nerval and Baudelaire. Professors Jean Pommier and Justin O'Brien have considerably lengthened the list. M. Pommier quotes a striking example from Musset's *Confession* of a memory felt as submerged but struggling to rise like a cork held below the water, where the image and the dramatic presentation are very close to Proust's images and style in the narrative of the *madeleine* incident. But the most interesting name on Proust's list is Baudelaire's.

For Baudelaire had said both that genius was the power to recover childhood and that literature was the gateway to heaven. He had exalted memory and writing as means of returning to a lost paradise; and for Proust, as he wrote in *Le Temps retrouvé*, our true paradises are always those we have lost. So when Marcel, after his 'revelation', looks to the romantic literature he knows so well for confirmation of the value of his new 'knowledge', it is to Baudelaire he turns. But he is interrupted —conveniently for him, exasperatingly for the reader— in his meditation. It will be suggested later that Proust never found a satisfactory theory to explain how his own 'vision-through-memory' could be equated with the supernaturalism of the Romantics. But he did find a way of conveying the feelings to which it gave rise and the sense of certain correspondences which eluded intellectual analysis. What *Jean Santeuil* lacks, and *A la recherche* has, is the construction of experience into a philosophical drama, which involuntary memory as the *deus ex machina*. Everything which Proust says about memory in *A la recherche* is explicit or implicit in *Jean Santeuil*; but not surrounded with the mystery of sleep and the unconscious, preceded by presentiments, struggling free of enchantments, suddenly appearing with a preternatural vividness of sensation to raise a past self from the dead. The old grandfather, M. Sandré, lives in a past which, for him, is the true present; and his mind moves to events in the past in a flash. 'The genius of memory which, faster than electricity, goes round the world, and as quickly goes round the world of time, had set him down before he could even tell if a second had passed.' Who does not recognize, in this banality, the thought which, surrounded with the mystery of sleep and coming after a carefully dramatic preparation, was to give the rich suggestiveness of 'A sleeping man has round him in a circle the succession of hours, the order of years and worlds'? M. Sandré triumphs over time through memory, but his triumph looks pale in the light of common day.

The theme of aesthetic decline, for which memory is the only compensation, is clearly stated. But again it is not dramatized, no conclusions are drawn, and much of the novel is quite without relation to it. The beauty of lilacs comes to be felt by *Jean Santeuil* as the beauty of his own childhood; and, in the long section of the novel which describes Jean's summer holidays at Etreuilles Proust is evidently searching his memory for the impressions which lie at the root of his own

17

aesthetic preferences. Apple blossom is more satisfying than the finest flowers in the world because its colours and shapes and textures have in them the feeling of the past in which they were first known. But most of all Jean is moved by pink hawthorn, the essence of spring and centre of many memories, ranging from the decorated altar of the church to the appetite for cream cheese with strawberries crushed in it. The sheer animal pleasure of food and bed, post-prandial torpor and hot water bottles is much more in evidence in *Jean Santeuil* than in *A la recherche*. In the latter, the number of images which take their effect from the simpler sensualities is striking; but their pleasure is carefully worked into contexts more sublime. *Jean Santeuil* shows sensation in the raw state, a crudely functioning imagination and the aspiration to transcendence through literature. The three have still to fuse.

In the last three chapters of the sixth part of *Jean Santeuil* Proust tries to come to grips with the peculiar experience of happiness which memory brings him, and in the last of the three the distinction between memory in the ordinary sense and memory stimulated by renewed sensation at last becomes clear. At Begmeil, in Brittany, Proust writes, Jean felt pleasure at the sight of the sea, but no real sense of its beauty. 'The mind seeks in vain, the eye looks in vain; it seems it is not by them that aesthetic enjoyment can be felt. Can it be felt even by memory? No. Next year Jean tried to remember these drives and describe them, but felt no pleasure.' But if, long afterwards, he goes to stay in Switzerland and drives by the lake of Geneva at a moment when it has a look of the sea, the magic of that past and apparently wasted time is felt at last. 'Between the lake and himself, what is there that was not between the sea and himself, which would not be between the lake and himself if he had not seen the sea in the first place?' Imagination, perhaps, which Proust thinks of as an 'invisible substance' only to be applied to a past recovered; and we are off on a rambling speculation which covers some of the ground of *Le Temps retrouvé* but is a good deal more naïve and more consistently centred on the century's clichés about imagination, conceived as the organ which serves the external and gives us glimpses of our spiritual home. The final exhortation, full as it is of the real pathos of Proust's inner life, is comic literature: 'So let us love, let us know all the times of our life, let us be sad in bedrooms, let us not even be too downcast that we have lived in elegant carriages and in drawing-rooms. We do not know on which of the days when we look for beauty in a mountain or a sky we shall find it in the sound of a rubber wheel or the smell of a material . . .' As a view of human happiness this Micawberism of the emotions is limited indeed; Proust was to learn to make better dramatic use of involuntary memory, and to build round his private and eccentric gospel a work of more universal acceptance.

What he had to discover was not so much the metaphysical explanation of his joy in memory as his own power to create. *Jean Santeuil* is preceded by an epigraph. It occurs to the reader that Proust may have intended this as C.'s epigraph for his book, but as now printed it refers to Proust's. 'Can I call this book a novel? It is less perhaps and much more, the very essence of my life collected with no admixture, in those times of agony when it is distilled. This book was never made, it was garnered.' Having been garnered, it had still to be made.

But if Proust, like C., felt he had little power of invention, the narrator's scepticism about the exact relation of C.'s life to his narrative warns us that, already in *Jean Santeuil*, we must expect reality to be adapted. No doubt Proust, like C., wrote 'nothing but what he had personally felt'; no doubt also he wrote about those feelings both as they arose in life and as they in turn gave rise to those crude imaginative constructions which are wishful fantasies.

There is a good deal of wishful fantasy in *Jean Santeuil*. The story of Jean's friendship with Henri de Réveillon bears the stamp of daydream elaborated on a real foundation. Henri de Réveillon is obviously the prototype of Robert de Saint-Loup; Robert is generally considered to have been modelled, at least in his virtues, on Bertrand de Fénelon and his friends, the Duc d'Albuféra and the Duc de Guiche. Henri de Réveillon is, in one chapter of *Jean Santeuil*, referred to as *Bertrand de Réveillon*. But, though the chronology of Proust's life has been uncertainly established by his biographers, it seems unlikely that Proust knew Fénelon at the age when Jean knew Henri. On the other hand Proust did, at that age, stay with friends in the country—at Chantilly, for instance, and at L'Isle-Adam with one Joyant. It seems probable that his imagination was already working up reality into something more satisfying; that, here, it was projecting his aristocratic acquaintances back into less aristocratic acquaintances and building up a situation which he would have liked to find himself in. Henri is the only son of the first Duke of France, and a schoolfriend of Jean's. In temperament he is the opposite of Jean, both active and disciplined, frank and straightforward. He has never known the meaning of snobbery and scorn, writes Proust with significant envy and admiration, never felt the need to hide snobbery or the wish to express scorn. Jean's schoolmaster, a Republican—not, of course, the beloved M. Beulier

—persuades Jean's parents that his friendship with Henri is a bad moral influence; which is the opposite of the truth. There is a violent family quarrel, after which Jean manages to repress his feelings of violent hatred for his parents, reminds himself that his mother will not always be with him, and makes it up in a flood of sentimental righteousness. This may well be a true account of one of the family explosions in which Proust was sometimes involved by his pursuit of acquaintances and a way of life outside his class. The friendship with Henri, however, continues; the Duke and Duchess are delighted with Jean; he becomes a second son and stays with them for long periods in the country. The account of these visits to Réveillon in some ways parallels the earlier account of summer holidays spent at Etreuilles; but the 'poetry' it expresses is that of utter privacy, complete liberty and unlimited creature comfort. There are no cousins to hide from, no *real* parents to moralize and harry; none of the drawbacks of family life but all its cosy security. It is, in fact, very much what the naïve young mind assumes the lives of the rich and powerful to be. The ideal parents of this dream-world are the first Duke and his lady, the ideal brother is both complement and friend. There is also a buxom servant who creeps to Jean's bedroom at night. Between them, the Réveillons shepherd Jean through the perils of high society, bolstering his self-assurance and avenging the snubs he suffers.

The account of Jean's entry into society gives some insight, though it must remain conjectural, into the timidities, wounds and frustrations which underlay the easy superficial success of which Proust's biographers make so much. The chronology of his conquest of society remains a little hazy. His biographers divide his life into successive periods without breaking these down into successive details, and indeed in a life consisting chiefly of an alternation of social engagements and secluded privacy it is difficult to do otherwise. From the salon of Mme Straus, mother of his schoolfriend Jacques Bizet, widow of the composer of *L'Arlésienne* and daughter of Halévy who composed *La Juive*, Proust moved on to the salons of Mme Aubernon, Mme Gaston de Caillavet, Mme Loynes, and perhaps to those, more socially distinguished, of the Comtesse Greffulhe and the Baronne Aimery de Pierrebourg. He met the Comtess d'Haussonville, the Princesse de Wagram, the Princesse Mathilde. In 1893 began his curious relationship with the Comte Robert de Montesquiou-Fezensac, compounded of genuine regard and sycophancy which could suddenly turn to respectful firmness when Montesquiou shared the anti-Semitism of most of his kind at the time of the Dreyfus affair.

In friendships with people of his own generation he added, to his middle-class schoolfriends of the Lycée Condorcet, the Duc de Guiche, Antoine and Emmanuel Bibesco, the Duc d'Albuféra and the Comte de Salignac-Fénelon. But if, as Derrick Leon wrote, 'by the time Proust was twenty-five, he had penetrated into almost every stratum of the social sphere', he was still, in two senses, an outsider. He was a learner longing to be assimilated, and he was an observer fascinated by observation for its own sake. *Jean Santeuil* suggests that Proust never forgave the Faubourg Saint-Germain for the slights and humiliations attending a social progress which itself troubled his conscience, and never forgave even the friendliest of his most aristocratic acquaintances for the distance by which they fell short of the Duke and Duchess of his first dream. For the closest friends of his own age he seems to have had a genuine feeling of warmth, and the feeling glows in his portrait of

22

Robert de Saint-Loup. But Proust could no more be assimilated into their world of values and habits than he could be assimilated into that of his own family; of the two environments, both incompatible with himself, he fell back on the more familiar. In so far as he concerned himself at all with moral judgments, he came to put the virtues of his own family, 'les vertus de Combray', above the virtues of the Faubourg, and retreated to the conviction that he carried, within himself, values superior to both.

But until he reached this position, and broke with both worlds after the death of his parents, Proust was no doubt divided, in his curiosity about genealogy, protocol and convention, between the detachment of the zoologist and the desire to perform faithfully the carefully regulated movements he was observing. He questioned the old Comtesse de Beaulaincourt about the manners and customs of the past, and Prince Antoine Bibesco about precedence, relationships and titles. He gently reproached his mother for addressing a letter to 'Fénélon' with a superfluous acute accent and spelling Bibesco's name with a 'k'.

In his social ambition he had, like Balzac's climbers, a model; his was Charles Haas. Haas, the Jewish stockbroker's son, appeared to be thoroughly at home in high society; he was a member of the Jockey Club and a friend of the Prince of Wales. When Proust found that he could not achieve the satisfaction which he imagined success had brought to Haas, but saw how to achieve his own in another way, he made Swann out of what he knew of Haas, what he remembered of his former self, and perhaps the culture and learning of Charles Ephrussi, founder of the *Gazette des beaux arts*, and something of the character and mannerisms of his own Jewish uncle, Louis Weil. Swann is a social success and an artistic failure; Marcel renounces social success, becomes a creative artist, and cruelly satirizes the denizens of the social zoo.

If, in *Jean Santeuil*, the dream of the happiness to which social success was to open the door is still intact, however crudely expressed by Jean's relations with the Réveillons, the bitter satire occasioned by the impact of hard reality has already begun. Though Jean enjoys the full sunshine of the Réveillons's affection and esteem, when he begins to make his way in the Paris salons he is blinked at by lesser lights and snubbed. Being more sensitive than vain, writes Proust, he feels hurt rather than resentful; yet somehow Providence, in the persons of the Duke and Duchess, manages to avenge his hurt and inflict more than compensating wounds on the unfortunate women who have offended him. The chapters in which this pattern is worked out can scarcely have been intended as consecutive; it looks rather as though Proust, finding a special attraction in the theme, had worked over it several times to try out the effect. As the passages are now printed, the effect is one of obsession with the sweetness of revenge, disguised as providential justice. To measure Proust's progress as an artist, we have only to compare these narratives to the scene in *La Prisonnière* where Charles, humiliated and shattered by the outburst of revolt which Mme Verdurin has inspired Morel to utter, is protected and reinstated by the sympathy and regard of the Queen of Naples, who gives him her arm and bears him proudly off with words of contempt for the *canaille* among which they find themselves. The emotions are the same; but now Proust has invented a situation in which the reader is prepared to share them.

In *Jean Santeuil*, invention on the narrative level scarcely rises above wishful fantasy. But the subjective preoccupation in no way inhibits Proust's strikingly shrewd observation of manners; and he is already taking another kind of revenge in caricature. The Réveillons are idealized figures and exempt from satirical comment, but every formula and gesture through which the Duke expresses one or other shade of aloof politeness is catalogued like the habits of an animal in a natural history. Mme Marmet, the third-rate, snobbish, ambitious and vulgar hostess who more than once hurts Jean's feelings and is as often confounded, is cruelly and contemptuously portrayed and treated. So is M. Guéraud-Houppin, an uncle by marriage who pretends, at a reception, not to have heard of his nephew until Jean's arrival, in the company of the Duchess, plunges him in an agony of embarrassment. More gratuitously cruel is the portrait of Henri de Réveillon's aunt, an inoffensive old maid whose only crimes are literary snobbery combined with utter ignorance and her pride in a vague acquaintance with Sully-Prudhomme. These sketches are amusing as well as cruel, and the savagery would be less perturbing if it were not camouflaged behind the 'beautiful, thoughtful eyes' and the sensitive, well-meaning nature of Jean Santeuil himself.

Personal impressions, impressions of reading, the tendency to live in the past, the experience of revelation through memory, the invention of social situations, observation of manners, caricature, the psychology of sexual passion and snobbery—all these are to be found already in *Jean Santeuil*. In spite of the epigraph and C.'s remark that he has no powers of invention, some degree of invention there undoubtedly is. But the elements of the book are not correlated. The last chapters speak of the ageing of Jean's parents and play on the theme of time and flux, and there the book simply peters out.

Proust is casting about for his own material and manner, and testing his own powers against a number of models. His literary ambitions seem to have canalized themselves into three tendencies, and as he explores each there are echoes from his models amounting to pastiche. The first and most central of these three tendencies is the 'mystical', drawing its nourishment from the idealism of romantic literature from Rousseau to the Symbolists, and philosophy from Kant to Bergson. The second is the ambition, centred on Balzac and Saint-Simon, to write the sociological history of a period in terms of personalities and, closely related to this, the ambition of a pure psychological analyst, a student of the general characters of human behaviour, centred on La Bruyère and the great moralists, and stimulated by the positivism of Proust's own century and the prestige of science. *Contre Sainte-Beuve* confirms our sense of Proust's uncertainty about the line he should follow, and some of the notes quoted in Fallois's preface show that Proust was at once genuinely at a loss and inclined to blame himself for irresolution. The decline of spontaneous lyrical feeling in himself led him to think he must give up the Romantic vision in favour of observation and analysis: to a landscape which no longer moved him, he wrote: 'You have nothing more to say to me; it is people who interest me now'. Yet when he read Sainte-Beuve, the transcendental idealism in himself was fanned to a flame of revolt against Sainte-Beuve's systematic confusion between the artist and the man, and went on burning on its own with a fresh creative light. Proust was, at this stage, swinging between feeling and analysis. The problem set by his manifold gifts and interests was that of finding an artistic unity for the material they provided, of bringing feeling and analysis together in a single conception.

26

2

REFERENCE-POINTS

Over a quarter of a century ago Ernst-Robert Curtius wrote that Proust's style is an intricate combination of intellectualism and impressionism, of rigorous logical analysis and the recording of the finest shades of sensation and feeling; these two modes of experience, he suggested, were inseparable in Proust's mind.

Many critics since then have puzzled and fought with each other over the way in which these two modes are related, and Bergson's name has figured largely in the discussion. There is no doubt that to compare Proust with Bergson is to arrive at a better understanding of both, but too much attention to the comparison has sometimes obscured Proust and his novel behind a fog of philosophical polemic. At one extreme Fiser assumes that Bergson said the last word about art and that Proust is the supreme example of a Bergsonian artist; at the other, Benda sees Bergson's philosophy as pernicious and proclaims that Proust is a great novelist because his work shows the traditional virtues of the novel, observation and the capacity to analyse the structure and motivation of the behaviour narrated. Such extreme views often imply a distressingly oversimplified idea of what Bergson said art ought to be and of what art, in fact, is; of what Proust said about his novel and of what the novel, in fact, turned out to be.

The mind which sees Bergson as *a* revelation but not *the* Revelation, which sees Proust as *an* artist but not *the* Artist, will approach their relationship differently from critics like Fiser; will see them as two major intellectual phenomena obviously related, yet as obviously distinct. Related first by their historical situation; and, in this respect, not only to each other but to a host of others. To Ruskin, first; we have studies of Proust's affinity with Bergson, of Proust's with Ruskin, of Bergson's with Ruskin. Still to be studied in detail is Proust's affinity with Emerson, quotations from whom appear as epigraphs to parts of Proust's first book, *Les Plaisirs et les jours*. There is the transcendental idealism which unites Emerson to Carlyle and Ruskin, and all three to the French Symbolists, and all these to Proust. But turn the leaves of Emerson's essays and you will come across many correspondences with Proust more particular than the conception of life as symbolizing a dimension outside life; for instance this:

> When the act of reflection takes place in the mind, when we look at ourselves in the light of thought, we discover that our life is embosomed in beauty. Behind us, as we go, all things assume pleasing forms, as clouds do far off. Not only things familiar and stale, but even the tragic and terrible are comely, as they take their place in the pictures of memory . . . In these hours the mind seems so great, that nothing can be taken from us that seems much. All loss, all pain is particular: the universe remains to the heart unhurt . . . For it is only the finite that has wrought and suffered; the infinite lies stretched in smiling repose.

With the word 'involuntary' added to memory, with the 'act of reflection' suitably defined, and with some

28

adjustment of the style, this passage could take its place in any one of the dozen contexts in *A la recherche du temps perdu*. Yet one remains convinced that when Proust read passages like this in Emerson, he was reading of states of mind which were already familiar or, at most, feeling his familiar states pulled into a particular focus and invested with a particular significance. This does not mean that Proust, when he came to fix his own focus and suggest his own significance, would not return, by way of reference, to Emerson's. Influences of this kind play their part in the formation of a sensibility, if only by reinforcing tendencies already present or bringing out the latent. But they are diffuse and overlapped with others, and if Proust's sensibility was to some extent modified by prose like Emerson's, the ideas which Emerson's prose implied had to run the gauntlet of Proust's intelligent scrutiny and be modified in turn, as far as was necessary for them to fit Proust's philosophical and artistic scheme.

What overlap is there in Bergson and Emerson? To state what common ground they might appear to Proust to occupy is to recognize how, in the manner of such affinities, intellectual rigour gives way to feeling, and metaphysical propositions to the *sensibility* of transcendence. Proust, metaphysically baulked, eventually made his clearest statement of his central proposition in an inconclusive form: 'One's real life is elsewhere, not in life so-called, nor yet in what we think of as the after-life, but in some dimension *outside* life, if a word that draws its meaning from the conceptions imposed on us by space can be said to have any meaning in a world freed from spatial disciplines . . .' This is intellectually vague enough to accord with both Bergson and Emerson; yet in their interpretations of the 'otherness' of the 'real' life, the life of the spirit, Bergson and

Emerson diverge. For both, 'real' life is life when it is properly known; and the proper knowledge of life primarily depends not upon reason but upon a faculty whose operations the untimely intrusion of reason is likely to hinder. But Bergson's 'otherness' is immanent and Emerson's is transcendent; and if, on that issue, Proust never made up his mind, he took refuge in thinking and valuing as if the ideas for which he felt devotion were, in some way, transcendent.

Baudelaire, when he found his mind could encompass no system adequate to the complexity of his experience and the strength of his intuitive conviction and values, took refuge, as he wrote himself two years before the publication of *Les Fleurs du mal,* in 'l'impeccable naïveté'; in the untutored vision of the artist, in the poetic expression of his intuitive values as their only pure expression and, consequently, for him, the only final truth. Proust was less willing than Baudelaire to take refuge in 'l'impeccable naïveté'. He might have been content to do so if his own naïve genius could have produced Baudelaire's results; but like other successors of Baudelaire he found that the sympathy of his feeling with Baudelaire and the transcendental tradition was, in itself, artistically sterile. As far as we know Proust never made the mistake of thinking himself a poet, unless in those verses included in *Les Plaisirs* which might be taken as a feeble attempt to exploit the vein of Baudelaire's 'Les Phares'. The poetry of which he was capable went eventually to nourish his prose, but only when 'naïveté' in Baudelaire's and the more current sense had been supplemented by sophistication. Proust's intellectual curiosity was as persistent as his aesthetic sensibility was delicate, and the speculations of his intelligence were not, as Baudelaire's, carried on outside the work of art but as part of its very substance. The coherence of *A la recherche* is planned and established by the intelligence.

Yet the coherence is not itself purely intellectual, not philosophical, for the materials which Proust's planning intelligence had to deal with had been secreted naturally and without premeditation by his temperament in a hard and, at first, quite unsuccessful struggle to come to terms with life. The hardness of that struggle opened Proust's sympathy to much of the pessimism of the century in which his mind was rooted; to Hardy's, for instance, to the very sense of fatality that Bergson strove against, in which time is the leading agent, and scientific determinism the principal mental component.

Mention of this sense of fatality reminds us of the precariousness of defining and attributing paternity to literary influence. The pessimism centred on time, on the cyclical view of history, on the insignificance of the individual span in the aeons—this pessimism is part of the spirit of the age. Proust's obsession with time has been attributed to the influence of his philosophy master, Darlu, of Bergson, of Ruskin, of George Eliot, as well as of Hardy. But he lived in a century whose poetry begins, in the anthologies, with *Le Lac,* and abounds in references to the relentlessness of clocks, a century divided between historicism and escape into eternities which sometimes appear synthetic, between the majority outlook of confidence in progress and ultimate happiness and the minority refusal of the values of life in favour of art. Bergson's philosophy was an attempt to resolve these dichotomies, in terms of which Proust, meditating on his own predicament, could respond to some but not all. For the rest he was very much a man of the century to which Bergson strove to point out the errors of its ways.

So, whenever we set about estimating an influence,

or even an affinity, we must keep our eye on the background. If we fix our eyes only on the pair of minds we are considering, and conscientiously tabulate every parallel idea, feeling, value and belief, we shall find, when our glance is lifted, that a good many items appear to need to be struck out as property common to more than our pair. Even in these cases, one particular formulation of a generally held idea, one particular expression of a widespread feeling may prove to have attracted particular attention; and then it may be illuminating to discover why. But it is equally illuminating to discover why what is not assimilated has been rejected.

This is the case with Bergson and Proust. Related first by their historical situation, which relates them both with many others, they are seen to be related in a closer way, by parallel observations of detail and even parallel images. There seems now to be little doubt that Proust borrowed ideas, sometimes slightly transposed, from Bergson, and even borrowed, with transposition as slight, Bergson's means of expression. But to move from this observation to the conclusion that the novel is to be interpreted and assessed in Bergsonian terms is hazardous; Bergson's ideas were by no means the only ones Proust found it convenient to adapt to his own purpose, not even, perhaps, the most fruitful. The evidence now available suggests that what there is of Bergsonian optimism in *A la recherche* is superimposed on a pessimistic ground, or on a ground in which pessimism about life is complementary to optimism about art, in which art, or the 'ideas' which art expresses, is the only intimation of a transcendent and entirely satisfactory state of being. Bergson's contribution to Proust's *summa* could only be accepted when Bergson's sense of the meaningfulness of life was matched by Proust's clear notion of his own purpose and the way to set about it, and even then much of what Bergson had to say was stubbornly rejected. To interpret Proust's novel, we must look at the novel and at Proust. We must bear in mind every influence we can discover, but keep our eye on the receiving end. And then we shall discover that, if Proust has had no imitators, it is not only because he was so original; it is also because he sucked so much nourishment into his own great plant that his successors had to grow roots in other ground. Few minds have been more generously nourished than Proust's upon the substance of other minds.

And we shall do well to bear in mind Curtius's terms: intellectualism and impressionism, analysis and sensibility, rejecting the over-simple views of those who would persuade us that the impressionism is all part of the analysis, or the intellectualism an unavoidable aberration from the impressionistic ideal (a view which Proust himself was too ready to foster); we must defend ourselves from the temptation to describe the work in terms of what an ideal work ought to be, and provisionally at least, turn a sceptical eye on programmes; even Bergson's; even Proust's. The study of a century and a half of romantic programmes suggests that the complexity and subtlety of artistic achievements are often more than doctrine can encompass, and raise more questions than theory can answer. But there is little doubt that Proust studied both the programmes and achievements of writers who caught his imagination, and that they were many.

During the years when Proust's still blurred conception of his novel was hovering between a poetical expression of intimate spiritual states and a more objective treatment of the passions of social ambition and love, moving on (as we shall see) to contain the latter while keeping its centre of gravity near the former, his literary culture seems to have developed in a corresponding way. Jean Santeuil and Marcel, like Proust and his schoolfriends, become period-conscious, modernity-conscious, first of all in terms of loyalty to the poetry of the Parnasse; Leconte de Lisle was still in the ascendant, while Symbolism, as a movement, was still in its heroic period. But all three loved books, and enjoyed the intimate delight of reading, before they were caught up in the collective and more dubious exaltation of being up-to-date and snobbish about the past. Jean Santeuil learned a good deal of Musset and Hugo by heart before the literary snobs converted him to Verlaine and Leconte de Lisle and taught him to feel contempt for the Romantics; Marcel, willing at first to listen seriously to Bloch's statement that Racine and Musset had managed to write one good line each which fulfilled Leconte de Lisle's requirements, later restored Racine and Musset to his literary pantheon and scourged the Blochs of this world with both mockery and argument. He had accepted the truth of a lesson which Baudelaire had taught; that beauty is eternal but that the way of perceiving beauty and the forms of its expression must continually change. He studied the new ways and forms of his time in Symbolism and Impressionism, and allowed Impressionism, in particular, to open his sensibility to the spectacle of contemporary life; but he also looked for the beauty reflected in the different sensibilities of other ages. His taste moved forward with the present but also enveloped more and more of the past.

And steadily, in his culture, the classical writers—to whose work Jean Santeuil was, at first, indifferent —came into their own. Racine, like the Renaissance painters, is a little too marked by the pomps and affectations of a splendid era not to contrast humorously with Proust's sometimes mischievous (and limited) sense of reality. If, at twenty, he had sometimes cast himself for the role of Phèdre, his production of himself in that role never went beyond the creation of the tempted and fallen young women of *Les Plaisirs*. As we saw earlier, on second thoughts his favourite heroine was Bérénice—not the most typical of Racine. His sense of sin shifted from sexual guilt to procrastination; his favourite literary hero, at twenty, was Hamlet. The procrastination ended, the Phèdre theme (as we shall see) was introduced into *A la recherche*, but ironically. The repressed guilt and its attendant feelings which, perhaps, superficially, Proust had outlived, spent its deeply accumulated forces in projecting the circumstances of its original formation into an imagined world, in which they were shown to be normal and as cosmically innocent as Leconte de Lisle's rapacious shark. And otherwise Racine is quoted in contexts where the prestige of his verse clashes amusingly with the trivial incident which brings it to Proust's mind; as when Françoise's emotions about Eulalie are likened to Joas's when he proclaims, with Athalie in mind, that 'Le bonheur des méchants comme un torrent s'écoule'.

Fascinated as he was by aristocracy, Proust paid more attention to the moralists and memorialists of the seventeenth century than to its drama; most particularly dear to him were La Bruyère and Saint-Simon. Apt always to assess life and literature in terms suggested by his own emotional predicament, his preferences embraced the lyrical and the cruelly if finely positive.

If, in the adolescent Proust, Leconte de Lisle—called, in *Jean Santeuil*, 'the last of the Romantics'—flattered both the cult of art and the enjoyment of disillusion, as Proust matured both pleasures were refined. Both became more intellectually fastidious, more subtly inter-fused with irony and humour. There is a comparable development of sensibility in certain Symbolists—in Laforgue and Corbière, for instance. But in no other writer, certainly no prose writer, do we find quite the same knitting together of strands which nevertheless remain distinguishable, the quite so happy coexistence in one mind of the double vision—the vision of a man accustomed to perceiving the sensuous beauty of the world through the imagination of a great century of poetry, and the vision of a classical observer of man-kind who has lived on into a century of scientific de-terminism.

But Proust was out to write a novel; his problem was to steer, between poetry and satirical observation of manners, a course proper to the novel. And he knew his novelists as well as his poets and moralists. 'The proper understanding of Proust's social world', wrote Ramon Fernandez, 'begins with the observation that in *Le Temps perdu* are to be found the traces and filiations of nearly all the great novels of the nineteenth century'. Just as the story of Jean Santeuil's first adult love affair with Françoise, otherwise called Mme S., is introduced by a discourse on the nature of love, in which Proust is quite obviously setting out to translate Stendhal's theory of crystallization into the terms of his own 'subjective idealism', the story of Jean's friendship with Henri de Réveillon is introduced by a psychology of snobbery where the literary association is with Balzac. Proust does not mention Julien Sorel here, but there is a paral-lel in his mind between the *arrivisme* of Jean Santeuil (and himself) and that of Rastignac and Rubempré. The narrative of the social rise of Antoine Desroches, a painter who marries Jean's cousin, begins like a pastiche of a Balzac novel and illustrates its philosophy of the contemporary form of social ambition with parallels from *Le Père Goriot*. But the Desroches soon disappear from the scene and play an episodic role.

There seems little doubt, too, that Flaubert offered Proust points of reference for the diagnosis of his own predicament and the construction of his own destiny. It must have occurred to Proust that he was related to a younger and immature self much as Flaubert was related to Mme Bovary. Emma's 'days of reading' in her adolescence at the convent are as important in her destiny as Jean's and Marcel's in theirs, and her tragedy is shown to be due to her spiritual obtuseness before a problem which Flaubert and Marcel saw as the central problem of the artist and believed themselves to have solved. She confuses literature and life, the exaltations of the spirit with the ecstasies of the flesh. We shall have to return to her later, and ourselves make use of her as a reference-point to clarify Proust's ideas.

For Fromentin Proust must have felt both sympathy and antipathy. Dominique, with gifts and problems of temperament not unlike Marcel's, takes what Proust, in his moral incapacity, must have felt to be an abysmally philistine course, rejecting the riches of his sensibility for the well-ordered but morose and half-frustrated life of a gentleman farmer. *Dominique* is indeed far less exhilarating than *A la recherche;* it stands for the more dismal renunciation effected not as the joyful choice of a greater good but as the repression of a feared indiscipline. If Marcel never quite grows up into an adult world, he at least finds his own issue from the dullness of middle age. But if, in reading *A la recherche,* one is rarely reminded of Fromentin except when he is mentioned by name, as he is once or twice as painter and author of *Les Maîtres d'autrefois,* and when, in Proust's pastiche of the Goncourt diary, it is revealed that Mme

Verdurin is none other than the Madeleine of Fromentin's novel, there are passages in *Jean Santeuil* which directly recall *Dominique*. Both boys, writing essays for their tutor or schoolmaster, read their own emotions into the historical situations they are writing about. Dominique writes tenderly about Hannibal's defeat because he is about to leave home to go to school; Jean identifies himself with Joan of Arc. Dominique, like Jean and Marcel, is emotionally dependent on sense impressions and has a memory which retains sense impressions more easily than facts. The seasonal and atmospheric impressions of his boyhood home are recorded with remarkable sensuous vividness.

Proust's work, then, is firmly rooted in the French literary tradition. But it is not merely literary. It is rooted in his personal experience. We have seen that Stendhal was absorbed and transmuted. And Fernandez, after noting that all the themes of the century's novels are picked up again in *A la recherche*, goes on to say: 'If these traces are not always recognizable (except to a few initiates) it is because Proust's intelligence, sensibility and imagination have submitted these traces, these elements, to greater pressures, like the high temperatures or chemical agents which distort certain metals. One must always bear these great themes of the novel in mind, and then one realizes what they could become in certain specific psychological conditions.' What, for Proust, built up these imaginative temperatures, precipitated these chemical agents? We have said that his work is not merely literary; it is rooted in his own experience; but if we ask where he found the tools to shape other men's writing to his own imaginative needs, we must answer that it was in other regions of literature. He found his tools in one literature, refined and improved them, and used them to adapt another literature to the purposes proposed by his own experience. Proust's work is not *merely* literary; but it is predominantly so.

He wrote to a friend in 1909 or 1910: 'It is curious that in all the different *genres*, from George Eliot to Hardy, from Stevenson to Emerson, there is no literature which has as much hold on me as English and American literature. Germany, Italy, very often France, leave me indifferent. But two pages of *The Mill on the Floss* reduce me to tears. I know that Ruskin loathed that novel, but I reconcile all these hostile gods in the Pantheon of my admiration.'

The most interesting names in that list are those of George Eliot and Ruskin. For *Jean Santeuil* confirms what L. A. Bisson had already more than half suggested; that George Eliot played as large a part in helping Proust to self-awareness as any philosopher. Her work encouraged him to clear his mind about the 'specific psychological conditions' within which, for example, Balzac's social climbers, Stendhal's lovers, Flaubert's romantic dreamers became distorted, and in their common distortion united, into the Proustian world.

As for Ruskin, another penetrating remark made by Fernandez, writing of Proust's style, will help us to see what he gave to Proust: 'Slowly and harmoniously Proust's sentences tend to poeticize the real *without transforming it*, the imagination working up every scrap of sensation which the real provides. The precision of the impressionistic notations is, as it were, the security for the graceful or piquant vagaries of the imagination.' The tendency to poeticize the real without transforming it is eminently French; but Proust seems to have learned his impressionistic precision from Ruskin. And from Ruskin he derived a lesson complementary to the one he learned from George Eliot. She helped him to the notion of an imaginative capital laid up in childhood, providing in later life diminishing means which only memory could subsidize; from Ruskin's thought and Ruskin's prose Proust forged an instrument whereby he could reinject imagination into a dreary world.

Of all the correspondences with his own sensibility which Proust must have found in *The Mill on the Floss,* the chief can be summed up in a theme to which George Eliot more than once returns: 'Childhood impressions are the mother-tongue of imagination.' This theme is paralleled in *Jean Santeuil:* 'They say that as we grow older sensations grow weaker; perhaps, but they are accompanied by the echo of former sensations, like those ageing primadonnas whose failing voice is supported by an invisible choir.' George Eliot prefers an elderberry bush to the finest fuchsia because of the memories it stirs; Proust is moved by may blossom for the same reason. But when we compare the formlessness of *Jean Santeuil* with the design of *A la recherche,* we notice that the coherence of the latter is in great part due to the fact that not only Marcel's love of may blossom but every aspiration of his life is referred back to the patterns which his imagination began to assume in childhood, influenced by natural beauty but also, and even more—which is characteristic of Proust—by the books with which he spent the most delightful part of his life. Proust tried to turn George Eliot's idea into a system, basing upon it the account of a fictional life in which romantic love and social ambition are seen as the pursuit of a poetry already and more fully known in the past.

But, in the latter novel, this account of an emotional decline takes its place in a more complex emotional pattern. The falling rhythm of the loss of childhood impressions is counterpointed by the rising rhythm of the growing sense of vocation; the loss of imaginative spontaneity is counterbalanced by a gain of imaginative insight, culminating in the 'revelation' provided by involuntary memory. This final upward swing is fore-shadowed in a recurring local pattern: imagination clashes with reality and disintegrates; then, usually under the guidance of an artist, it reawakens in forms compatible with reality. For instance, Marcel goes to Balbec with his head full of the romance of Gothic churches and primitive seas; he is disappointed in the church, until Elstir teaches him to read in its fabric the very spirit of the age which created it; he shades his eyes from the unprimitive yachts and bathers until Elstir teaches him to find beauty in images of contemporary life. No doubt these upward movements, which more than compensate for romantic disillusion by cultivated insight, reflect similar movements in Proust's sensibility between *Jean Santeuil* and *A la recherche*; in life, the man who did most to stimulate them was Ruskin.

Ruskin preached an idealism like Emerson's, but it was an *applied* idealism. He showed Proust exactly how certain works of art could be said to reflect the inner and transcendent life. Proust turned from *Jean Santeuil* to the study and translation of Ruskin because, as he wrote, he sometimes felt that he was piling up ruins, like Casaubon in *Middlemarch*. Ruskin taught him how to set about a real building. He showed him how familiar things become strangely interesting when they are resolved into their complex details, and provided the example of a style in which such details are precisely noted. He suggested a way of according to the dull world of natural experience a prestige reflected from the more satisfactory and exciting world of art, or of viewing the world with a humorous sense of its contrast with a world of art which some of its features recall.

Ruskin's influence is reflected in Proust's minute account of Aunt Léonie's dried lime-flowers, of the rise and change of feeling, of motives, of how milk looks as it comes to the boil. And there is to be noted in both writers a sense of the enduring combined with the evanescent, of the perspective of history and the precariousness of the moment. Ruskin sought a particular fall of sunlight on a building made solidly meaningful by the stretch of its history; at the climax of *A la recherche*, after watching the different momentary lights falling on different aspects of people's characters, we see them solid, and, it seems, fixed at last with the depth of their past behind them.

3

THE PLAN

In 1906 or thereabouts, Proust had come to a number of interesting but unrelated conclusions about life as experienced by himself; and he had a message, which was that 'real life is in some dimension outside life'. In the literature of the century he had come across this same message in many forms, and in Symbolism particularly he saw an aesthetic ambition directed towards the expression of the experience of this ideal dimension to the exclusion of those of everyday. He had explored philosophy, and found a number of ideas which corresponded with his own intuitions, but he had found no system which could comprehend and account for all his own intuitions, and had been unable to invent one for himself. And so he set about inventing a world in which all that he believed himself to know about human experience could be exemplified, and from which everything of human experience which was irrelevant to his own discoveries and opaque to his understanding would be omitted. In a sense every novelist does this; but few, if any, novelists have done it with the same clarity of intention and the same cerebral method as Proust's. In what E. M. Forster calls novels of prophecy—*Moby Dick* for instance—the novelist, we imagine, is at least in part discovering his purpose as he goes. Not so Proust. He had amassed a number of observations of detail; he was convinced of one 'truth' which was a matter of his own feeling that there was no happiness for him outside himself, no happiness the world could give him other than what he himself had contributed to the world through his own spiritual spontaneity. Baulked of coherence of a purely philosophical order, he interrelated his materials in every possible way, weaving in thread after thread so that each appeared to be related to the others by an internal necessity. In part the plan was determined by the material, by the need to present and justify certain modes of experience valued in a certain way; but the internal necessity of the plan in turn affected the material—its selection, its ordering, its transmuting—and gave rise to the invention of new material. Proust wrote that his book was part memoirs and part novel, and it is in this respect that it left the domain of memoir behind and entered the realm of the novel proper. He invented events, characters, landscapes, artists, works of art to carry patterns of feeling which were felt in that particular way and perceived as or arranged in patterns only at the time of writing the novel. If *Jean Santeuil* seems to be a mixture of tentative and puzzled reporting of actual experience with wishful fantasy, in *A la recherche* the two have fused into an imagined world dominated and ordered by the mind of Proust, where the groping and uncertainty of the young Marcel are always seen against the background of his later conviction and certainty; every apparently shapeless fragment is ready to click into place at the touch of the appropriate spring; the mechanisms are all prepared, and in *Le Temps retrouvé* the sections consisting of groups of fragments were all to fit together into the final pattern. The book represents the creation of a destiny. In the event the final fit is not exact; there are rifts in the mental fabric of Proust's novel. And the individual

44

destiny there portrayed has to be adapted by the reader to provide a conception of the destiny of humanity as a whole. But one has to press to find the cracks, for they are effectively papered over. The rifts are philosophical; they are papered over by the cunning devices of the novelist.

'Man's vices', wrote Baudelaire, 'contain the proof . . . of his inclination towards the infinite . . . In this depravation of the sense of the infinite, in my view, lies the reason for all culpable excesses . . .' Proust, in retrospect, saw his final success as an artist—and at the root of his notion of the artist lies the romantic-symbolist ambition to make the infinite perceptible, to move out of time to eternity—as a precarious victory over the forces of two 'culpable excesses', eroticism and snobbery. He lived first in a state of conflict between these and the attempt to write; the conflict was resolved, and the spiritual calm, content and purposeful assurance reflected in *A la recherche* were made possible when the experience garnered from sexual passion and social ambition was made the very stuff of the book itself, the springboard from which Marcel, like Banville's clown, was to leap into the infinite. By 1906 Proust could feel that he had renounced the world, if not the flesh. He could look out from his ark on the society he had abandoned, about to be engulfed by the rising tide of democracy, with, superficially, the tolerance born of assurance, of confidence in his own kind of superiority. Writing, he behaved towards the aristocrats of his created world as he had seen some of the real aristocrats behave towards himself, with the apparent humility of those who are entirely sure of themselves. But he also avenged his earlier, humiliated self, and appropriated the naked arrogance of some of his creations for his own —and his readers'—satisfaction. In his Balzacian psychology of social ambition in *Jean Santeuil,* Proust remarked: 'Either because his perspicacity takes pleasure in cruelly punishing in other people the shame of feeling these effects (of snobbery) within himself, or rather because writing of his morbid passion even to stigmatize it is another way of cultivating and satisfying it, the novelist who is also a snob will become the novelist who treats of snobs.' These observations are true of Proust himself, and no less in 1906 than in 1896; valid also is his principle that the artist who is the victim of a passion will rationalize his predicament and pretend that he has chosen the way of life to which his passion has condemned him. What has changed is the reason given for the extended study of high society and snobbery. Marcel's social ambition is to be shown as a mistaken pursuit of poetry, an idealist's mirage imaging more substantial spiritual states to be traced back to childhood and Combray; it is in other characters like Legrandin and Mme Verdurin that snobbery appears as a crude and selfish vice, the shamefully unspiritual character of which is imaged in Legrandin's quivering buttocks.

Sexual desire and social ambition Proust felt to be, or rationalized into, the pursuit of something spiritually valued, in the purest sense loved. Romantic love is involved in both; in one case rooted in a subsoil of pure sensuality but rising into successive and fragile flowers of imagination—Gilberte and Albertine; in the other radiating from a more ethereal centre—the romance of history and the stability of tradition merging into maternal protectiveness—and finally dispersing into the void when Oriane de Guermantes is seen as herself and not as the incarnation of an imagined Geneviève de Brabantes and all the mother-mistresses who inhabit the faery landscapes of romantic prose. Beauty loved and betrayed first through desire and then through social ambition; beauty finally abstracted from the experiences of these and fixed in the enchantment of style; this is the foundation pattern on which the book is built. 'And even in my most carnal desires, always pointing in a certain direction, concentrated about a dream essentially the same, I might have recognized as the first cause an idea, an idea to which I would have sacrificed my life, and at the most central point of which, as in my reveries during the afternoons when I used to read in the Combray garden, was the idea of perfection.'

The symmetry of the pattern is clearly to be seen in the early draft of the passage on the two 'ways' published by *La Table ronde* in 1945.

'On the Méséglise way I learned that to awaken love in our heart it is enough for a woman to have looked long at us and made us feel she might be ours; but on the Guermantes way I learned that sometimes to awaken our love it is enough for a woman to have looked away from us and made us feel she never could be ours.' These two women were to become Gilberte and Oriane. The situation was to be changed—Marcel was to misinterpret Gilberte's gesture of amorous invitation for one of contempt, and the look of kindness and promise was to be given to Mme de Guermantes. But the principle of crystallizing the imaginative experience of early life round two centres, represented by the two 'ways', was to be maintained and to provide the main articulation of the novel's skeleton.

This same draft goes on to describe an experience of involuntary memory. On the way to Combray one year, the narrator hears the clink of hammer on steel as the gangers work on the railway lines. It is a moment of spiritual depression when he has lost all sense of beauty or desire. Later in his holiday, picnicking with his governess in the woods, the sound of a fork striking a plate

47

recalls the earlier moment; again he sees the landscape from the train window, but differently. Seen by the intelligence or remembered by the intelligence the view had been 'insipid'; re-created through sensation, nature seemed 'alive, lived, past, intoxicating and lovely'. And Proust offers his explanation; the sense of beauty is dependent on the apprehension of an 'extra-temporal truth' arising from the exact correspondence of a present moment with a past moment.

This incident and the explanation offered by Proust subsist in the later novel, but they are postponed to Marcel's middle age. This postponement is the first and most important of the steps by which the embryo plan grew into the final design, and it is worth tracing the other steps as far as we can. Not in the order in which they were made; the evidence is lacking, and it is more revealing to follow rather their logical order.

In the later plan the revelation of a kind of eternity through involuntary memory is postponed, multiplied into a series of instances, and shown as the culmination of a more sustained and more dramatically effective rhythm; for the moment of spiritual impercipience is no longer an isolated moment, a mood, but the nadir of a slow spiritual decline. The reader has been prepared long since for the idea of this spiritual wasting, for it figures largely in the explanation of Swann's artistic infertility in the first two volumes, and it was perhaps with the introduction of this scheme of decline, death and resurrection that Proust came to see how certain religious notions could be adapted to his purpose and how some ready-made patterns of emotional response which, in so many contemporary minds, were inhibited by the intellectual refusal of religious experience could be released in the more acceptable context of the religion of art. 'Resurrection', he wrote in *Sodome et Gomorrhe,* 'is perhaps a phenomenon of memory.' Not only did he splendidly recapture the sublime of the perennial notion that an artist lives on in his work, the notion which had obsessed Mallarmé and which Proust expresses in the passage on the death of Bergotte; he imported reincarnation, successive deaths and final resurrection in the eternal into the scheme of life itself as lived by a creative artist, by emphasizing the discontinuity between the different epochs of Marcel's affective life—Marcel before and after his grandmother's death, Marcel in and out of love with successive women—while showing the spiritual continuity which underlies the epochs and finally abstracting and systematizing their spirituality in the 'resurrection' of *Le Temps retrouvé*.

The moment before the revelation, when Marcel hears the ganger's hammer ringing on the metal of the carriage wheel and thinks dispiritedly of the beauty he ought to be seeing in the dappled trees, is the end of his spiritual decline; the peak from which life falls away is Combray and childhood, the time of greatest spiritual vitality, imaginative spontaneity and confidence in life. Between these two terms come the repeated attempts to convert into the acts of living, into immediately real and solid substance, the spiritual experiences glimpsed through literature or in the solitary enjoyment of natural beauty. Each attempt is frustrated; after each Marcel is thrown back upon his solitude and the increasing conviction that spiritual value is nowhere to be found outside himself except where his own imagination has projected it. But imagination itself loses its conviction and its power; Marcel is less and less convinced that there is any transcendence to be hankered after, and less and less able to bring about the illusion whereby it may be pursued in a woman or a landscape; in the last stage of imaginative debility he cannot even find it in art itself. As imagination fades faith and the intuition of purpose fail with it. This withering ends in what is virtually a spiritual death; and in the first of the two volumes of *Le Temps retrouvé* the theme of decay and disintegration, of a world grown dreary and passionless, is sustained and amplified until, at the end of the volume, the curve begins to mount rapidly towards the counter-theme of revelation and resurrection, while the sense of transformation and renewal is heightened by the continuing, in counterpoint, of the theme of decadence pursued now in connection, not with Marcel's spiritual life, but with the effects on other people of the time from which Marcel is on the point of escaping into his own kind of eternity.

This brings us to the (logically) next step in the elaboration of the novel's plan; for the revelation, though it is dramatically important for it to present itself in a rapid series of lightning-flashes, must be prepared if it is to win the reader's assent. It must be prepared, and the preparation must be, as far as possible, clandestine. Illumination must be retrospective; the light of the flashes must irradiate the country over which the reader has travelled; mysteries must be made plain, but they must first of all be mysteries. And so firstly, Marcel's spiritual decline is accompanied by a frustrated and declining sense of literary vocation. Secondly, this downward curve is offset by another—the curve of Marcel's understanding and appreciation of literature, painting and music through contact with the works and personalities of artists, which rises steadily until the approach to the moment of crisis. Then it reverses its direction, to move steeply downwards with the other curve towards the stay with Gilberte de Saint-Loup at Tansonville, when the two 'ways' with their individual auras of magic are shown to have become one stretch of dreary countryside, and a passage supposed to have been found among unpublished portions of the Goncourt diary finally shakes Marcel's belief in his own vocation and faith in art itself. Thirdly, the essential characteristics of the predestined artist in Marcel are thrown into relief, when they are at last revealed, because Proust has drawn in a number of near-artists and shown (though this is apt to be unnoticed except in retrospect or perhaps more often, in practice, on a second reading) the elements which these incomplete artists lack and which Marcel is eventually shown to possess. The most important instance of this is Swann. Marcel is able to grasp firmly and finally a spiritual reality which had dangled just outside Swann's reach.

This design gave Proust complete liberty to introduce into his book every feeling and every idea derived from the dialogue between his own spiritual self-exploration and the various forms of the romantic-symbolist mysticism of art. Under the guise of showing love as an illusion, a debased ideal, he could exercise to the full his capacity for the lucid, detailed and most unmystical observation and notation of the movements of his own emotions; the meticulous detail could be fitted (though not without a certain amount of intellectual evasion) into the grand pattern, richly related to traditional religious patterns, of spiritual destiny conceived in terms of the gulf between the eternal and the temporal and culminating in the redemption of the temporal through art. Time becomes the key to destiny, becomes fate itself; everything connected with the effects of time and change becomes relevant to the general scheme; man is great because he bears the weight of time and twice great when, as artist, he can create his own means of salvation.

Just as the idea of love as illusion allows Proust to extend his clinical study of its emotions and link the tradition of Constant and Stendhal to that of Chateaubriand, Baudelaire and the Symbolists, the idea of social ambition as the pursuit of poetry allows him to satisfy his ambition, based on his admiration for La Bruyère, Saint-Simon and Balzac, to survey the society of his day—or that region of society which was all he himself could pretend to know. And here, moreover (and in spite of Proust's careful distinction, in *Le Temps retrouvé*, between the truth of art and the truth of science), Proust unites in himself the two great intellectual trends of the nineteenth century, Idealism and Positivism; for he is at once an Idealist expressing his own Idealism and a Positivist dissecting and explaining his own Idealism, though always, if not always consistently, explaining it in terms which leave the way open for a spiritual rather than a materialistic interpretation of ultimate reality. A. N. Whitehead observed that since the Renaissance the idea of scientific determinism has taken the place of the Greek fate. Nineteenth-century writers had various ways of dealing with the increasing sense of imprisonment in mechanical process. Mallarmé admitted that there was no place for the spirit in the natural cosmos and affirmed that humanity had created spirit and could learn to make its own world of it. Proust portrays a similar dichotomy in terms of the hostility between subjective spirituality and reality outside the self; a reality which, he appears to believe, we can never know in itself, but which, whenever illusion fails, we must always realize to be at best indifferent and at worst hostile to the subject. The process of human destiny, seen from the outside, is repetitive and meaningless. But Proust, like so many of his contemporaries—like Hardy, for instance—is fascinated by the circling juggernaut of time; and just as in Greek tragedy the greatness of man is measured by the greatness of the forces which oppress him, in the final volumes of *A la recherche* we hear more and more of the 'great laws' which govern those patterns of human vicissitudes from which art is the refuge. There are laws which apply to individual experience—the laws of love, the laws which govern all the relationships between imagination and reality. But laws apply also to the evolution of groups; groups decline and are renewed, and with renewal comes change. The *grand monde* declines and is renewed through an infiltration of the *bourgeoisie* which changes its character—superficially at least, and perhaps only superficially. None of these changes is progressive; within groups the lives of individuals follow the same basic patterns; behind every individual is massed a great thrust of determinism. Heredity, for instance, loomed almost as large in Proust's mind as it did in Zola's, different as his treatment of it is. Swann, as he grows older, falls into the habits and ways of thought of his Jewish ancestry; Marcel feels his father's character growing again within himself.

The difficulty was to assimilate these 'laws' into the philosophical explanation of art which was to follow the revelation and crown the work. For this explanation was to be in essence anti-intellectual, or at least (since the intellect is allowed a large part in the act of writing) anti-conceptual; and the laws in which Proust was so interested are, however arrived at, conceptual. The reconciliation was difficult and no doubt accounts for much of the confusion of ideas in *Le Temps retrouvé;* in so far as it can be said to have been effected at all, the trick depends on the ambiguity of the word 'idea'. One sense is that of the Symbolists, where the idea is the abstraction from lived experience of certain affective components which can be held in the mind apart (to some extent at least) from the particular occasions which gave rise to them. In this sense lyrical art can be held to be the expression of 'ideas', of the aesthetic essence of experiences, and the notion can be given a Platonic or Hegelian or Bergsonian twist. The other sense is that of the idea as an intellectual pattern in which relationships are logical and in no degree affective. Here, to arrive at the idea of a process is to understand its nature; and Proust justifies the need to arrive at such ideas within his scheme of salvation by proposing the notion that to understand the nature of one's suffering is to escape from it. Schopenhauer wrote of the 'ideas' of art as an escape from flux, but he used the word in the first rather than the second sense. Spinoza had said that an emotion ceases to be an emotion as soon as we form a clear and distinct idea of it. Proust proposes two kinds of enjoyment: the perpetuation of transcendent pleasure through involuntary memory and the escape from remembered suffering through understanding. Both are, in a sense, abstractions from experience; but the one is the abstraction of feeling, the other of principles. Both abstractions are functions of the intellect; but in the first case the intellect must be prevented from abstracting its own aesthetically irrelevant patterns and omitting the concrete and intellectually irrelevant detail of the impression.

So far we have seen the plan in the abstract, built on the foundation of Combray and the two 'ways'. In the imagination of Marcel as a child, Swann's way stands for a world beyond the familiar world of family life. Outside, unknown, existing as a steadily growing set of imaginative assumptions is a world of artistic culture, which is closed to Marcel's family, and of romantic sexual love frowned on by the *vertus de Combray*. The imagination of a world of artists and artistically cultured people is centred in the unknown figure of Bergotte; the imagination of sexual adventure in the unknown figure of Swann's daughter, Gilberte. Swann is, at first, the only contact with both except for Bergotte's books; and both are interrelated by the thought of Gilberte's friendship with Bergotte. In the imaginative halo which surrounds the unknown Gilberte are reflected the colours which glow in Bergotte's prose; later, when Marcel has met and fallen in love with the real Gilberte, Bergotte's halo reflects the colours of Marcel's romantic passion. Marcel, through his acquaintance with Gilberte, explores the reality of the Swann *milieu*, and begins to explore the experience of love on the mental and physical planes; the world of literary culture, Bergotte and all, is, as a way of life, disappointing, and so is love.

Similarly, the Guermantes way is associated with the poetry of history, lineage, aristocracy and a more rarefied, more maternally protective, less sensual love. Marcel again makes his way into the corresponding reality and is disillusioned.

The two ways are made the assembly-points, as it were, for the features of Marcel's imaginative life, and organized into two sets of ambitions, each of which is to be realized. They are distinct, and stand for two socially distinct worlds into which Marcel successively penetrates. At the end of the Combray episode they divide, and we move first into Swann's world, then into the Guermantes'; but they are connected in their division by a complicated web of individual relationships which multiply and pull them together again in *Le Temps retrouvé*. When Marcel goes to visit Gilberte and her husband at Tansonville, he realizes how the two ways, so distinct in his childish imagination, connect on the map—sees, too, how empty they are of the poetry with which in childhood he had invested them; until at last these two kinds of poetry themselves draw together in the beatific vision of Combray re-created in art. Their distinct poetries meet in Marcel's subjectivity as their geographical realities connected in gloomy reality on the map. And the two social worlds for which they stand are united; Gilberte, whom, in Swann's lifetime, Oriane de Guermantes refused to receive, is married to Oriane's nephew; the Princesse de Guermantes is now Mme Verdurin, the apparently inverted snob of Swann's own social stratum; and the guests are a motley collection of aristocracy, bourgeoisie and nondescripts.

If the middle sections of the novel had not been so inflated during the years of the war when publication was suspended, the abstract symmetry of the plan would have been reflected in the physical symmetry of the divisions of the book; distributed over two or three volumes, we have had *Du côté de chez Swann* and *Le côté de Guermantes* in roughly equal dimensions, preceded by Combray and rounded off with the account of Marcel's revelation, originally to be called *L'Adoration perpétuelle*.

The movement of Marcel's consciousness of experience is, generally speaking (to use the expression applied by Ramon Fernandez to the development of Marcel's notion of the Guermantes) that of a 'poetic nebula which slowly crystallizes and cools into ideas'. The aesthetic satisfaction Proust proposed to himself was to recover, as far as possible, the nebula and to illustrate the ideas. To concentrate the nebula, he arranged the memories of his own childhood and filled in the gaps in the pattern, wonderfully re-creating within himself the eye and soul of a child, but never losing the lucidity, critical power and irony of an adult intelligence; to demonstrate his laws, he stylized his psychology of the passions he knew best, arranging and creating according to the principles he set out to demonstrate; with a marvellous fidelity of detail, but omitting whatever of human love did not fit his pattern and, *a fortiori,* whatever of human love did not come within the purview of his own experience.

4

COMBRAY

In *Le Temps retrouvé,* Proust complains that the critics who read the first part of his book spoke of his microscopic scrutiny of his mind 'whereas I had, on the contrary, used a telescope to descry things which were indeed very small, but because of their great distance, and each of which was a world'. Marcel, looking backwards, sees a succession of different selves, and each of them inhabiting his own world, with its own particular atmosphere and key sensations; the word itself connects with the famous sentence of the introduction: 'A sleeping man has round him in a circle the succession of hours, the order of years and worlds'. The epoch when he first explored the Faubourg Saint-Germain was one of these worlds; Balbec was another; the Champs-Élysées and Gilberte's home were another. The most self-contained, the brightest, the sun from which all other worlds borrowed some degree of reflected light, was Combray. Whenever Marcel looks for the origin of those values, attitudes and expectations which set the course of his life and determine the measure of his happiness, it is to Combray that he must return; and when he comes to present his past in the radiance of involuntary memory, it is round Combray that the halo shines most convincingly.

Combray, with its two ways, was artificially constructed

out of the significant features of Proust's childhood. Into it went memories of his life in Paris itself, at his uncle's house at Auteuil and at his Aunt Amyot's house at Illiers. Illiers played by far the largest part. P.-L. Larcher, in *Le Parfum de Combray,* shows just how much (and how little) the actual topography of Illiers contributed to Proust's reconstruction; the rest was invented by Proust to correspond with what he remembered of his imaginative life and with the pattern of this as he ordered and completed it in transforming his own past into Marcel's. According to Léon Pierre-Quint, Proust could never spend his summer holidays in the country after his first bad attack of asthma at the age of nine, and went instead to the coast. But memories of sea, coast and seaside resorts were reserved for the second 'world' of natural impressions, Balbec, which was to show the second of the two most creative phases in Marcel's spiritual history. Into the stylized topography and partly imagined family and inhabitants of Combray, Proust packed all his childhood memories, up to early adolescence, which in retrospect appeared to be connected with his moral failure and artistic success. The year is limited to late spring, summer and early autumn. Marcel's is a life of freedom from school and social contacts with people of his own age. The surroundings which reflect and stimulate his imagination are natural instead of urban. Leisure, in independence and solitude limit the story of his growth to the story of the use he made of the freedom of his imagination.

People are part of the child's background. Proust had a brother, Robert; Marcel has none. He is dispensed from the frictions and adjustments which Proust had known. Elisabeth de Gramont wrote of the division of Proust's family into two clans: Marcel and his mother, sensitive and easily moved; Robert and his father, sane, stable, conventional and impatient of the hyperaesthesia of the others. In *Jean Santeuil* there is no brother, but there are distractingly normal cousins, from whom Jean Santeuil has to shut himself away in a manner which, to the unsympathetic reader, might appear frowsty and perhaps disagreeably unsociable; in *A la recherche,* the room with drawn blinds or the deep hooded chair in the garden are part of the idealized and dreamlike privacy of Marcel's natural solitude, accepted and savoured in isolation from the world of social obligations. Most of the people who live close to Marcel are two generations away in time: the grandmother and her two sisters, Céline and Flora, the grandfather, his brother Adolphe (soon cut off from the family by his supposed indiscretion in introducing Marcel to his flighty mistress, Swann's future wife Odette de Crécy) and his cousin, Marcel's great-aunt, who owns the Combray house. The others are a generation away: his parents and Aunt Léonie, great-aunt's daughter, who becomes a permanent invalid from the time when her husband, Uncle Octave, dies.

If, to the child, these people are part of his background, the moral forces with which he has to reckon and from which he draws his first impressions of the world of adult responsibilities and relationships, to Proust they are puppets in the human comedy. They share with the dreamlike quality of a world supposedly recovered by involuntary memory the shadowy yet over-rigid, inconsequential yet over-typical character of their words and habits; they are not quite in tune—the grandmother particularly—with the moral exigencies and ideals which for the child they represent. For they and the whole of the Combray episode are seen with the double vision which, in one form or another, is characteristic of Proust. One form of the double vision here is that the child's divinities are felt by the child as divinities and seen and appraised by the grown man as equals (or, subtly, as inferiors); another is that Proust, always capable of seeing his own character sympathetically from the inside and critically from the outside, condemning his vices while he was frustrated as a writer but more inclined to rationalize them when successfully writing because he saw the interconnection between his weakness and his genius, tended to reserve for Marcel all of himself that could be idealized and connected with genius and to project into other characters, sometimes recommended for tolerance and sympathy but sometimes mocked, gently or cruelly, the comic or more obviously morbid or vicious sides of himself. And so illness and solitude, in so far as they mean sensitiveness, contemplation and reflection, are given to Marcel; in so far as they stand for hypochondria, self-indulgence and the shelving of responsibility they are indulgently caricatured in Aunt Léonie, 'perpetually lying in a vague state of sorrow, physical weakness, illness, obsession and devotion', Aunt Léonie to whom Marcel, in *La Prisonnière*, finds himself growing closer in temperament and habits as his illness increases its hold upon his life.

If, for Proust, these adult characters are the butts of his indulgent humour, the childish perspective of them which he attributes to the young Marcel is dominated by three impressions: the love and solicitude of his grandmother and his mother, their moral rectitude and even, in his grandmother, idealism, together with the guilty sense of how far he falls short of the standards they propose, and the gratuitous cruelty which these grown-ups sometimes show each other. Céline and Flora bate their sister by offering her husband forbidden brandy and calling her to see him drink; Françoise is as brutal to the pregnant kitchen-maid as she is to the chickens she enjoys killing. Happiness and security depend on the affection of his mother and grandmother; and the symbol of this too close dependence on maternal protectiveness is the good night kiss of which he is deprived on the evenings when Swann comes to dine. There comes an evening, no doubt real enough in Proust's life, for it begins *Jean Santeuil* and figures again in the draft published by *La Table ronde,* when the child must at all costs have his good night kiss. Since the greatest suffering of an otherwise secure and happy life is the nightly separation from his mother, the ideal is to force the issue and demand the viaticum. Which he does, only to discover that he has ruined for himself another ideal by failing to control one of those nervous impulses which those who most care for him see as the most pressing danger to his moral life and future happiness. The child takes what solace he can from the notion that his defection comes more from his nerves than himself, but cannot rid himself of the guilt of disappointing his mother. Calm, escape from guilt and quiet enjoyment of his mother's presence come only when George Sand's *François le Champi* has put a veil of lively if, to the child who only partly follows the story, obscure patterns of imagination between reality and himself. This is Marcel's first contact with romantic literature; the incident of the good night kiss is the first instance of the escape from reality into imagination which is the direction of art, the direction of life being, in general, the fall from imagination into the desert of reality. The anguish of the child, moreover, is connected, by Proust, with the anguish which for Swann, and an older Marcel, is an essential part of the experience of love.

Proust, since he paid so much attention to this incident, seems to have remembered it more readily and vividly than any other part of his childhood. It is a perfect introduction to the temperamental qualities of the narrator, and it is magnificently dramatic writing. What might, in cold blood, appear a molehill makes a most convincing mountain; and the moral dilemma it symbolizes must indeed have been crucial for Proust himself. Over-sensitive and suffering children have lately infested literature, but impatience can hardly project itself back on to Proust. Whatever may now seem banal in the situation is redeemed by many things: the obvious artistic sincerity which marks successful communication of feeling without sentimental comment; the distance which the narrator puts between the experience and his present self, the cool detachment with which, paradoxically, the drama is conveyed—another aspect of that duality which is characteristic of Proust's attitude to his material; the emotional subtlety of the presentation, assuming guilt, yet forcing sympathy and the reader's connivance—Baudelaire's 'hypocrite lecteur' less brutally and more insidiously proposed; above all, perhaps, the sense of revelation of intimate mysteries which has been built up by the introduction. This crux of Proust's moral failure, this epitome of the moral drama diluted in the narratives of *Les Plaisirs et les jours,* is bathed now in a serenity reflected from Proust's sense of his achievement of *l'adoration perpétuelle.* He has won his battle on ground of his own choosing.

In *Le Temps retrouvé,* Proust wrote that the deeper the artist has to plunge within himself to recover the impressions to be recorded, the denser will be the poetic atmosphere with which they are surrounded. It is in his introduction, leading into the world of Combray, that Proust makes artistic use of the mystery, effort and final sense of reward which attend the recovery of past impressions. At the outset, we wait outside the Ali Baba's cave of the unconscious. Humblot, the manager of the publishing house of Ollendorff, waited impatiently, unable to understand, he reported, why a man need take thirty pages to describe his tossings and turnings on the verge of sleep. The more patient reader, catching the rumour of intriguing doings within, is given glimpses of the range of partial consciousness from civilization to brutishness and back, mentions of the riches which, later, he is to possess—Combray, Balbec, Paris, Doncières, Venice—then a full view of one moment of the Combray ritual, the incident of the good night kiss. After the mounting tension and release of the child's anguish, the assault on the door of Marcel's past begins again; Marcel, at some undefined moment in middle life, tastes the *madeleine* soaked in tea, and slowly the door moves, to open wide at last on the vision of Combray seen from the approaching train, with the church in the foreground.

The atmosphere of apocalypse generated by the superb narrative of the *madeleine* incident and the introduction surrounds the whole of the Combray episode. The imperfect tense lifts even specific and apparently singular happenings out of the world of temporal succession; events and scraps of conversation are reported in this tense of habit and extension, of actions and feelings which are never thought of as ending in a recordable achievement; which, as parts of life, are irremediably lost, but, recovered in words, are the significant extensions and dimensions of the past's substance. 'I confess', wrote Proust, 'that a certain use of the imperfect— that cruel tense which shows us life as at once ephemeral and passive, which, at the very moment when it retraces our actions, marks them as illusions, annihilates them in the past without leaving us, as the perfect tense does, the consolation of activity—is always, for me, a source of mysterious moods of sadness.' Many events are thrust back into the pluperfect; seen, that is, not as part of the succession of a moving life but as subsisting only in their effects, in their lasting contribution to the tensions and assumptions which are part of Marcel's background.

The anguish of bedtime is the first sign of the serpent in Marcel's Eden, the first instance of the way in which events refuse to adapt themselves to wishes. There are other foreshadowings of a future to be lived in a fallen world. Yet Combray is stability and security, with its limitations offset by the freedom of a vivid and lively imagination nourished on books, and not yet aware that its failure to be self-sufficient promises disillusion. At this stage we are given the delight in the illusions themselves, the promises later to be betrayed.

Stability, security, tradition, habit, all these are summed up in the church solidly and comfortably ensconced in time, a visible and permanent past. The church is the first part of Combray to be seen, after Marcel's bedroom, and if we leave it to meet Aunt Léonie drinking her lime-flower tea we soon return to explore its detail. For it is a symbol of what the novel sets out to be; in *Le Temps retrouvé,* at the very end of the book, it reappears: 'This dimension of Time, of which I had had a presentiment in Combray church, I would try to make continually perceptible in a transcription of the world which would have to be very different from that provided by our misleading senses.' For Proust the only essence is that of destiny completed, the only contemplation of essence is the contemplation of the essence of a completed past. In *Le Temps retrouvé* his white-haired and wrinkled characters have achieved a kind of grandeur by achieving a past, their only real dimension. Combray church and Balbec church, symbols of Amiens and all the mediaeval churches to the significance of whose iconography Proust had been awakened by Ruskin and Mâle, are, like Proust's novel, means of renewing in contemplation a lost spiritual vigour.

The past is solidity; it is also romance. Every symbol of the past is a window for the imagination on to the glamour of legend. The ancient porch of the church gives access not only to the finger-worn holy water stoup, the tomb covering the noble dust of the abbots of Combray and the peacock colours of the windows, but, by suggestion, to a grotto hung with stalactites, a valley visited by fairies and the mystery of a Merovingian darkness. Stimulating to the imagination, yet static, familiar and unthreatening; offering the rich essence of time with none of time's menace of change, the church has the degree of its past extension marked in the varieties of its architecture and ornament, reflecting the preoccupations, tastes and spiritual qualities of many periods. And its steeple is the symbol of a world clear of Proust's oppressive sense of guilt, the centre of the *vertus de Combray*; they, the steeple and Marcel's grandmother are grouped together in Marcel's memory.

It is the privilege of childhood to combine routine and freedom, security and imaginative adventure; Marcel is so morbidly dependent on the familiar that he is a little afraid even of the freedom and adventure of imagination. The magic lantern which covers the walls of the bedroom where he suffers the prospect of the nightly separation from his mother with coloured pictures of Geneviève de Brabant's castle and Golo on horseback 'filled with dreadful purpose' is an intimation of supernatural mystery and beauty, but also an uncomfortable intrusion into the world of comfortable habit. There are, in the last event, only two ways in which Marcel can adjust imagination and reality; by dulling imagination through habit, or by escaping from reality into books. Habit is the drug which deadens the pain experienced by the imaginative self in a hostile reality.

But imagination is not to be denied; and between habit and art there lie the alternately ecstatic and dispiriting rhythms of illusion and disillusion. In the Combray episode, almost the whole of the child's world is caught up in the tide of poetry, as the doorknob and all the natural irregularities in the walls of Marcel's room are caught up out of their material function by the light of the magic lantern and absorbed into the 'supernatural essence' of Golo and his horse; this complex of the sensuous pleasure of colour, historical exoticism and the emotions connected with Golo's vaguely ominous descent on Geneviève's castle is one of the determinants of Marcel's imaginative life; it connects directly and in all its elements with suggestiveness of the stained glass windows in the church, and the double complex is the source of the poetry which marks the beginning of what Marcel, using one of Bergson's terms, calls the 'durée' of the name Guermantes in his own mind—for Oriane de Guermantes is a descendant of the historical Geneviève. Elements drawn from his later imagining as stimulated by books gravitate towards and crystallize round this double nucleus; and before this particular poetic world is thrown off its orbit by the first sight of Oriane in the flesh, he is already more than half in love with her as he has created her for himself.

In the draft of *La Table ronde,* where the river Vivette, later to be the Vivonne, has already changed in character from the more realistic Loir of *Jean Santeuil,* Proust confesses that what he looked for in the Guermantes way was the magic country-side suggested by books like *Le Lys dans la vallée.* He looked, he said, in vain. Nature could not live up to the combined creativeness of Balzac's novel and Marcel's imagination. In *A la recherche,* the Guermantes way is made to the measure of the spiritual reality. In the draft, Proust wrote: 'In the characteristic colour assumed in memory by each separate year of my life, I cannot distinguish whether it was desire for the landscape which made me link a woman with it or whether it was love for the woman which made me desire the landscape.' In *A la recherche,* he refers often to that fusion of erethism with the sense of natural beauty which makes him long to possess the country-side physically in the person of a peasant girl who sums up her background in herself; but in the case of the imagined Oriane, where the notion of love is most rarefied, the poetry of the woman and of the 'way' with which she is associated has its earliest sources in colour, legend and books. Marcel's spiritual progress is from the Eden of reading to the fallen world of living and back to the paradise of a literature created, this time, by himself. It seems, moreover, that if the real Oriane de Guermantes was based on people like the Comtesse de Chevigné and Mme Strauss, the Oriane of Marcel's imagination may have been a relative of Balzac's Mme de Mortsauf, perhaps also of Stendhal's Mme de Rênal; and that the faery beauty of the Guermantes way was created by Proust's imagination dwelling on memories not only of Illiers but of the landscapes he read of in books—the river landscapes of *Le Lys,* of *Le Rouge et le noir,* of *Mademoiselle de Maupin.* Proust's notebooks, as they have so far been reported on, do not provide, like Coleridge's, the clues needed to investigate such imaginative transmutations in detail; but comparison of all these landscapes shows suggestive correspondences which it would take too long to detail here, and leads to the conclusion that Proust finally created in his own words the magic which other men's words had suggested to him and which, even to his childish and willing eyes, the real landscapes had appeared to lack.

And this suggests a reason for the main differences between the landscapes of *A la recherche* and *Jean Santeuil*. Jean's Etreuilles, like Marcel's Combray, is based on memories of Illiers—indeed sometimes Proust forgets himself and writes 'Illiers' instead of 'Etreuilles'. Etreuilles is, in fact, nearer the reality. Compared with Combray, Etreuilles is one-sided. The prosy river Loir is the forerunner of the Vivonne, but there is only one 'way'. There is a Méséglise; there are long descriptions of hawthorn and apple-blossom; these flowers are already surrounded with significant emotional associations which Proust is exploring. But the hawthorns are not balanced by the waterlilies, and there is no question of the symbolic geography of the two ways. Of all the choice of explanations offered in *Le Temps retrouvé* for the transcendence of experience relived in memory, the most likely seems to be the freedom which memory leaves to the imagination to transpose the past as it will.

In *A la recherche*, too, the feeling of yearning after the past is kept within narrow bounds. It breaks through sometimes in a shaft of emotion which has gained in poignancy from its containment, as when Marcel suddenly leaps forward in time from the description of the Combray church to a moment when, in Paris, the sight of a spire recalls it, and he forgets the purpose for which he had asked a passer-by the way, to stand dreaming at the view and the memory: 'and no doubt then, and more anxiously than a moment ago when I asked for information, I am looking for the right way, turning down a street . . . but . . . that street is in my heart'; or when, at the end of the account of Combray, he speaks of its beauties as the foundation of his aesthetic life: 'When on summer evenings the resounding sky growls like a wild beast and everyone is depressed by the storm, it is to the Méséglise way that I owe the ecstasy I alone know of breathing, through the sound of falling rain, the perfume of invisible and everlasting lilacs.'

The poignancy here is felt by a reader who has just seen and smelled the lilacs and known their beauty in the terms Marcel proposes. The vision which in *Jean Santeuil* is merely hinted at is here created. In *Jean Santeuil* the sea which, remembered, is beatitude, is, as described, a less-than-ordinary sea. The reference to it is brief; the novelist is concerned with the disembodied emotion of the experience, ineffable and only to be hinted at in terms which are little more than the abstract signs of feeling. Etreuilles is described in detail, and the poetry of the hawthorn and lilacs of Combray is there in germ. But it is a daylight and unframed picture of Jean's early summers. The 'worlds' of *A la recherche* which are to correspond most closely with the evocations of unconscious memory, and which are also to be shown as the occasions and crystallizers of the narrator's awareness of his own poetry—Combray and Balbec—are created in sensuous terms and bathed in a dreamlike atmosphere which carries over something of the mystery of the introduction.

And with the satisfaction of creating an ideal world, the yearning passes into the background of Proust's mind. His imagination is no longer dispersing itself painfully into the void, but exercising itself to make good the gaps in the writer's present world. Not merely remembering, with whatever kind of memory, a past as it *really* was, in whatever sense of 'really', but shaping an ideal present in terms of the best of the past. At last Proust is not crying for the moon, but making his own, in his own—the artist's—way.

A la recherche, then, adds to the earlier Etreuilles the

Guermantes way with its complex of associations—the magic lantern, the church windows, books—all concentrated into a magnetic attraction towards Oriane. It also develops and organizes the complex of associations centred on the Méséglise—later called Swann's—way. Books again—Bergotte's here, with ironic but significant overtones of *Phèdre*—the hawthorns of Tansonville; the magnetism of the image of Gilberte. The central image here is the hawthorns, which draw their power from an associative complex of their own. In *Jean Santeuil* their associations are lucidly probed and baldly stated; in *A la recherche* merely suggested. But the early version confirms the importance of the suggestions and the deliberation with which they were worked into the pattern.

The hawthorns are white and pink; the order of impact in the main passage to which we must refer is white hawthorn, pink hawthorn, Gilberte. Pink had a particular and particularly important emotive power for Proust; *Jean Santeuil* shows how clearly he realized it and how curious he himself was to know why. In this early book pink is first singled out for attention in connection with the magic lantern. In *A la recherche* the magic lantern, appropriated to the Guermantes complex, has another colouring; Geneviève wears a blue sash, Golo is dressed in red; but the striking colour is yellow—the yellow of the *landes* and of Geneviève's castle—and yellow the name Guermantes will always be for Marcel. Yellow, it naturally is, he further claims, playing in symbolist fashion with the notion of fixed correspondences between sensations of different orders and their significances; but the private mental association is established by the magic lantern. In *Jean Santeuil*, the pink of the magic lantern is connected with the pink biscuits served after lunch at Etreuilles; it is the colour associated with things which the child thinks delicious and exciting to eat; it is eminently sensual.

It returns, in *Jean Santeuil,* in the pink hawthorn. For Jean, as far back as he can remember, pink hawthorn is the epitome of spring, and its beauty the symbol of spring's sensation and the focus of his earliest desire. He proposes a choice of explanations without himself choosing. Were they really more beautiful than others, these flowers, so delicate in structure and vivid in colour that they seemed made for festive occasions— were indeed massed on the altar for the festive Month of Mary? Was it the intellectual pleasure of comparing them with the white variety, the double with the single, and noting at once the analogies and the distinctions? Hardly this, since he had seen dogroses before seeing roses proper and had felt no comparable delight in that case. Was it because the white and pink hawthorn reminded him of cream cheese plain and cream cheese flavoured and coloured with crushed strawberries? Was it because, when he was ill in bed, his mother had brought him branches of pink hawthorn which had to stand for the spring landscapes he could not go out to see?

This method of probing is familiar even in *A la recherche,* where it subsists chiefly in the analysis of psychological motive, all possible explanations being mooted but none finally and exclusively chosen. The associations of the hawthorn, however,—and of all the intensely imagined passages on Combray—are dealt with differently. The private associations are brought in, but they are made to bring with them a universal, perennial and sublimated spring. We are given, not the wherefores of the experience, but the experience itself, detached from the passing moments of its real possession and transformed into a climate and a place—into what

Mallarmé would have called a *région où vivre*, a dwelling place of the mind.

To trace the springs of the flood of feeling released by the main description of the hawthorns and transferred by Marcel to Gilberte we have to go back to the long passage on the pleasures of reading. We shall have to consider this in greater detail in the next chapter, when we come to consider Marcel's vocation. Here we need only note that Proust builds up the impression of an imagination which, stimulated by books, is confidently forward-looking and hopeful, and turned towards a future vague, but compact of pleasures known, pleasures unknown and anticipated, and pleasure and knowledge beyond what is already known or specifically imagined. 'My dreams of travel and love were only moments —which today I isolate artificially as if I were cutting sections at different heights in a fountain of water, rainbow-coloured and seemingly motionless—in an identical and inflexible upspringing of all the force of life within me.'

Almost immediately afterwards these pleasures of reading are attached to the name of Bergotte. What is particularly emphasized here is the notion of transcendence. In Bergotte, for the first time, transcendence is associated with style; for Marcel, as we shall see, has later to realize that transcendence can *only* be achieved in style. But, for the purpose we are now considering, Bergotte's name is firmly established as a password to the heaven of Marcel's imagining.

Bergotte has written on *Phèdre*. This is first mentioned quite casually, as one of the books and natural features of which Bergotte's style had 'revealed' the beauty to Marcel; but gradually, when Bergotte's name is mentioned, his pamphlet on Racine is brought into the foreground. One importance of this is in connection with the later development of the theme of Marcel's understanding of art; Phèdre is the chief role of La Berma, and after the pretentious nonsense talked about that actress by Norpois it is Bergotte who will reveal to Marcel the beauty of La Berma's acting. But Phèdre also provides overtones to Marcel's passion, first for Gilberte, then for Albertine.

Next, Bergotte's name is linked with Gilberte's; they go off together, as Marcel learns from Swann, to visit historic towns, cathedrals and castles which, for Marcel, add their romantic associations to the names of the two people. It is then that Marcel begins to fall in love with the unknown girl.

Soon afterwards the hawthorn theme is introduced; here they are white, and first seen on the church altar in celebration of the Month of Mary. But the images worked into their detailed description bring in a series of associations ranging from the religious to the frankly sensual: the church, the holy mysteries, festivity and marriage, nature and the life-force; the grace, liveliness and coquetry of girls; then, specifically, and by a cunning transition, Vinteuil's daughter; Marcel tries to enter by empathy into the very sense of the movement of the stamens, and finds in this the toss of the head of a 'white, careless and sprightly girl ('*fille*')'. The next sentence ostensibly changes the subject: 'M. Vinteuil had sat next to us with his daughter ('*fille*')'. By the repeated word, Mlle Vinteuil is connected with the flowers, and after the short digression on Vinteuil's modesty and shyness, hawthorns and girl return. The flowers, as Marcel leaves the church, suddenly turn from sight to perfume, the bitter-sweet smell of almonds; Marcel's fancy locates this perfume in little spots on the flowers' surface which are whiter than the rest, associates it with the taste of almond paste and with Mlle

Vinteuil's freckles, then with the imagined taste of Mlle Vinteuil's skin. From the holy mysteries we have run down a scale which ends in natural sensuality and the bite of instinct:

> For all the silence and stillness of the hawthorn, this intermittent ardour [of their perfume] was like the murmur of their intense life with which the altar buzzed like a hedgerow under the visitation of the living antennae of which the observer was reminded by certain stamens nearly red in colour which seemed to have kept the springtime virulence, the irritant power, of insects now metamorphosed into flowers.

Thus is established a scale of feeling on which Proust has learned to play at will, and the way is prepared for the main passage on the hawthorns and their association with Marcel's passion for Gilberte.

This passage is part of the section on the Méséglise way. From the beginning of the section, the impression is infused with sensuousness, with suggestions of the physically voluptuous; but this voluptuousness is idealized and caught up into the realm of poetry. Not, however, without a certain tension between the poetic and the physical, between the delight in the present sense of beauty and the pull of desire on the plane of instinct.

The first intimation of the essence of the Méséglise way is the smell of its lilacs. The leaves of the lilacs are hearts, but they are *les petits coeurs verts et frais*— little, green and all that *frais* suggests of youth, coolness and innocence. The flowers are exotic, oriental; they are minarets showing above the Gothic gable of the lodge; they are houris. But beside them the nymphs of a western spring would seem common—for the overtones of sensuality are immediately damped and modified by the suggestion that these houris are not divinized flesh as much as the figures fixed in 'bright, pure colours' by Persian miniaturists. Yet, in Marcel, the impression ends in the desire to possess, to embrace the lilacs as if they were women.

The lilacs are nearly over; from them we pass to the hawthorns, by way of the less obviously but no less deeply erotic images of the flower-fringed pool, dominated by the 'lakeside sceptre' of the gladioli, its sleeping waters 'irritated' by insects which remind the observant reader consciously and the rapid reader unconsciously of the 'springtime virulence, the irritant power, of insects now metamorphosed into flowers' attributed earlier to the scent of the hawthorns in the church. When, immediately afterwards, the main hawthorn passage begins, Proust picks up all the associations established before—the church, holy mysteries, festivity, nature, the grace and liveliness of girls. But here the idea of the transcendence of their beauty is clearly brought out. The white hawthorns, which Marcel sees first, are connected with the church; with decorated altars, stained glass windows, the traceries of the rood-loft and the window-frames. In the next paragraph comes the suggestion of a transcendent beauty of which these flowers are the obscure symbol, the intimation of a 'dimension outside life' the idea of which haunted Proust. And this ideal dimension is referred to in terms of music; the flowers are first perfume, then rhythm, then melody, with the inscrutable beauty of melody. Next, framed within Marcel's hands, they become a painting; and the lead into the passage on the pink hawthorns is a double comparison—that between the painter's sketch and the finished picture, that between a piece of music played on the piano and the same work played by an orchestra. The two comparisons are the more closely linked by the use of the word 'colour' to distinguish the richness of the orchestra from the clear tone of the piano.

The increased richness of the pink hawthorns as compared with the white is conveyed in terms of more frankly sensuous imagery. The associations Proust found in his mind during the explorations of *Jean Santeuil* are here lightly suggested, and their matter-of-factness is offset by a deprecatory irony. The pink biscuits are mentioned, and the bathos is cushioned by an indulgently slighting reference to the aesthetic values of Combray. The mature Proust is again double-sighted; aware of the emotional importance of the pink colour, aware also of the bathetic nature of its associations and that to sophisticated colour sensibilities pink is a little crude and common. He manages, subtly, to admit the validity of the memories of pink biscuits and cream cheese with strawberries crushed in it, while adopting a patronizing attitude to such naïve and materialistic associations: and this attitude, at once admiring and condescending, is extended to nature itself, 'nature which, spontaneously, had expressed [the festive intention] with the naïveté of a village shopkeeper working at a wayside altar, overloading the bush with these rosettes of too lush a pink, this provincial "pompadour".' And, from the idea of something exciting to eat in the eyes of a child, we pass to the idea of girls dressed for a ball. Just as, earlier, the transition was from the perfume of the hawthorn to the taste of Mlle Vinteuil's cheeks, here the transition is from the flowers as girls dressed in pink to Gilberte, with her reddish hair and her pink-freckled face. Just as at the beginning of the passage on the Méséglise way Marcel longed to embrace the lilacs, here he fixes on Gilberte a look in which all his senses urge the capture of her, body and soul.

All these impressions which have been linked together

are now concentrated into the image of Gilberte; her name becomes a magic talisman: everything that is mysterious in the impressions themselves is now placed within the mystery of Gilberte's unknown personality; every kind of desire, from the immediately sensual to the aspiration after the obscurely transcendent, is concentrated into the desire for Gilberte: and her name is left floating on the air, ready to be picked up, literally in mid-air, when the story of Marcel's acquaintance with Gilberte is resumed in the second volume, thus connecting the two parts of the love story with one of those links unconsciously operative before they are consciously perceived, in the use of which Proust is a conscious master.

And the last stage in the development of the hawthorn theme is a half-suggestive, half-ironic reference to *Phèdre:* Marcel, on the eve of his departure for Paris, is found by his mother embracing the hawthorns as he would have liked to embrace the lilacs, trampling his new hat and tearing his new coat as Phèdre tore off her *vains ornements*. The Phèdre suggestions move forward into the rest of the novel with the story of Marcel's passion for Gilberte and Albertine; the theme is wound up in *Albertine disparue* with an overt and detailed analogy between Phèdre and Marcel in which Proust interprets Racine's psychology in his own terms.

Thus both the 'ways' bring together impressions in which delight in the senses is both an immediate pleasure and the suggestion of a more mysterious pleasure to be attained, a transcendent pleasure with which the only communication is through the imagination. In both cases Marcel places this transcendent pleasure in a person, and the attainment of the pleasure in the future. In the case of the *côté de Guermantes,* the contribution of the imagination is greater, that of the senses less than in the case of the *côté de chez Swann*. To each of these poetic aspirations corresponds a lower reality: Marcel's longing for the Guermantes magic is paralleled by Legrandin's snobbery; his romantic love for Gilberte is paralleled by his own more grossly sensual response to the beauty of the countryside, by the lesbianism of Mlle Vinteuil and her friend, by the forward look to the time when women will be the 'interchangeable instruments of a pleasure always the same'. Like Musset, Proust was inclined to look at sexual passion with the eye of a Chamfort as well as the eye of a Rousseau.

5

SWANN

In *Un amour de Swann*, Swann steps out of Marcel's background into the foreground of the picture. The transition here is a kind of trick, a rapid glossing over of the inconvenient fact that involuntary memory can have played no part in Marcel's knowledge of Swann's past; Marcel casually mentions that, as he lay in bed— a reference, not to the *madeleine* incident which is supposed to have given rise to the vision of Combray, but to the very beginning of the novel—he used to think of what others had told him of Swann's past. Many critics have complained of this interruption of the narrative of Marcel's life, the dislocation of the chronology, the shift of attention from one person to another. The fact is, of course, that to Proust Swann and Marcel were intimately linked. They are related in much the same way as the novelist C. and Jean Santeuil are related, though with some relations reversed. Proust had snatched success out of the jaws of frustration: Marcel is the successful self, Swann the frustrated self. The things which distinguish Swann from Marcel are just those things which marked Proust's progress from sterility to productiveness. Between *Jean Santeuil* and *A la recherche,* Proust seems to have conceived the plan of telling his whole story as a biography of Swann in the third person: at that stage, the love affair of Jean Santeuil and Françoise was transferred to Swann. Whether Swann was to be successful or no we do not know; but eventually he was kept to serve as a foil to Marcel.

The temperamental affinities between Swann and Marcel are more than hinted at in the first volume; but if Swann, like Marcel, is based on Proust's knowledge of himself, he is also modelled, as we saw earlier, on other real people, chiefly Charles Haas.

Swann's gifts of sensibility are similar to Marcel's. He is open to sensuous beauty and keenly aware of sensual pleasure. Both work their way into the world of the Faubourg Saint-Germain without the advantages of birth and connection. Both suffer from a spiritual decline, a loss of aspiration, of devotion to an ideal beauty. Both are re-awakened from their spiritual torpor by the music of Vinteuil; but Swann is given only a partial and ineffectual reminder of the transcendent world, the dimension outside life; Marcel is given the full revelation which enables him to overcome the defects of character which make Swann a failure: hedonism, passivity, intellectual inertia, self-centredness. Marcel learns to transmute the 'impressions' provided by his sensibility into their 'spiritual equivalent'; Swann is a hedonist content with the passive enjoyment of whatever the chance of life provides. Marcel, by intellectual effort, understands his own suffering and the recurring pattern of his loves; Swann is obtuse and intellectually lazy, and *bears* his love affairs passively as outbreaks of an undiagnosed disease. Marcel willingly undertakes the painful effort of writing as an act of spiritual devotion and a sacrifice for the sake of mankind; Swann is mean in spirit and more than once behaves with a certain *muflerie*. Marcel sees the frivolity of high life and becomes an ascetic in order to write his book; Swann's ambition is reduced to that of introducing his daughter into the Guermantes circle. His attempts at creativity go no further than works like his little book on Vermeer, and he dies frustrated and unrealized. The parallel between Swann and Marcel is not blatant, but to the attentive reader it is pointed with precision.

From the moment when the conception of the novel took the form of the spiritual autobiography of a successful artist, Proust had left behind him a whole phase of his life, a phase marked by guilt and frustration: one can say perhaps that the leftovers of this phase are worked into the story of Swann, who, artistically speaking, misses salvation. He is given the destiny marked out for Proust by his friends and critics in the nineties —that of a dilettante. The phases of his love affair with Odette are almost exactly the phases of Marcel's; but he marries his mistress instead of art. *Un amour de Swann*, then, is tied in to the main structure; but it and the main structure could do without each other. It could have stood as a novel on its own: the rest of the book could have followed on without it. But as now arranged, the two are linked by innumerable cross-references connected with Swann, Odette and the Verdurins, and the foundations of the social history theme are laid in this part of the book; after which the emphasis shifts back to Marcel's spiritual autobiography.

In the Combray section Proust has set up the imaginative structures of the two passions which are to meet the check of reality. In Part III of *Du côté de chez Swann* he makes ready to introduce the theme of the disparity between imagination and reality explicitly, at first on a small scale. Having built up the complicated poetries of Oriane and Gilberte, he turns to the simpler images and associations of a number of place names, one of which is Balbec. These mental entities also are to meet the check of material reality. In the first plan of the book, the section called 'Place Names: the Name' was to be followed almost immediately by another called 'Place Names: the Place'. In the cutting and transposing made necessary by the inordinate size of the first projected volume, the original *Swann's Way*, and the redistribution and expansion which took place during the war, the second of the two titles disappeared. It is in *A l'ombre des jeunes filles* that the real Balbec comes to disturb Marcel's preconceptions.

Having set up the properties for this sequence near the end of the new *Swann's Way*, Proust returns immediately to the earlier sequence connected with his passion for Gilberte. And the continuity of this resumption with the earlier section is achieved with miraculous effect by a simple expedient, that of picking up Gilberte's name where, in the first part, it was left: floating in the air—of the Champs-Élysées, now, instead of the Tansonville garden. The correspondences between the two passages—of reflective comment, imagery, even phrasing—are striking; it is as though Proust were deliberately knotting the new thread on to the old— as, no doubt, he was.

Thus we begin the story of the reality of Marcel's love for Gilberte, which takes us over into *A l'ombre des jeunes filles*. The imagined Gilberte is detached from the real Gilberte and perishes, though ready for rebirth in a new shape and in connection with another girl. The imagined Bergotte is also detached from the real Bergotte. After the extinction of Marcel's love for Gilberte comes the journey to Balbec, and the imagined Balbec is detached from the real.

But these successive examples of the gulf between imagination and reality are not monotonous or uniform. If, in some cases, the reality is a dead weight of disillusion, in others there is a recovery. For instance, Marcel has romantic and sentimental notions of how charity, envy and justice should be represented in human form by a painter; when he sees Giotto's Virtues and Vices for the first time they seem to bear no relation to what they are supposed to represent—they are too solid, real and earthy to connect with his high-flown emotions. Later he comes to understand that their effectiveness as artistic expression lies in their very earthiness, their physical immediacy. Marcel goes to Balbec and is disappointed in its church and its sea until Elstir opens his eyes to their real beauty and significance. He goes to see La Berma play Phèdre, and is merely depressed by his own incapacity to be moved, until Bergotte has closed his mind both to his own irrelevant expectations and the would-be appreciative but equally irrelevant comments of Norpois.

In these cases, the sense of disillusion arises from a maladjustment which is to be blamed as much on a naïve imagination as on a defective reality, and to be corrected by the maturing of sensibility and understanding. Thus the older Marcel is able to trace the real connections between Bergotte the man and Bergotte the artist which, to his younger self, were at first invisible; and at the last he is able to see how art can achieve, in recorded contemplation, those states of mind which can finally satisfy the aspirations felt in childhood as a continuous upspringing of passionate expectation.

6

THE ARTISTS

To convey his own notions about art and to show how these ideas were gradually and, at first, obscurely planted in Marcel's mind Proust invented four artists. In fact, he invented a great many; but those responsible for Marcel's education are Bergotte the novelist, Elstir the painter, Vinteuil the musician and La Berma the actress. In the case of these as of other characters in the novel we can look for, and find, originals; but in their case it is more interesting to look for the originals of their works. As characters, they fit into the pattern of Proustian society, but their human interest is slight. As people they have the transparency of their premeditated meaning; it is on their works that Proust lavishes his creative effort; their works become for the reader dense, familiar and real. Bergotte's we know only in fragments, since we never really get inside the covers of the one work of his which is mentioned by name, the pamphlet on Racine; but Elstir's 'Port de Carquethuit' is almost as real to us as if we had seen it, and many of us are almost convinced we have heard Vinteuil's sonata and septet— perhaps that these are the loveliest things we have ever heard, which is at once ironic and tantalizing when we remember Proust's letter to Jacques de Lacretelle: 'The "little phrase" of the sonata is . . . the charming but infinitely mediocre phrase of a sonata for piano and violin by Saint-Saëns, a musician I don't like.' The passages on the 'little phrase' are based on the memory of a scrap of Saint-Saëns which *had once* moved Proust as the 'little phrase' in the novel moves Swann; but to this original impression Proust added others more recent and circumstantial—of fragments of *Parsifal* and *Lohengrin*, Franck's sonata and 'something of Schubert'. As finally presented, the account of Vinteuil's music is an attempt to concentrate Proust's sense of the very essence of music, felt in the mode of his time and interpreted according to the ideas of his time, ideas which he absorbed from sources as distinct as George Eliot and Schopenhauer.

Marcel's sense of vocation begins, naturally enough, with reading. In *Jean Santeuil*, reading is a pleasure which has to be defended against the pressures of a more active world; in *A la recherche* it is a part of the accepted ritual of paradise. True, Marcel's grandmother attempts to dislodge Marcel from the shuttered bedroom into which the disembodied essence of summer filters with the rays of sunlight and the sound of Camus's hammering away at his packing-cases, as the disembodied essence of travel reaches the narrator with the whistling of trains in the first pages of the novel, and the essence of the life of Balbec is to come to him behind the curtains of the Grand Hotel as he lies in bed, withdrawn, irresponsible and free to select and interpret sensation as his imagination wills; but grandmother's passion for fresh air has already been placed in the category of things to be laughed at and laughed away, and the vast hooded chair in the garden provides the essential amenities of inwardness combined with nearness to the concrete sensations of reality. This is Proust's ideal situation, the situation which his own style, 'poeticizing the real without transforming it', reflects.

But this 'poeticizing' itself is, in a sense, a transformation of the real; the real has to be filtered, concentrated and finally translated into language, into *cosa mentale*. Here, in these summer afternoons spent with books, withdrawal is a condition of the filtering and concentration of summer: 'The cool darkness of my room was to the full sunlight in the street as the shadow is to the sunbeam, just as luminous, that is, and offered my imagination the whole spectacle of summer which my senses, had I been out walking, could only have enjoyed in fragments.

For Proust, eventually, withdrawal into the cork-lined room is to be the condition of the filtering and concentration of his life. On the selected and concentrated substance intellect and imagination are to work, expressing, but also embroidering and heightening. Here, at Combray, the embroidering and heightening are provided by the books Marcel reads. Against the background of the withdrawn mind, blank except for its sensuous well-being, situate nowhere but at the heart of summer, are to be enacted the events of mind-made worlds. These ideal realities, for Marcel, are the familiar ones, and from the consciousness of them he looks out almost as a stranger upon the concrete details of the summer scene from which his own mind has abstracted the essence. Between observed reality and his mind there is always an opaque film.

The first lesson, then, is that the writer's purpose is to create a kind of reality which, because it is mental in its nature, the mind can assimilate. The writer's first step, moreover, must be to detach his creation from life as it is lived. Real people are as opaque as real things; the real emotions of other people can only reach us through an intermediary—Proust writes 'through an image', but what he means includes, no doubt, all the means of the language of art, which he is later to discuss in terms of metaphor. These images, unlike the emotions of real people, can become as meaningful as the images of our own dreams; the emotions they awaken, like the emotions of dreams, are in fact amplified beyond anything we experience in life; they can be modulated at a speed beyond the resources of life, and therefore can show us truths about our own life whose truth we could not otherwise have felt—for instance, that our 'heart', our very way of feeling and desiring, changes, but too slowly, in life, for us to notice it. Here, in fact, Proust is modelling a general idea into a particular shape, coaxing it into a form which will be seen to correspond directly with one of the characteristics of his own book.

He goes on to say that if people, in the novels Marcel reads, are at once unlike the real people one knows but significant of the essence of humanity, the landscapes they live in are different in quality from any Marcel knows at Combray, and seem to be a part of nature itself. What Marcel does not realize, at this stage (for in these passages on art, more obviously than in the rest of the novel, we are in the presence of two Marcels: the younger, amassing observations but only dimly understanding them, and the older who has finally come to understand and is explaining the younger man's observations as he presents them), is that the human experience he reads about seems to him more significant than his own, the landscapes more essential than his familiar ones, not because the characters are people of a kind he does not know, the landscapes of a kind he has not seen, but because they are being presented by an artist who has made their significance perceptible. At this stage, in fact, Marcel is prepared to (and will later) make the same mistake as Emma Bovary: to believe that there are people it would be as thrilling to know as to read his favourite books, places as satisfyingly beautiful as description. Later Marcel, like Flaubert himself, will maintain that these delights are never to be found except in the mind, never to be achieved objectively except in style, which is a record of mind and a means of communication with other minds. This analogy, already referred to, is perhaps worth pursuing here, for it illuminates not only the intentions of Flaubert and Proust but a whole region of romantic assumptions about the relationship between life and art.

Flaubert, like Proust, was intimately related to the chief character of his best book, *Mme Bovary*. 'Emma Bovary is myself.' Like Proust also, he approached this character in a spirit of detached and critical analysis. But the relationship is not quite the same in both cases. Emma Bovary is, in a sense, an incomplete artist like Swann. She is infinitely more crude in her tastes, ideas and feelings than Swann is, but she is a creature who experiences life through senses keenly alive and with a vivid imagination. She is Flaubert's 'lower self', the self which throve on the sensationalism and imaginative debauchery of romantic literature. 'I too', wrote Flaubert, 'have lived on my nerves . . . and like a convict I still bear the brand of it.' Flaubert shows how, at her convent, Emma's imagination was stimulated and nourished by romantic literature. She reads *Paul et Virginie* and imagines herself living their pure and innocent love, their idyllic passion combined with sentimental morality and modesty amounting to prudery. She also identifies herself with the great heroines of history, particularly with those who led a wild life before becoming heroines or nuns. She enjoys the mysticity of the religious life without any genuine religious feeling. She loves church for the sake of the flowers, and enjoys confession. On

Sundays Chateaubriand's *Génie du Christianisme* is read aloud; Emma is moved by Chateaubriand's romantic melancholy, and develops a longing for tempestuous seas and ruins. In Chateaubriand's prose she is aware not of its artistry but of its power of awakening strong emotions; and she seeks these emotions for their own sake. Later, after the disappointment of her marriage and the first abortive love affair with Léon, we see that Emma's mind is either full of imagined satisfactions or (as Flaubert says) empty as a disused attic. The rhythm of her progressive disenchantment is constant: a mind full of vivid images and expectations, an attempt to find these imagined pleasures in life, disappointment and disillusion or frustration and deflation, a mind empty and cold, the refilling of the mind with new images. What Emma was incapable of learning, as Flaubert shows her to be, was the essential lesson which Flaubert believed himself to have learned; that the imagination can never find, in life, the equal of its imagining. As Baudelaire put it, in this world 'action is not the twin of dream'. Flaubert wrote in one of his letters that he had found a great truth: that wine has a taste unknown to those who drink it. 'Happiness lies in the idea, and nowhere else.' And this 'idea', which satisfies the imagination and brings repose to the mind, can only be achieved and fixed in literature, through style. 'From form the idea is born.'

The correspondences between Flaubert-Emma and Marcel the older-Marcel the younger are fairly easy to see. Marcel, until Bergotte reveals to him the meaning of style, makes mistakes about the enjoyment of literature comparable to Emma's, though never quite as crude. Like Flaubert, he came to see true satisfaction for his own spirit only in the spiritualization of sensuous experience through adequate expression, through style.

True, this spiritualization is always associated with the pastness and recovery through memory of what is spiritualized; but he might have taken Flaubert's belief that 'wine has a taste unknown to those who drink it' and restated it in his own terms: perhaps 'life has pleasures unknown to those who live it'. True, between *Mme Bovary* and *A la recherche* comes the philosophy of Bergson, and Proust was prepared to suggest in *Le Temps retrouvé* that our spiritual awareness of life itself might be more acute and pleasurable if only the intelligence could be prevented from schematizing and desiccating the rich pulp of experience with which it has no business to concern itself; but the rich pulp itself, as Proust presents it, is almost purely sensuous. What has to be abstracted from experience to leave artistically transmutable 'impressions' is not only the utilitarian function of intelligence but the whole mechanism of moral responsibility—except the moral responsibility of the artist, engaged in the service of the amorally aesthetic. 'Aesthetic' here tends towards the narrowness of its etymology; and this is the sign of a spiritual limitation which deepens where it narrows, which produces a fictional world of unparalleled vividness from which so much of humanity is missing. In Flaubert and Proust we have writers assessing their experience in two modes, the lyrical and the pessimistically critical, and reconciling these two modes in novels reflecting the peculiar tensions, the irony, the sense of grotesque incompatibilities to which the two modes give rise.

The ideas contained in Marcel's first and other lessons, abstracted from Proust's narrative, appear nowadays to be platitudes; and in Proust's own day, if not quite the common currency they have become, they were already well handled and familiar to people who followed the aesthetic speculation of the century. But the narrative itself never loses its enchantment. Though its ostensible object is to lead us from observations about the pleasures of reading towards acceptance of conclusions to be clinched and interrelated in *Le Temps retrouvé*, when we return from a critical appraisal of Proust's ideas to the narrative (and others of the same kind) we return to the very essence of a pleasure; here, the pleasure of reading—at least a certain kind of pleasure we have all known in reading, and perhaps one which we may feel, with some regret, to be behind us. If we do, we shall find that Proust is still with us and has anticipated our judgment. For if Proust sometimes allows his desire to make art into an absolute to lead him into evasive tactics, he is at least honest when he does not evade. Art is made to the measure of mind, but Proust knows also that mind must be made to the measure of the kind of art it is to enjoy, and that if the immature mind misses the pleasures offered by, say, Stendhal, the mature mind misses the full glamour of the *Arabian Nights*. Part of Proust's ambition, in fact, is to create a work which will offer the mature mind the pleasures of both. But if Marcel read as he did, and aspired as he did to a future bright with the hope of what he read, it was, the narrator suggests, because he was not only less sophisticated but richer in potentialities than the narrator. There is in the narrator (and in Proust) a self who would give all the works of art in the world in exchange for these naïve dreams. At his moments of greatest frankness Proust is inclined to admit that art is not absolute, but only less relative than life, that the maturing of taste itself means loss as well as gain. Marcel will lose his capacity to enjoy Bergotte, will eventually fail to find in the enjoyment of any book the conviction that appears to be its own guarantee of value. His final word will be that books are only means of reading within oneself; that in certain states of the self there is nothing to read, and then books are useless; that there are certain parts of the self that no other man's book is adequate to make legible, and then one must write one's own; that, even then, there is in the true self an incommunicable residue. But this egotistic relativity, loyal to the detail of Proust's observation of his own experience, is constantly jarring with the wish to prove that art is absolute, that the 'ideas' which art reveals are not only intimately personal but also drawn from a common fund of universally valid 'ideas', and with the ambition to write the book which will be a universal instrument for all minds.

The first passage on reading in *Swann* leads almost immediately to Marcel's discovery of Bergotte and, through Bergotte, of the pleasure of style. Not until the end of his progress will Marcel realize that all other literary pleasures—including those of emotions and landscapes —depend on style; but already he realizes that through style literature becomes, instead of that pleasurable anticipation of what is to happen next which is, after all, too like the contingencies of living, a pleasure realized, held, and deepening rather than changing: a constant present. His notion of style is still insufficient; his mind separates, in Bergotte's works, the passages where 'style' is in the foreground from the narrative proper; he begins to prefer style to story and to mistake affectation for distinction. The style of Bergotte as Proust writes of it here is (as comparison with *Jean Santeuil* shows) compounded of the pseudo-archaic pomposity which Proust remembered enjoying in books which he later outgrew, like *Le Capitaine Fracasse,* and the more pretentious and sentimental phrases of Leconte de Lisle and Ruskin; it is the kind of style admiration for which makes literary-minded schoolboys speak as Bloch does and Proust once did. But the comparative crudity of the style which attracted the young Proust by its very extravagance is only forced on our attention when, with the aid of *Jean Santeuil* and some of Proust's early letters, we work back from *A la recherche* to the reality. Here we are given the boy's sense of adventure and discovery at the opening up of a fresh pleasure, intense enough to call for all the psalmody of heaven for its expression. Here, for the first time since the *madeleine* incident, the narrator speaks of a 'privileged moment' of plenitude and freedom. From that time onward Marcel feels every image of Bergotte to be a revelation; through Bergotte's style he feels for the first time the beauty of the things Bergotte writes of—forests, hail, *Notre-Dame de Paris, Athalie* and *Phèdre*. Some of Bergotte's 'revelations' correspond to Marcel's own 'discoveries'; occasionally he finds his own way of seeing things reflected in Bergotte's. In this Proust places the germ of Marcel's belief that he may be a born writer.

When, in *A l'ombre des jeunes filles*, Marcel meets Elstir, the latter's works take over the progressive education of Marcel in the Proustian aesthetic where Bergotte's left off. Albert Feuillerat has pointed out, after examining the proofs of the pre-war unprinted edition of this part of the book, that most of the account of the main Elstir episode was added as an afterthought; yet the ideas it conveys fit most wonderfully into the existing structure and improve both the pattern and the coherence. Again they are selected for a special purpose. It is useless to expect from Proust a complete aesthetic of painting or even of Impressionism, which is the kind of painting Proust obviously has in mind here. He is concerned to stress his favourite points; to use some very particular observations on painting to support his view of literature and to suggest, at the same time, that his view of literature fits into a comprehensive view of all modes of art. In fact, this more lately elaborated passage supports the main conclusions of *Le Temps retrouvé* in greater detail than the passages on Vinteuil and music, many of which belong to the period when Proust's general plan was not clear enough to force its pattern on experience. In writing of Elstir's painting Proust knows more exactly what he is trying to demonstrate, and the evidence is marshalled and presented accordingly. Elstir is often said to be based on the French impressionist painters, and different critics favour different names; what is too often forgotten—though it has been clearly enough demonstrated—is that much of the material of this episode is worked up from suggestions Proust noted in his study of Ruskin. Behind his comments we can see Ruskin's writing on mediaeval architecture, Ruskin's remarks on Turner, and Turner's remarks as reported by Ruskin or by Robert de la Sizeranne who wrote a book introducing Ruskin's 'religion of beauty' to the French. But Proust has shorn away whatever his critical intelligence rejected, and cut the remainder to his own requirement.

The first lesson Elstir's work teaches (though again it is only the older Marcel who has absorbed it and can formulate it clearly) is that painting is not the imitation of nature but the *metamorphosis* of nature. This links with the lesson to be drawn from Bergotte's writing that literature is not a transcription but a transformation and reordering of life. Proust drives home his point by stating that Elstir's metamorphoses are analogous to the metaphors of writing; in his 'Port de Carquethuit' land is painted in terms of sea, sea in terms of land. Each element appears, in this novel perspective, to have invaded the other. The intelligence knows this interfusion of the elements to be false as representation, but in its

95

misrepresentation lies its artistic effectiveness; its truth is of an unintellectual order; it is the truth of the impression. Not only is the impression *felt* as clarity and truth, distinct from the opaqueness and puzzlement of nature; it is also felt as *unity*, distinct from natural diversity and incoherence.

Again these ideas, abstracted from their concrete expression are seen to be the common currency of Proust's contemporaries; easily translatable, for instance, into the main tenets of Baudelaire's theory of correspondences, though reticent about metaphysical sanctions. But, unlike Baudelaire and the Symbolists, Proust is always anxious to preserve the status of intelligence and its operations in art. So Elstir's work, like Proust's, is made to exhibit laws as well as register impressions; his paintings show intellectual discernment as well as irrational sensibility. Not only do they make use of novel perspective to suggest a fruitful misrepresentation of reality; they force the scrutinizing intellect to acknowledge that the *apparent* misrepresentation is such as might be *observed* in reality if the observer chose the same point of vantage as Elstir; and thus, concludes Proust, they enlighten the observer about the laws of perspective. Here, however, we see signs of the strain and special pleading which appear whenever Proust attempts to unite his irrational transcendentalism and his intellectualism in a single conception. For the objections to the 'metaphor' analogy which arise from the outset—for instance that no painting achieves its effect merely, if at all, by novel perspective, that the unity of a picture is brought about by modifications of reality belonging to the painter's idea, as much as to his vantage-point and that his idea, if it is subject to any laws, obeys laws of personal psychology rather than of perspective—objections to which the reader has perhaps paid little attention because they seemed irrelevant to Proust's demonstration, now oppose the very union of ideas which Proust is trying to bring about. Proust's novel exhibits 'laws' which our intelligence can abstract because Proust has consciously and intelligently worked them into it; but there are other great novels, and certainly great paintings, which do not. We have to read Proust's aesthetic not as disinterested speculation but as a compromise between disinterested speculation and the kind of artistic creation to which Proust found himself suited. Reduced to plain language, what Proust is saying is this: our most valuable spiritual experiences are the result of illusions about objective reality; art can do two things —record and perpetuate the valuable illusions and make clear the laws according to which such illusions arise in the mind. The potentiality of the spiritual experiences can only be situated in the self; yet this potentiality can only, it seems, be realized by projecting itself into objects outside the self which are then pursued with a passion which *appears* to be directed towards qualities in the object. The artist, instead of passionately *pursuing* the object, makes use of it, translates it into the language of his art—the style of painting or of literature—and thus captures and holds for ever the values of which, through the object, he has become aware.

Provided we allow Proust to limit our own speculation where he will and to select his evidence, we can appreciate the ingenuity with which he constructs his ideas into his system and, above all, the subtlety with which he presents them. For instance, Marcel comes across a portrait whose charm seems to be in its subject rather than in Elstir's 'metamorphosis' of it. Does this mean that things (or people) really can possess a charm other than that with which the artist's mind endows them? The suggestion conflicts with Proust's 'subjective idealism'. We like to believe that such things can exist, he says, because we are natural materialists. But reason combats the belief. There the subject is dropped, the problem left suspended. Later the solution is given, but we have to discover for ourselves that it *is* the solution, for it is propounded in another context. Marcel meets Mme Elstir. He sees a correspondence between her type of beauty and the style of Elstir's early paintings and realizes that Elstir has fallen in love with her because she represents a ready-made plastic expression, provided by nature, for the inner, personal ideals for which, until he met her, Elstir had had to discover his own plastic equivalents. There, then, is Proust's answer: nature sometimes provides the forms which our own ideals require for their expression. All this is an ingenious and fascinating way of making Marcel 'discover' that beauty is in the eye of the beholder and that the beauty of nature can be given a place, in Proust's aesthetic based on 'subjective idealism', which is properly subordinate to the beauty of art. Not only is the main passage on Elstir more closely adapted to the theoretical account of Marcel's own novel as it is given in *Le Temps retrouvé* than either the Bergotte or the Vinteuil material; it is also thinner in texture and more frankly expository. Proust is thinking more and feeling less. He is working on comparatively recent layers of feeling; the roots of his meditations on reading and music are growing strongly in *Jean Santeuil,* but painting as yet shows no signs of awakening a comparable interest.

There was in Proust a nostalgia for an absolute sanction for art, but his intellectual scepticism made it increasingly difficult for him to accept any philosophy which could provide it. His mind revolved like many nineteenth-century minds round the notion of transcendent 'ideas'. In *Jean Santeuil* the work of the novelist Traves expresses 'ideas' which 'no doubt had their home in heaven', ideas which find their way into his work in spite of the materialism and scepticism of Traves's consciously held philosophy. Jean Santeuil himself professes a kind of idealism which seems as eclectic and vague as Victor Cousin's but is obviously attached to experiences of Proust's which contained a true sense of devotion to overriding value. This same vaguely Platonic idealism permeates Proust's account of Vinteuil's music in *A la recherche*; like the literature of the nineteenth century according to Jean Santeuil, it is 'the expression of the mysterious truths which were for him the only truth'. To music, the most privileged and quintessential of all the arts according to the Symbolists and the philosophers dear to the Symbolists, Proust eventually accorded its privilege. But he found it more intractable than impressionist painting when he came to the task of presenting it in such a way that it could fit and support his explanation and justification of his own novel. So the older Proust gathered and concentrated the century's literary and philosophical account of music, which at one point he had been prepared to make his own, turned it into a concrete experience elaborated round a remembered experience of his own, the phrase of Saint-Saëns, and ascribed the philosophical commentary to Swann. 'Swann took musical themes to be real ideas, of another world, another order . . .' Proust could thus draw on whatever ideas he needed to characterize and reinforce the impression of the music, without intellectually committing himself to those ideas. The comments which he takes upon himself are more guarded: Swann, they suggest, was fundamentally right, but a little credulous in the detail of his account. He was, in fact, nearer the truth then than after his marriage, when music lost all value for him except as a sen-

99

sation reminding him of his own past (this personal valuation of the mnemonic effect of music above its intrinsic expressive contents, in *Jean Santeuil*, precedes the recognition of the Saint-Saëns fragment as at once recording and transcending the experience of Jean Santeuil's love for Françoise, the prototype of Swann's for Odette. Once more Proust is attributing to Swann's state of spiritual apathy an attitude he had himself adopted before he saw the light).

When, in *La Prisonnière*, Marcel himself takes over the commentary on Vinteuil's music, his emphasis is different. In *Swann*, Vinteuil is shown to have captured 'invisible ideas' which are the common spiritual heritage of humanity; in *La Prisonnière*, Vinteuil's ideas are 'irreducibly individual'; each artist's ideas come from a heaven, but each artist has his own heaven. It is useless, here, to look for a philosophy. Proust is simply stating his conviction of the transcendence, universality and uniqueness of the work of every great artist. These were things he had felt, and perceived more sharply when he read, in *Sesame and Lilies*, Ruskin's statement that beauty is an absolute existing outside individuals though perceived by each artist in an irreducibly individual form. He might equally have found the paradox implied in Baudelaire's *Salons*; Baudelaire, too, claimed that beauty is eternal and absolute but expressed by every age and country in its own way. Or he might have found the same idea in Hegel. Neglecting the background, we might judge that the first account of Vinteuil's music was Platonic, the second Bergsonian. In fact, the paradox itself is part of the thinking of the nineteenth century. The metaphysical trimmings are vehicles for the expression of aspects of the experience of works of art; the experiences are recognizable, but the comment takes us nowhere. Philosophically Proust, in the last event, is as puzzled as we are, though in his early volumes he has provided a wonderfully suggestive psychological account of the way in which the mysterious values to which Marcel is devoted first crystallized in the depths of his mind.

The philosophical discomfort is most apparent in *Le Temps retrouvé*; it is a carefully prepared explosion which sputters a little as if the powder were damp. The preparation for the final blaze is magnificent; Marcel touches the rock-bottom of disillusion and goes through a dark night of the soul, until a series of chance sensations open up visions of his own past which carry with them the sense of plenitude and freedom he had sometimes previously known but never explored or exploited. But after the first vigorous movement the rhythm flags. The long meditation on literature and art is sometimes confused in exposition, repetitive in its ideas and even in the very sentences which express them.

Some of this is accounted for by the lack of revision, since Proust died before he could prepare the end of his novel for the press. But there is another reason; the very difficulty of picking up all the statements about art made throughout the novel, accounting for every feature of the novel itself, relating these two sets of ideas, and showing how this complicated system was revealed to Marcel as the result of involuntary memory. Proust's efforts reveal the most astonishing intellectual resourcefulness, but he does not always play fairly. He shifts his viewpoint and changes his terms of reference without warning; there is a good deal of intellectual sleight-of-hand and more than a suspicion of sham profundity. The reader finds his feet caught in tangled coils of explanation when he should be flying; he may feel inclined to wish that Proust had been less anxious to explain. In matters aesthetic, Proust is always least authentic in abstraction; it is the impressions of real experience, or based on real experience, which are convincing and perennially fresh.

But even the intellectual conjuring tricks are stimulating and challenging, and they have been prompted by a genuine sense of correspondences which even Proust's intelligence has not been able to make manifest as clear intellectual relations; correspondences between that aspect of the expressive power of painting which Impressionism isolated and concentrated and that aspect of the expressive power of language which Symbolism isolated and concentrated; correspondences between language, so specialized, and music; correspondences between the kind of lyricism which Symbolism selected from the romantic range and the kind Proust experienced through involuntary memory; the importance to this specialized symbolist language of the fusion metaphor. All these offer problems enough; but to those problems which belong to the fashionable speculation of his age Proust added others. Where Mallarmé, for instance, was content to depreciate all poetry which did not fit his own aesthetic as diluted and debased, Proust, infinitely more catholic in his appreciation of literature than most of his contemporaries, was looking for an aesthetic which could comprehend Classicism as well as Romanticism, memoirs as well as poetry. The range of his speculation is such that he may be forgiven some confusion. It is as well to recognize that any full account of the power of literature would have to take note of factors to which he, as well as his contemporaries, was blind; but he had the courage and independence, in an age of literature almost entirely devoted to the exploration of feeling and the exercise of imaginative freedom, to recognize that intellectual power is an asset even for the artist, and that we ought to be able to look to art for understanding as well as rapture.

7

FREE FANTASIA

Proust's account of Marcel's vocation as the expression of ideals realized in impressions and of ideas reflecting the understanding of laws governing human behaviour left him free to construct a fiction which is not only the creation of a subjectivity but the creation and explanation of the world in which that subjectivity exists. Proust's theory was based on aesthetic ideas produced by the romantic tradition to account for and assure the philosophical prestige of the kind of lyrical ecstasy which Baudelaire called 'rapture of the soul'. Baudelaire felt something of the mystery and wonderment which he associated with the supernatural when he read Balzac's novels as well as when he read the more romantic poems of Gautier, and thought of both writers as *voyants,* as revealers of a transcendent world. Flaubert, concerned with his own purely literary, metaphysically agnostic kind of transcendence, proclaimed that happiness lay in the 'idea' of satisfactions rather than in the achievement of satisfactions in experience, that the 'idea' was to be realized by literary style, and that ideally he would like to write a novel which had no plot and no characters, nothing but style. But he admitted that this kind of 'pure' novel was a chimera, just as Proust had to admit his kind of 'pure' novel was a chimera. If we think of the larger conception of style, the style of which plot, character, and style in the narrower sense are all part, then the style of *Madame Bovary* is the equivalent of an 'idea'; Flaubert has achieved a means of holding certain regions of experience in the mind in a satisfactory way. This notion of 'style' however is applicable to any work of art, irrespective of the importance given to 'style' in the narrower sense, the sense in which we say that Gide is a stylist, or that Flaubert took pains over his style which Balzac did not. Running through the century, we find the concern with style in the narrower sense, from a moment marked approximately by Hugo's essay proclaiming that 'the nature belongs to style'; and within this current of speculation on style we find a continuing preoccupation with metaphor (not restricted to France, and coeval with Romanticism in all its manifestations throughout Europe) and with the belief that the experience of the transcendental in literature arises from the fusion, in metaphor, of logically disparate elements; that the Idea arises from the imaginative fusion of ideas which, naturally, are related in such a way that reason is incapable of apprehending the significance of that relation. Baudelaire, whose theory of correspondences centres on such a notion of the metaphor, could admit Balzac to the company of *voyants* unreflectingly. Reason, for him, always went down in matters artistic before intuition. He had little tendency to dilate on technical problems, and little occasion to dwell on problems specific to the novel. He was not hag-ridden by the kind of scepticism which made Proust test the ideas that won his emotional assent against his own intelligence, and made him finally condemn Ruskin for intellectual dishonesty. Proust must both have felt and partly understood what linked his own sensibility with Baudelaire's, Emerson's, Ruskin's and others like them; he must have looked in the philosophers he read (or read about) for a more complete theory, and found many variations or alternatives all centred on oneirism and transcendence, the subconscious, the subrational, dream, instinct, intuition; and states of consciousness which could be called beauty, a consciousness of plenitude, freedom and devotion. Proust seems to have accepted, from all sides, observations of detail which fitted his own experience, but rejected all systems with sceptical irony. His own attempt at an aesthetic, richly suggestive and stimulating in the detail of its own observations, is disappointing as a system; most suggestive in the course of the novel where it applies itself to a number of independent subjects, most disappointing in *Le Temps retrouvé* where all the fragments of explanation ought to be brought together into a system to provide the key to Marcel's vocation. Proust had set himself an enormous problem. He had to adapt the interrelated ideas of Baudelaire, Emerson, Ruskin and so on to his own case, which meant refusing a too-easy reliance on the idea of supernatural revelation, attempting to give a 'rational' explanation without falling back on religion and an after-life (here Bergson, with his importation of the eternal within time, within the limits of human life, had hints to offer), bringing 'memory' and not 'vision' into the centre of the picture, and adapting to prose style a theory of metaphor first applied to poetry. Proust had also to extend the symbolist aesthetic to cover aspects of his work which had manifestly nothing to do with dreams, visions and revelations, and he could do it only by grafting on to it a quite distinct and even alien claim for the artistic importance of intellectual understanding.

This 'aesthetic' is a kind of trick. But having performed it tolerably, Proust was free to include in his novel the most varied presentations of experience and attitudes to experience. When the foundations of the book's structure had been laid, and the two pillars of the first and last volumes constructed, Proust was left with a good deal of liberty in the elaboration of the superstructure; whatever he found it interesting to add could be tied in to the relevant supports, or even carried as inessential ornament on the components which did carry the architectural stresses.

Proust made full use of this freedom. The progress from the formlessness of *Jean Santeuil* to the organic structure of *A la recherche* involved first selection and pruning of the autobiographical material until the main stems were growing in the right direction. Marcel's personality was to be shown rooted in childhood impressions, and these impressions had to be concentrated, reinforced, stylized; the movements of the imagination had to be centred in dominant symbols. Fantasy had to be disciplined within the bounds of the demonstration. The stages of Marcel's spiritual growth had to be clearly marked, the climax carefully prepared. But once this discipline was accomplished, Proust was free to embroider at will, and he embroidered so lavishly that his plan was all but obscured for any but his most attentive readers. During the war years, when the publication of the book was held up, the matter proliferated steadily, as it had done from the moment of its planning, but now there was no printer to arrest the process.

In *Le Temps retrouvé*, at a moment when Proust is least philosophical, least bound by the need to fit his comment on his own work into a metaphysical demonstration, he compares his book to a cathedral, a frock pinned together piece by piece, and one of Françoise's best dishes, the *boeuf mode* so much appreciated by Norpois. All those images are suggestive and revealing. The book is planned as a cathedral must be planned,

planned as a shrine to the religion of art, as a monument piled up by the past and a means of recovery of the past's spirituality. But it was not built as a cathedral must be built, stone on stone; it was put together as a designer puts together a frock, pinning his ornaments on the first drape and standing back to look at the effect. And the parts fitted into the whole were chosen as the best of their kind. Just as Françoise chose the best meat for her *boeuf mode*, Proust chose the best and most interesting experiences of a rich if inwardly bitter life. Yet something must be added to these images to complete the picture. As Proust wrote and added he had less and less of rich and strange impressions to draw on, and more and more of shrewd, detached observation. He could remake the magic of Combray, with a great creative effort, by supplementing memory and imagination with Gaston Bonnier's *Flora*; he could ask his women friends to bring out their old hats and frocks to help out remembered atmospheres with descriptive fact; but much more easily could he move on occasions from his cork-lined room into the still active outside world and, turning his developed and specialized vision on to the social antics from which he had now withdrawn, add incident after incident, fresco after fresco to the human comedy whose vanity points up the drama and reward of artistic vocation. And so, more and more, the aspects of the book which are tied into the fundamental structure by the thinnest stays, or resting merely on its surface, were developed in their own right, for their own intrinsic interest. In a narrative stretched over half a century, half a volume out of fifteen is devoted to a single dinner-party.

From the beginning, scenes from the human comedy are slipped into passages whose chief concern is the life of Marcel's imagination. Characters slip from the background to the foreground and begin to exist in their own right: Aunt Léonie, as a variation on the perennial theme of the hypochondriac; Françoise who, like the figures carved on the porch of Saint-André-des-Champs which bring her to Marcel's mind, in her mixture of superstition and shrewdness, cruelty and devotion, snobbery and independence sums up virtues, failings and oddities which Proust felt to be characteristic of the uneducated servant class in the France of his time; Legrandin, the first of the lay figures which Proust is to use to record his anatomy of snobbery. The Swann love story brings in Mme Verdurin. She is multipurposed: an important agent in the narrative of Swann's love for Odette and Charlus's for Marcel; an illustration of the transformation of society, since she is to expose the sham of her own inverted snobbery by marrying the Prince de Guermantes; but also a great if exaggeratedly caricatured comic figure. In her salon are set the first of the elaborate conversation pieces which, as Mansfield has pointed out, can be detached as self-sufficient comic interludes, and from which, as Fernandez writes, the narrator seems to be as detached as if he were a folklore expert or a student of dialects playing the records he had collected of the speech habits of an alien people.

The introduction of the 'little phrase' of Vinteuil's sonata, itself integral to the 'vocation theme', is the pretext for one of the great set-pieces, Mme de St. Euverte's reception. It is interesting here that Swann is said to be able to see the pretentious elegance of this particular stratum of the Faubourg Saint-Germain because he has become detached from it by his devotion to Odette and returns to it with eyes cleared of the film of long habit and unquestioning acceptance. He returns to it, in fact, like Proust emerging from his retreat. And Proust uses the opportunity to exercise his talent for transforming human beings into specimens, to offer the reader a peep at his human zoo. Metaphor, here, is abundant; not the fusion metaphors of the romantic tradition but metaphors underlining the grotesque disparity between the people and the things they recall to Proust's mind. Footmen and guests are thrust out of their normal context and placed in the contexts of animal nature or Renaissance painting, and the mockery spills over a little on to the inflated humanism of the paintings referred to. The comic climax is achieved when M. de Palancy, whose name constantly calls out fishlike imagery, becomes a carp, and his monocle a symbolic fragment of his aquarium.

In *A l'ombre des jeunes filles* we are carried into a new complex of spiritual and erotic associations, parallel with and to some extent growing out of the earlier Combray pattern. Instead of the hawthorns, Combray church, Bergotte and Gilberte, we have the sea, Balbec church, Elstir and Albertine. And, as previously, the novel's rhythm proceeds by a complicated process of overlapping. The Albertine story is left in suspense while the Guermantes story is picked up again, for at Balbec Marcel meets Oriane's nephew, Robert de Saint-Loup, and her brother-in-law, Palamède, Baron de Charlus. From the Faubourg Saint-Germain we move to Sodom and Gomorrha, the underworld of sexual perversion in which all classes are united by their senses and instincts. Then the Albertine story is resumed.

In the meantime, the procession of characters in the human comedy continues.

With *A l'ombre des jeunes filles* comes the Baron de Norpois, who at one time had made one character with Charlus, now separated off as the type of the long-winded, cliché-ridden diplomat with no qualification but the hidebound conviction which hides his spiritual

obtuseness and timidity; Mme de Villeparisis, a particularly interesting social type because, as a *déclassée*,
she cuts across the normal stratification; the Bloch family, another collection of caricatures comparable to the
clan Verdurin. But it is in the middle section of the
novel—*Le côté de Guermantes* and *Sodome et Gomorrhe*—that the human comedy comes to and stays in the
foreground. The shattering of Marcel's dream of the
name 'Guermantes' is effectively dealt with in comparatively little space; through it, and constant references to
Combray, the earlier themes of the novel are kept in
mind. There is a long section on Marcel's visit to Doncières, where Saint-Loup is garrisoned. No doubt this
originated in a cherished memory of Proust's real life,
since there is a very long section in *Jean Santeuil* about
Jean's stay with Henri de Réveillon in similar circumstances. But here, as elsewhere, the comparison of *Jean
Santeuil* with *A la recherche* shows the degree of imaginative transmutation undergone by the autobiographical
material. The story of Marcel's ephemeral and absurd
passion for Oriane de Guermantes is told, and that of
Saint-Loup's for Rachel (which illustrates the same
Proustian 'laws' of love as Swann's and Marcel's) is
begun. But more and more space is given to the broad
frescoes, the satirical observation of character and manners, the impact of the Dreyfus affair on individuals
and groups.

Then Palamède de Charlus advances to the centre of
the stage, to dominate, as a character, the whole book.
He is the personification of arrogance—arrogance of
the kind Marcel's grandfather found so fascinating in
Saint-Simon's story of the commoner who, 'through ignorance or as a try-on', offered his hand to his sons. He
is, further, a sometimes comic and eventually nightmar-
ish projection of the frightening and shameful perver-

sion which Proust knew within himself. But he is also a sensitive and vulnerable creature, and the arrogance itself gives the measure of his humiliation at the hands of Mme Verdurin and of his abjection when he last appears as a decrepit and dependent old man. He is grandiose, grotesque and infinitely pathetic. Of all the characters Proust used to put his own vices at a distance and establish a tenable attitude towards them, Charlus is the richest and most subtly drawn.

To the successive subjective 'worlds' of Marcel's imagination are added, then, the objective 'worlds' or social groups into which human beings become organized, the astronomical system of which Marcel, like a social Newton, has 'discovered' the laws of motion. Here, as in the subjective scheme, Proust's observations have been stylized and, as far as possible, arranged in a system; again the creative process is marked by three stages: observation, abstraction of general principles, the imaginative re-creation, round these abstract principles, of human reality. But here, far more than in the case of Marcel's subjective life, one is aware that the re-created reality is not quite human. The account is given not by a humanist but by a naturalist, and by a naturalist whose field of speculation and categories of systematization are limited by his personal obsessions. Like Descartes' whirlwinds, Proust's social astronomy is impressive but obviously false; its correspondence with our own experience is close enough to allow us to admire the mental powers which have exercised themselves in the perfection of its internal coherence, but not close enough to convince us that its coherence is adequate to the complexity of the world in which we are involved. Proust's world is not quite our world, but it is imaginatively authentic. When Marcel reduces his haloes to ideas, these ideas are still part of Proust's imaginative construction. They are sufficiently based on lucid observation to help us to order and clarify our own experience of ourselves and others; but they need supplementation to become fully human. In the last event Proust's world is arranged in superficial and delightful pattern rather than penetrated in tragic depth.

Marcel the child sees two social spheres outside his own—Swann's and Oriane's; about these and his own he entertains illusions, among them being the belief that the two unknowns are intrinsically superior. Having penetrated their mystery he can be 'objective' about all three. The superiority of the Guermantes' world, its highest poetry, he annexes to his own idealism; there remains a lower poetry, an irreducible individuality, a fascination exerted by the Guermantes in their own right. The halo proper belongs elsewhere, but there remains the harder, colder radiation of *l'esprit des Guermantes*. What Proust takes most pleasure in making plain, however, is the system of laws which binds all three social worlds together, and within them smaller worlds, and, within these, individuals. Marcel's subjective 'worlds' were individual and distinct, but linked by the same underlying patterns. The same is true of social groups.

Mme Brée has remarked that the shadow of Louis XIV and Saint-Simon helps to pattern Proust's world. There are a number of 'courts' gravitating about their sovereigns—the Faubourg Saint-Germain round Charlus (more truly, perhaps, round the Guermantes as a family), Eulalie and Françoise round Aunt Léonie, the lower servants round Françoise, the staff of the Grand Hotel at Balbec round the manager. We can add the 'little clan' formed round Mme Verdurin. Each court has its own ritual and its own mechanisms for the preservation of self-esteem. Each member has to put on the appropriate mask and dance the ritual dance; to fail to conform is to risk extrusion, as Swann and Charlus are extruded by Mme Verdurin. There is a hierarchy of courts; one of the conventions of each is its exclusiveness—real when directed downwards, sham as regards those above. The generality of these principles is demonstrated, and all societies shorn of their pretensions, by their application to the 'Marquise' who looks after the public lavatories in the Champs-Élysées; for she also has her standards, and is particular about whom she admits.

We, endowed with the narrator's omniscience, are pleasured with the spectacle of all these people shut within their ignorance and unconscious of it. We know that they are moved by the same futile motives as the 'Marquise', and they do not. We see when they are behaving incongruously, unaware of the ritual which is expected of them, of the essential differences between their own and that of other groups. We hear them repeating in all seriousness the enormities which they are made to utter by their ignorance, or their total inability, under the stress of unconscious inhibitions, to allow themselves to see the truth. Nobody can truly know anybody else—that is a fundamental proposition of Proust's 'subjective idealism'; but to this philosophical veto is added, in the general run of humanity, a positive unwillingness to know what *can* be known. The humour of this spectacle of human beings enclosed within less-than-human limitations—blindness, stupidity, ignorance, prejudice, vice—is in the comic tradition. But compare it with Molière's, where there is the assumption of a norm from which the inhumanity is seen as a deviation; here there is no norm except the figure of the artist, no remedy except withdrawal into disinterested contemplation, composed of sensuous lyricism, the bitter-sweet of understanding, and (though the aesthetic theory makes no mention of this) a humour sometimes bordering on cruel contempt.

Whatever the character of the subject-matter, Proust the narrator is continually present as the presiding intelligence. Even when Marcel is not present—as when Swann's story is being told and Marcel has not been born, or when Marcel effaces himself behind the narrative of scenes in which he is not personally concerned— the narrator, Proust, the older Marcel of the fiction, is passing the substance of his sensibility and imagination through the filter and mould of his intelligence. Even in passages which the theory of involuntary memory seems most satisfactorily to account for, those passages of impressions which seem most truly 'outside time'—almost the whole account of Combray, in which happenings are dissolved in states, (in particular, the account of the two 'ways'), the less sustained notations of the very 'feel' of Balbec and the sunlit sea, the increasingly fugitive statements of climate and atmosphere—the narrator is there not only to create the past but to point, comment, deprecate, patronize and lighten with irony and humour. What varies is the relation between the delight of what is felt to have been (or what is now projected into) the past, and the delight in the narrator's manner of presentation, between sensibility and shrewdness, tenderness and malice, compassion and humour. Too often Marcel has the lion's share of the first of these pairs of terms, and the rest of the world is the victim of the second; though Marcel, too, in his young and naïve days, comes in for his share of mockery. But even when Proust is living in Marcel's lost paradises, his joy is as much in the present act of creating with words as in the delight of what is in part recovered and in part created. With him, the rapture of the soul never means the rape of the intelligence. Like others of his contemporaries, he belongs to the latter stage of a long romantic tradition, where one part of that tradition sweeps on into the convulsions of Surrealism, and another sweeps back towards the perennial virtues of the French mind—lucidity, delicacy and sureness of touch.

In respect of his detachment as a writer from what he is writing about, even when what he is writing about is himself, Proust may be compared to Lautréamont. Each, in his time, had nourished his imagination on books rather than on active experience and had sensed reverberations from romantic literature to his own deep-lying but not suppressed, controlled, or organized unconscious movements. To what extent irony played a part in Lautréamont's use of the shadier romantic themes we can only speculate, and it would be unprofitable to compare his exploration or exploitation of the oneiric with Proust's. But each, in his way, was consciously using his awareness of oneiric experience, and, in the work of each, part of the individuality of the work and the peculiarity of its pleasure (keeping the necessary proportions between a minor and a major writer) comes from the parallel awareness of oneiric power and intelligence. It is worth while pressing the point a little further, for the suggestion that the act of creating any considerable literary work can be lacking in conscious control and criticism is likely nowadays to offend. The point is that whereas, when the critic is studying the creative process of, say, Baudelaire or even Rimbaud, he may maintain that the choice of the means of expression is always a consciously critical act, he must admit that the reader's awareness of the work itself may involve a greater or less degree of self-awareness with respect to the experience proposed. Baudelaire and Rimbaud propose a surrender to the incantatory power of the style and the affective impact of the images, and one aspect of the development of Symbolism was the sacrifice of logical and (to some extent) syntactical coherence to 'supralogic'. Proust and Lautréamont both have a classical respect for the logic of language.

Only through long acquaintance with the work is the subtlety of Proust's style, and the attitudes it communicates, apparent. One critic will deprecate for its pre-Raphaelite affectations and preciosity a passage in which another will see a redeeming irony; one will point to the pathos of an event or character which to another seems comic. In general (and one must make this limitation because there are occasions when technique becomes empty mannerism) the subtlety bears a direct relation to the syntactical complication. If Proust never depends in true symbolist fashion on the supralogical clash of impression-laden images, the effect of his complicated constructions is that the images strike first and the precise relations between the images emerge afterwards, and only as these relations are taken by the mind do the exactly relevant impressions from the images oust the irrelevant. The proper appreciation of Proust's attitude to what he is putting before the reader depends not only on a minutely adjusted awareness of local style but on bringing to bear on particular instances impressions derived from the book as a whole, on the cross-reference of attitudes. Even then, there is sometimes an ambiguity of feeling which turns his prose into shot silk traversed by change. Less, however, than the obtuseness of some of his commentators would give one to suppose. Let us look at an instance of how a translator has failed to take Proust's mood.

In the main passage on the hawthorns, there is a patronizing reference to nature to which we referred earlier. Here is the original text, with the operative words in italics:

> Et certes, je l'avais tout de suite senti, comme devant les épines blanches mais avec plus d'émerveillement, que ce n'était pas facticement, par un artifice de fabrication humaine, qu'était traduite l'intention de festivité dans les fleurs, mais que c'était la nature qui, spontanément, l'avait exprimée avec la *naïveté d'une commerçante de village* travaillant pour un reposoir, en *surchargeant* l'arbuste de ces rosettes d'un *ton trop tendre* et d'un *pompadour provincial.*

The mood here is complicated. There is tenderness as well as patronage, of the sort which the older Marcel extends to his earlier self and to the past in which the other self lived. Scott-Moncrieff, unable no doubt to admit emotions which seemed irrelevant to the context, simplified the attitude in his translation:

> And, indeed, I had felt at once, as I had felt before the white blossom, but now still more marvelling, that it was in no artificial manner, by no device of human construction, that the festal intention of these flowers was revealed, but that it was Nature herself who had spontaneously expressed it (with the simplicity of a woman from a village shop, labouring at the decoration of a street altar for some procession) by burying the bush in these little rosettes, almost too ravishing in colour, this rustic 'pompadour'.

'Simplicity' distorts 'naïveté', 'burying' attenuates 'surchargeant', 'little rosettes' is gratuitous, 'ravishing', though not too far from the dictionary meaning of 'tendre', substitutes new overtones to those given to the word here by its context.

Proust's method of writing, then, bears out his theory to the extent that impressionism is served by intelligence in the shaping of its 'spiritual equivalent'. What the theory does not admit is that to the 'spiritual equivalent' of past impressions is added a present attitude.

Fernandez, in his own summing-up of Proust's qualities, quotes a passage written by Jacques Rivière on the relaunching of the *Nouvelle revue française* in 1919, which looks forward to a new phase of literature applying a lucid intelligence to the inventory of the sensations and emotions brought into literature by Romanticism and Symbolism. No author has done more to bring about that dream than Proust. His book is a philosophic mystery—some have called it a 'metaphysical detective story'—to which the key is provided in the finale. The creation of the 'vision' is the work of the imagination, but the elaboration of the structure on which it is created is the work of a keen and powerful intelligence analyzing and synthesizing in the service of imagination, working on an amazingly wide culture apprehended by a fine sensibility and recorded by a quite exceptional memory biased, like Stendhal's and Fromentin's, though less exclusively, towards impression rather than facts. What gives the mystery and the key their authenticity, the validity which suspends disbelief at least to the extent of providing aesthetic satisfaction is, besides their internal aesthetic coherence, their close correspondence with those of the nineteenth-century attitudes to art to which we are now inclined to attach most value. *A la recherche* is a human comedy, but it is also the Divine Comedy of the religion of art; it is the bodying forth in an imaginatively created world of the aesthetic idealism underlying romantic and symbolist literature, as Dante's poem is the bodying forth of the abstractions of Aquinas, the breath of life coming from a lyrical tradition both sensuous and mystical.

Paradoxically, perhaps, Proust's originality depends

in part upon his own catholicity and powers of absorption, upon the richness and variety of the substance he drew from others. But it also depends on his powers of digesting and transmuting. When he accepted and absorbed ideas, it was because he had lived the experience to which the ideas referred, or could refer it to his own and translate it into his own terms. We mentioned earlier that in *Jean Santeuil* Proust notes an idea which much preoccupied Baudelaire and other students of the imagination—that of the analogies and distinctions between the ecstasies of art and drugs. In *A la recherche,* the idea is translated into the terms of Proust's subjective idealism and presented in concrete images when Marcel drinks too much in the restaurant at Rivebelle; alcohol provides him with a precarious and caricatural correspondence of the sense of plenitude and freedom which his art is to create and fix. Similarly, the banal romantic obsession with the gulf between imagination and reality is turned into specific experiences, the most strikingly vivid of which are the account of the pleasures of reading and the scene where Marcel stands nonplussed before the distressing solidity of the figures carved on the façade of Balbec church, reflecting that he could write his name on the status of the Virgin already desecrated by having an existence in spatially extended—and limited—matter. The passage from general ideas to concrete realizations of the corresponding experience allowed innumerable variations on the same theme.

Nor are the pleasures of the 'metaphysical detective novel' to be despised. Clues are planted everywhere like needles in a haystack, threaded and interconnecting. When we read the book first it is often difficult to put our hand on the clue we need; but continually, as we go back over supposedly familiar passages, new clues unexpectedly prick our attention and add their quota to the intricate pattern.

There are passages which are tedious; there is a good deal of repetition. But Proust is so successful a spell-binder that even tedium is felt rather as the willing wait for the next confidently expected stretch of amusement or delight. Even when we are slightly bored, we are still living in another world, a world commanded by the steady, meticulous, apparently dis-interested voice of the narrator, so finally convinced of the ultimate importance even of his own platitudes that the reader does not recognize their familiarity until he has disentangled an abstract idea or general observa-tion from the sinuous rills of a style which keeps the garden bright even when it is enfolding no sunny spots of greenery. At his artistically feeblest, Proust is a great conversationalist of whom we are willing to miss very little; even a long discourse on the art of warfare, a sub-ject on which we can hardly expect Proust to provide anything but the most bookish information, may yield a gem or two of comment, some outside slant on the world to which not only Saint-Loup belongs but Gen-eral Froberville with his monocle fixed in his eye like a shining shell fragment.

And so, unless we dislike Proust and are looking for a stick to beat him with, we do not ask too pertinaciously, as we read, to what purpose we are being told what Proust is telling us. The plan of the book is there, and can be exhibited to refute the critics who said that Proust's work is amorphous; but the amount of work which must go to its exhibition gives some point to the criticism. If Proust found it difficult to leave anything out which he could possibly fit in, it is because of his un-bounded curiosity and interest. Like Marcel's grand-mother, Proust talks of the objects of his interest 'with that detached, smiling, almost sympathetic benevolence with which we reward the object of our disinterested observation for the pleasure which it procures us'.

If his undoubted pessimism about human relations is so rarely depressing, it is because he communicates, at least to the sympathetic reader, his delight at finding people out, at finding life out, his exhilaration at 'blowing the gaff', to borrow Professor Empson's name for a stock literary process. Such determined deflation relieves, for us, the strain of maintaining our own optimism, like Voltaire's 'bon père de famille est capable de tout'.

Too often, in romantic writing, we find such stock literary processes isolated and exalted into philosophies. Thus marks a disequilibrium which has its serious implications in so far as it reflects the disequilibrium of our culture; but when the irony and humour go out of such attitudes they can become wearisome personal complaints, and often the depression and discouragement they represent is offset only, apart from a delight in destruction grown lyrical, by the sense of value and purpose represented by the form in which the complaint is cast. Even the most pessimistic work of art, as Valéry observes somewhere, is never merely depressing; it contains its own dose of exhilaration. In nineteenth-century writing about the status of literature, the exalting of art is often balanced by the disparagement of life; but never, before Proust, has the disparagement of life been so successfully shouted down within the work of art itself, by the triumphant cry of purpose achieved, of destiny worked out in the teeth of despair and to the point of death. *A la recherche* does not contain the whole truth about human life, but it does contain some essential truth about Proust's.

In part it is false even to Proust's, however. Not simply because Marcel is a simplified and idealized Proust, the simplification and idealization being part of the creative effort by which Proust finally achieved his purpose, part of the imaginative rectification of his world. This kind of insincerity can sometimes be exacted by some greater consideration of artistic sincerity. Rather because in the account of Marcel's success the given is emphasized at the expense of the won, revelation at the expense of effort. It has often been admitted that the novel shows no awareness of any morality but that of the creative artist; what it does not sufficiently bring out within itself is the importance, even for the artist—and particularly for Proust—of an effort which is itself fundamentally moral. It is nearer, in feeling, to a fairy tale for very sophisticated adults than to a mature and tragic awareness of human responsibility.

One can see what Bergson meant when he said that *A la recherche du temps perdu* fails to exalt and brace the spirit. One can see the point, too, of the adverse English criticism collected together by Floris Delattre. D. H. Lawrence said that Proust's novel was made of water-jelly. George Moore said Proust reminded him of a man trying to plough a field with knitting-needles. Desmond McCarthy said he was completely and extravagantly romantic, a kind of Lady of Shalott who never lifts his eyes from his magic mirror. F. L. Lucas called his philosophy 'a muddled idealism' and the author a cross between Mephistopheles and Machiavelli. Cyril Connolly said that in Proust the terror of having to make a decision and the fear of leaving something out have put on the masks of love and truth. To all of these criticisms Proust is vulnerable. He tried to stretch an inadequate philosophy too far. He had the good sense to avoid the more extravagant of the conclusions which his over-simple idealism implied, as when, having been led to the point of making the notion of German war guilt a nationally subjective valuation on the part of the French, he saw the moral nihilism which such a theory of valuation implied, and stopped short. There were problems of and about human life which Proust never touched on because they were not his, and some of these omissions bear on his treatment of the problems which he felt to be peculiarly his. It has been said that he de-dramatizes society and de-dramatizes love. It has also been said that his very originality and, partly, merit, lie in having de-dramatized the French novel, casting off from it the shackles put on it by the prestige of classical tragedy and making it free of its own dimension, which is feeling rather than deeds. Yet it is difficult to see how any account of feeling can be complete without taking account of such feelings as are concerned with the interchange in reality, meaning here the sphere of behavior as distinct from the sphere of subjective flux, between the self and the non-self. It is one of the limitations of Proust's gifts that he cannot take seriously any passion which is not the pursuit of a state of mind; his pathological self-reference has enriched his presentation of life in some directions and impoverished it in others.

But to condemn a work because it fails in some particular respect is to fail to heed the warning of artists as different as Hugo and Mallarmé, who both pointed to the critical error which consists of expecting fruit from a flowering tree—or, to adapt the image, potatoes from a peach. Rebecca West once compared *A la recherche du temps perdu* to a velvet-gloved hand stretched out to grasp a peach, and contrasted its leisurely movement with the convulsive clutch of James Joyce in *Ulysses*. It is useless to ask Proust for the sense of discovering or recovering our own inner energies and convictions which Dostoevsky and Melville can awaken; Proust's spirit is not the breath of life itself, but a refinement and enrichment of life. A peach, perhaps even a little soft in places, but carrying no threat to sound digestions. The book carries its own antidote; its range of sensation is from the sensuality of Petronius to the devoted sensuousness of Keats.

BIOGRAPHICAL NOTE

1871 (10th July) Proust born at Auteuil, near Paris.

1880   First attack of asthma. According to Léon Pierre-Quint, Proust was no longer able to spend his summer holidays in the country, and went instead to the sea.

1887–1888 Proust contributes articles to reviews founded and edited by his school-fellows at the Lycée Condorcet.

1889   Military service with the 76th Infantry Regiment at Orléans.

1892   Contributes society notes and book reviews to *Le Banquet*, a review founded by the Lycée Condorcet group.

1893   Meets the Comte Robert de Montesquiou-Fezensac.

1894   Proust obtains an unpaid post as assistant at the Mazarine Library, but does not assume his duties.

1895–1900 (about) At work on a long novel, eventually abandoned (posthumously published as *Jean Santeuiil*).

1900   Begins serious study and translation of Ruskin.

1903   Death of Proust's father.

1905   Death of his mother.

1906(?) Proust begins to write the novel which will eventually become *A la recherche du temps perdu*.
        Leaves his parents' house and moves to 102, Boulevard Haussmann. Lives in increasing solitude in his cork-lined bedroom.

1908–1910 Turns aside from novel to write a critical study of Sainte-Beuve (posthumously published as *Contre Sainte-Beuve*). This work leads to a further exploration of memories of his own past, and to the development of themes and narratives later to be incorporated in *A la recherche du temps perdu*.

1911   First 700 pages ready for printing. Proust in search of a publisher. *N.R.F.* (advised by André Gide) rejects the manuscript, but takes over publication from Grasset after the appearance of the first volume.

1913–1922 Proust continues to revise and expand the later parts of his novel as the earlier parts are published.

1922   (18th November) Proust dies, with the last five volumes still unpublished.

BIBLIOGRAPHICAL NOTE

WORKS

1896   *Portraits de peintres*
        Les Plaisirs et les jours

1904   *La Bible d'Amiens* (Ruskin). Translation, preface and notes by Proust

1906   *Sésame et les lys* (Ruskin). Translation, preface and notes by Proust

1913   *Du côté de chez Swann*

1919   *A l'ombre des jeunes filles en fleurs*
        Pastiches et mélanges

1920–27 Remaining volumes of *A la recherche*

1927   *Chroniques*

1952   *Jean Santeuil*

1954   *Contre Sainte-Beuve*

WORKS AVAILABLE IN ENGLISH TRANSLATION

1922–31 *Remembrance of Things Past.* Translated by C. K. Scott-Moncrieff (*Swann's Way* to *The Sweet Cheat Gone*) and Stephen Hudson (*Time Regained*)

1941   Uniform Edition

1948   *Marcel Proust: A Selection from His Miscellaneous Writings.* Translated by Gerard Hopkins.

1950   *Letters of Marcel Proust,* Selected, edited and translated by Mina Curtiss

1955   *Jean Santeuil.* Translated by Gerard Hopkins
        In preparation *Contre Sainte-Beuve.* Translated by Sylvia Townsend Warner

SOME WORKS ON PROUST IN ENGLISH

1940   Derrick Leon, *Introduction to Proust*

1948   Harold March, *The Two Worlds of Marcel Proust*

1949   F. C. Green, *The Mind of Proust*

1950   André Maurois, *The Quest for Proust.* Translated by Gerard Hopkins

1950   Martin Turnell, *The French Novel*

1952   P. A. Spalding, *A Reader's Handbook to Proust*
        In preparation Germaine Brée, *Marcel Proust and the Deliverance from Time*

André Gide

For Evangeline and James Olmsted

A small token of friendship in gratitude for many things

INTRODUCTION

André Gide was not only one of the greatest European
writers of our time, he was as well one of its main forces.
He touched the literature of every country at many
points, and not only the literature, but the individual
as well, all over the world, even in countries so far distant as Japan. 'There are writers', says François Mauriac,
'the meeting with whom can decide the course of a
whole life'. Gide was one of these and I myself can still
remember vividly the spiritual shock I received when,
at the age of fifteen, I picked up one of his works in a
second-hand book-shop on the quays in Dublin. It was
the sudden opening of a door, an immediate liberation.
It seemed to me that, in a single day, I had been completely transformed. I had never heard of Gide, and
only learned of his significance years later when I became a student in Paris. Then I discovered that that very
book, *Les Nourritures Terrestres,* had exercised the
same influence on most members of my generation in
post-war France. In those days Gide's influence was considered pernicious, but since then he has been sanctified
by being granted the degree of Doctor of Letters, *Honoris Causa,* by the University of Oxford in 1947—the
first honour he had ever received though he was seventy-
eight at the time—which was followed in the same year
by the Nobel Prize for literature.

It would seem at first sight that it should not be an
arduous task to produce a study of Gide, an author who
has written nearly a million words of an intimate Jour-

nal, as well as several volumes of autobiography, and whose every work was moreover undertaken with the avowed purpose of discovering himself. But, in spite of his frankness and outspokenness, Gide leaves many important episodes so shrouded in a haze of vagueness and uncertainty that it is very difficult to be sure of what has really happened, and diverse interpretations are possible. Indeed he says no less than the truth when he declares 'it is my reticences that are most passionate'. Significant amongst these are those concerning his relationship with his wife, which he calls 'the secret drama of my life'; and he admits that because of his reticence on this important subject his Journal is blinded, with only a hole where the heart should be. This is indeed a tragic admission from a sincere diarist. He calls his attachment for her the secret of all his indecision. In spite of the new light thrown on this subject by the posthumous work, *Nunc manet in te,* the mystery remains as impenetrable as ever.

He has told us much about his homosexuality, but I have never felt personally that this problem is as serious as he thought himself, or would have us believe; not as serious as it need have been if his emotional experience had been different at a critical stage in his development. Later it was as if, deliberately, he sought to be a martyr for this stronghold of prejudice and hypocrisy, the martyr and not the unwilling victim as Oscar Wilde had been. He has told us much about this topic but, on the other hand, he has given no clue to his feelings for the mother of his child, and he has destroyed much of what he wrote about his wife. Normally such questions would not concern the critic, but with a writer like Gide who professes—and indeed practises—frankness in other equally delicate matters, this mixture of reticence and outspokenness is intriguing, and is significant and revealing psychologically.

Although he has written so much about himself, I have never felt that Gide wanted his readers to know him fully; or rather he became afraid and anxious when people began to interpret him—as indeed who does not —and he cries 'Do not understand me so quickly!' In these confessions that he pours out to us he does not provide us with ammunition to use against him, but rather builds up ramparts against us. He wants us to know only the picture that he himself paints. I remember the first time that I went to see him, and he was as charming as I subsequently discovered he was always to everyone. He sat there bending forward with eagerness and sympathetic understanding, anxious that I should feel completely at my ease with him. His smile was of the kindest as he talked freely to me and answered all my questions, but I felt, nevertheless, that I was getting nowhere at all. He seemed to be vanishing further and further behind that smoke-screen of sincere and friendly words and charm, until I felt that I could no longer see him. I tried to resist the overwhelming charm of his personality, to peer into the mist and to seize hold of the elusive figure which seemed to appear and disappear like the Cheshire Cat in *Alice in Wonderland*. In the same way as the smile sometimes appeared without the Cat, I felt that Gide's charming smile was hovering disembodied before me. All my will-power was concentrated in a desperate effort to keep him before me in a concrete form, when suddenly I heard the door behind me open and an old friend of his appeared. This put an end to our conversation. I have often wondered since whether he might not have, like officials in their offices, a hidden bell beneath the ledge of the desk which, on being pressed, rang in another room, whenever he felt that he was slipping out of his own control, and into someone else's nets.

On that first meeting what struck me most about him was the serenity of his expression, and this surprised me, for the picture I had formed of him from his books was of a tormented and anxious being. His works had become for our anguished generation of the post-war years the expression of the new 'Mal du Siècle'. This psychological climate—often called 'angst'—is typical of the Gidian atmosphere and could be called 'Gidism' just as "Rousseauism' is the influence of Rousseau during the early years of the nineteenth century. This was, however, not the atmosphere radiated by Gide when I met him first twenty years ago, but an earlier one. There was in him the paradox that, at the very moment when he had achieved serenity in himself, his earlier works were beginning to exercise a deep influence over the youth of the country. After the First World War, in the general shipwreck of old values, the world was facing the same problems which had preoccupied him when he began to write as a young man, and then the works which he had written thirty years before became widely known and were the most vital influence on the rising generation; Gide himself by that time, however, had left that phase far behind him and was displeased whenever it was recalled to him.

In spite of its many contradictions there is one striking characteristic which runs through Gide's work in all its many phases, a deep embedded shining seam; his quality as a moralist, passionately interested in the problem of sin, what it is and where it hides itself, especially in the apparently virtuous and complacent. He describes himself as watching people coming out of Church on a Sunday, and he says that their thoughts are freshly washed and ironed by the sermon they have just heard and put away tidily in their minds, as in a cupboard. 'I would like to rummage in the bottom-drawer', he declares, 'I've got the key'. This bottom-drawer is the hidden part of man's nature. As a young man, when he looked at civilisation, he was appalled by the pressure of outworn codes on the individual personality—the Church, society, political theories—, and he considered that, in his attempt to conform, the individual was obliged to develop an outward personality, a counterfeit personality. Discovery of our unacted desires, emancipation from the counterfeit personality, Gide thought, would bring freedom and fulfilment to the individual. It is the inner personality, beneath the counterfeit one, which he always tried to reach; that inner reality where good and evil overlap as in a marriage of Heaven and Hell. In reaching that inner personality he stirs up its troubled depths, drags up from the thick overlaying mud the hidden motives. This is for him the really fertile soil, the one which, in a state of nature, is overrun by exuberant vegetation and which must be cleared before it can be cultivated. He considered that those who had first studied man's nature did so only where it was most easily accessible and that only very gradually did psychologists come to realise all the hidden possibilities in man. All the troubled, tortured and distressed beings are those who interest Gide because he believes that more can be expected from them, when the subterranean forces have been liberated and subdued, than from the complacent. So he studies cases of disconcerting behavior, cases of apparent wrong-doing; he observes all the idiosyncrasies, the nervous tics, as signs which reveal the hidden obsessions; he studies all these unconscious gestures as evidence, just as a detective might look for fingerprints, or analyse grains of dust or tufts of hair. Most of the characters in Gide's writings have some maladjustment, or psychological flaw, which drives them to their doom, and often to the destruction of others as well.

It is impossible, in a short monograph, to give a satisfactory full-length portrait of Gide and of his works. He was in his eighty-second year when he died; his first work appeared in 1891 and following it he published eighty odd volumes. There are many aspects which might be considered. He could be studied as a novelist, a short-story writer, a dramatist or essayist; he could be analysed as an accomplished prose artist or a humourist; as a diarist he has no peer and he is important also as a moralist and psychologist. Any one of these aspects could become the subject of a whole book. To attempt to deal with all at once—as indeed one must if the picture is to have verisimilitude—is to produce only a tangled skein; but then Gide is a very tangled skein, the biographer's despair, the most baffling and fascinating figure in modern literature. 'Is it my fault', he asks, 'if God took great pains to have me born between two stars, fruit of two races, of two provinces and of two creeds?' He means to indicate that his father was a protestant from the South and his mother a Catholic from Normandy; but this suggestion is, however, not quite accurate, for his mother was also a protestant by breeding though from Catholic stock. He was born, as he says, between two stars, on November 22nd, when Scorpio yields the place to Sagittarius.

This little monograph, promised before Gide died and finished in May 1952, the publication of which has been unfortunately delayed through unforeseen circumstances, is intended only as a preliminary sketch for a later full-length portrait. The time is however not ripe for that; we are too near the subject as yet, and the dust from Death's chariot wheels, which still obscures our vision, must first be allowed to settle. It has moreover stirred up all the vicious blowflies which always swarm round the remains of the illustrious dead, and only when they are sated will it be possible to gauge what will survive.

1

NARCISSUS SPEAKS

André Gide was born on November 22nd, 1869. His father, Paul Gide, a professor of Law at the University of Paris, was appointed to the Chair of Roman Law three years after the birth of his only child. He came of protestant stock from Uzès, near Nîmes in Provence, which, since the Reformation, had been a strong centre of Huguenots. His own father, Tancrède Gide, an austere and devout man who devoted his life to good works, did not live to know any of his grandchildren; he died prematurely, refusing to call in a doctor because it was, he declared, contrary to God's intentions. He had been greatly admired and respected by all those who came into contact with him, and his son, Paul, was said to resemble him in many respects—he certainly shared his reputation for honour and integrity and was called 'vir probus' by his colleagues at the École de Droit. One summer, when on holiday in Normandy, he was introduced to a rich heiress called Juliette Rondeaux. She had the reputation of being a spoilt young woman who was very difficult to please since she had refused many eligible suitors and was now no longer young, but she fell passionately in love with the earnest young professor who seemed to share her serious view of life and of its duties and responsibilities. They were married in February 1863 when he was thirty-one and she twenty-eight, but they were to wait six years for the birth of their only child.

Juliette Rondeaux came from a long established bourgeois family in Rouen—there had been Rondeaux of substance as early as the seventeenth century who, by degrees, had accumulated a large fortune through their shrewd business sense and thrifty ways. Edouard Rondeaux, Gide's grandfather, although born a Catholic, was himself a liberal free-thinker who married a protestant and then allowed his children to be brought up as protestants, but one of his sons eventually became converted to Catholicism. He had five children of whom one was Gide's mother and another the father of his cousin Madeleine, his closest friend in childhood and eventually his wife, who remained, to the end of his life, his only great love.

Thus André Gide, on both sides of his family, came from austere, Godfearing protestants whose religious fervour was coloured—or discoloured—by puritanism.

He was born in Paris, in a top-floor flat in the Rue de Médicis, near the corner of the Boulevard Saint Michel, where he could peer, from his window, into the depths of the Luxembourg Gardens and launch paper-darts right over the intervening square, which used to become entangled in the branches of the chestnut trees in the Gardens. He remembered little of his life in that flat, he tells us in his autobiography, little except the reprehensible habits he indulged in with the concierge's little son, hidden under the long, heavy table-cloth of the dining room table; he remembered also the sandcastles made by some children in the Gardens, which he had stamped underfoot one day when he had refused to play with them. These memories remained deeply burnt into his memory as signs of early depravity—though no rational reader would regard them so seriously.

He was six when his parents moved to the Rue de Tournon, to a big flat on the second floor in a house at the corner of the Rue Saint Sulpice. There his chief memory was of his father's large study which he always entered as solemnly and as seriously as if he were going to Church; he remembered the thick pile of the carpet which mysteriously deadened his footfalls, and the calf-bound volumes with their gold lettering and tooling. His father there began to take an interest in his progress and used to read to him, not the insipid children's books current at the time, but Homer, Molière and the *Arabian Nights*. He read him also *The Book of Job* and thus started his son's life-long passion for the Bible. Gide also remembered walks in the summer evenings with his father, when work was over and supper had not been too long delayed. They walked through the Gardens in the dusk, until the roll of the drum gave notice that the gates were closing. He remembered afterwards looking through the railings at the empty park shrouded in mystery.

With so many uncles and aunts on his mother's side there was a great choice of places where he could visit during the holidays. The summer was spent at La Roque, a property inherited by his mother from her father. It was a castle, some parts of which dated back to the sixteenth century, but most of which had been re-built in 1803 in the same style. It was surrounded by a moat and he liked to imagine that he was living on an island. He used its setting in two of his novels—in *L'Immoraliste*, and more fully in *Isabelle*. The New Year's holidays he used to spend at Rouen with his Catholic uncle, whose children were much older than he and so no use as playmates, but he played with the daughters of his uncle Émile—Jeanne, Valentine and Madeleine. They were his closest friends and he went often to visit them in their country house at Cuverville, which their father had inherited from his father, and which was to become Gide's home for many years when it belonged to his wife. It is a pleasant well-proportioned eighteenth-century house with romantically laid-out gardens, and Gide used it as a setting for his most perfect work, *La Porte Étroite*. At Easter he used to visit his paternal grandmother in Uzès, and his most vivid memory of that house was connected with a marble which he discovered one day embedded in a knot-hole in a door, and which the maid told him his father had put there as a child and had then been unable to remove it. Gide brooded over this for a whole year before he went there for his next visit; he had allowed one of his finger-nails to grow unusually long and, as soon as he got to his grandmother's house, he inserted it into the hole and levered the marble out. But, as soon as he had succeeded, he was bitterly disappointed for it was only an ordinary black marble, without any mystery or romance, so he slid it back into its cavity and told no one of his exploit. He cut his nail, feeling a bitter sense of disillusionment.

At the age of eight Gide was sent to the École Alsacienne, but his parents were later requested to remove him for a time on account of what were called his evil habits, which he made no attempt to conceal since he did not know that they were wrong.

In 1880, when Gide was eleven, his father died of intestinal tuberculosis and henceforth he was left to his mother's care, whose chief joy and concern he became, her most precious treasure. She had, to help and advise her in this task, her own governess, Anna Shackleton, the daughter of a Scots engineer who had helped to build the Paris-Havre railway. Later Gide bore in his character and personality the stigma of a man brought up exclusively by women. Anna Shackleton encouraged his taste for natural history and botany, which he revealed as early as four years old—; for his mother, once writing to his father, described his habit of standing stock-still deep in contemplation of the behaviour of snails. This interest for botany and zoology lasted him all through his life and many traces are to be found scattered through his *Journal.*

After the death of her husband Madame Gide moved again, to a larger flat in the Rue de Commailles, because one of her sisters told her that she owed it to herself, and to her son, to have a carriage entrance.

Gide's school life was much interrupted during his mother's widowhood. He spent most of one year at Rouen where he shared his cousins' tutor; the following year, perhaps because his mother did not want him to forget his father's family, he lived with his uncle Charles Gide who was a professor at the University of Montpelier, and he was sent to school in the town. Then, for the first time in his life, he became aware of the differences between various religious persuasions and of the bitterness of religious strife, for he was mercilessly bullied by the boys on account of his protestant faith. To avoid returning to school he simulated illness, and it was diagnosed as a nervous ailment; but it is not certain that he was really malingering since various doctors pronounced his complaint authentic and he was henceforth treated with added care so that, even after his return to Paris, he was kept away from school and taught by a succession of inefficient tutors.

When he was thirteen he experienced the great shock which altered his life and gave it a new orientation. He had always played with the daughters of his maternal uncle Émile, but hitherto it had been Jeanne whom he had preferred, since her hobbledehoy ways were more in sympathy with his own. Then one evening, after he had gone home to his uncle Henri with whom he was staying, he did not find him there and returned to his uncle Émile's house, intending to take his cousins by surprise. He found no one about in the house but he crept softly upstairs to the girls' rooms and discovered Madeleine kneeling, weeping by her bedside. He was about to run away but she called to him and then revealed the cause of her grief. She had discovered the infidelity of her mother, she alone of all the family knew it, and she had to keep this secret to herself. It was a grievous burden for an innocent and sensitive child of fifteen to bear, and Gide then suddenly realised why, for so long now, she had seemed unhappy and grave beyond her years. He fell in love with her immediately, although he was only thirteen, and felt that the whole of his life and love should be devoted to curing the intolerable sorrow which dwelt in her. He realised, in a flash, that up to that day he had only been wandering in the outer darkness, but now he discovered the aim and the devotion of his whole life, its mystic orientation. He hid his love for her, but knew that it would never die and that one day he would marry her. He used this scene twice, first in *La Porte Étroite* and then in his autobiography, *Si le Grain ne meurt.*

Shortly after this event one of Gide's older cousins managed to persuade his mother to allow him free access to his father's library and he began to develop his own taste in literature. But, whatever he read, the thought of Madeleine always followed him, and against the passages which he thought would please her in the books he read, he put her initials. He began to correspond with her and to make her the confidante of his deepest thoughts and preoccupations. She encouraged him to read the Bible and his love for her became blended with his love for God. He appears as a grave and innocent youth who read his Bible whenever he could and carried a New Testament everywhere with him. He used to mortify his flesh in order to make himself more worthy of her. He would lie at night, like a Carmelite, on bare boards, and rise in the dark to pray. He used to get up at dawn, bathe in ice-cold water, and read some chapters of the Scriptures before he went to his studies.

Even as a small child Gide had shown aptitude for music, and after his mother had taken him to Rubenstein's recitals in 1883, when he was fourteen, and to the Pasdeloup orchestral concerts the following year, he became passionately interested in music—especially in the piano—and, under the teaching of La Nux, whom he portrayed in the person of La Pérouse in *Les Faux Monnayeurs,* he seemed bent on making music his profession. When he was eighteen, after intermittent attendance at school, Gide returned to the École Alsacienne for his final year, to work for his Baccalauréat. In his class there was the future poet Pierre Louys. Up to the time of Gide's arrival Louys had always been first in the literature class and he was held by his schoolmates to be a genius. One day, however, the master, to the great surprise of everyone, announced: 'First in the class Gide, and second Louys'. All the glances of the boys were fixed on Gide in amazement and he blushed with embarrassment. However, what worried him most was how Louys would take his deposition, for he had felt drawn towards him for some time and had been trying to gather the courage to approach him. Now there was this unfortunate episode of the change in the class order, and he felt that he could no longer take the first step.

It was Louys himself, however, who made advances by

coming up to him and asking him what he was reading. It happened to be a book of poems by Heine and this broke the ice, for Louÿs's ambition was to become a poet. Thereafter they became friends, and he was the first close friend that Gide had ever had, except his cousins. They exchanged poems as they walked together in the woods of Meudon and Chantilly, and Gide confessed to his friend, what he had never yet told anyone, his love for Madeleine and his ambition to write a work which would enshrine that devotion; how he would show it to her, and how then she would love him and consent to marry him.

In July 1889 Gide sat for his Baccalauréat and failed, but he scraped through in October, at the second attempt, and then signed on as a student at the Sorbonne with the presumed purpose of reading for the Licence of philosophy. His studies were, however, the least of his preoccupations. He describes in the first entry of his *Journal* how he climbed to the sixth floor of a house in the Rue Monsieur le Prince, to seek suitable accommodation for a literary Cénacle, and how, looking out of the window into the street, he had thrown down the same challenge to Paris as Rastignac in *Père Goriot* when he had gazed over the city from the cemetery of Père Lachaise.

Gide however found that he could not work in Paris, and he retired to a village near the Forest of Compiègne and later to Lake Annecy; but by the summer of 1890 he was back again in Paris, having almost completed his first work which was finished by the autumn. This was *Les Cahiers d'André Walter*. A recent biographer of Gide, George Painter, has given a new explanation of the name of 'André Walter'. He derives it from the name of a prominent protestant evangelical worker,

Henriette André-Walther, who lived from 1807 to 1886 and whose biography was published in 1889, just at the time that Gide was planning his own work.

André Walter is a pious young man, innocent and in-experienced, deeply in love with his orphan cousin Emmanuèle, who is also his adopted sister. Most readers have concluded that this name is that of Gide's own cousin, since in his *Journal* he always refers to her as 'Em'. But this abbreviation is only a pun on the pronunciation of the first initial of her name. André Walter's mother is opposed to a match between her son and her niece and, on her death-bed, she makes him promise to renounce her and betrothes her to another young man. All three young people kneel and pray at her bedside. Six months after the death of her adopted mother, Emmanuèle marries André Walter's rival and, in order to forget his grief, he begins to write a book. It is written in two note-books—hence the 'cahiers' in the title—one of which is white and the other black. The white one is the colour of renunciation and chastity, and in it André Walter retraces the development of his love for his cousin, many episodes of which recall Gide's own life. He decides then that he will write a novel—many of Gide's works deal with characters who are also writing books which will relate the story of their lives. He hopes that, since he must lose Emmanuèle, he will find God. Just as he is on the point of beginning his novel, news is brought to him that his cousin has died. His sacrifice, he thinks, has been in vain. He begins the black note-book, the colour of mourning and despair. His novel will now be the story of an inner conflict, the conflict between the soul and the body, and it will end with the hero's insanity. It is then a race between André Walter himself and his creation Allain as to which of them will go mad first. Allain wins by a neck, but his creator is not far behind, for he falls ill of brain-fever—that complaint so favoured by inexperienced novelists—and dies on finishing his book.

The *Cahiers d'André Walter* was a book into which Gide poured himself, his reading, his ideals, his struggles and aspirations. It was intended to be a statement of his love for his cousin, a declaration to her, but also a warning of what might happen if she refused him. In this book became focussed and crystallised his view of love for a woman, and it is possible to believe that here begins psychological trouble for him, in his obsession with disembodied and spiritualized love. It was the passionate and adoring love of a young man for a woman somewhat older than himself, whom he idolised but to whom he was rarely able to draw near, through timidity and diffidence. Emmanuèle-Madeleine became the ideal towards which he looked; but she crystallised also for him the idea of the perfect woman, and that was a pity for she, as well as he, was not emotionally stable or normal—she had her own inhibitions and obsessions, for she had been too deeply branded, when a child, by the circumstances of her mother's infidelity, to accept love easily; she remained frightened of it as a force which would wreak such destruction, and for her passionate love was always Racinian. *Les Cahiers d'André Walter* is a young man's romantic and subjective first work, filled with renunciation and tragic death. It is a promising work but is not, naturally, without the faults of youth and inexperience. Its chief interest today is that it tells us much of Gide himself during this formative period of his life, tells it first-hand and not, as in his autobiography, with the mature reflection of a middle-aged man looking back on his youth.

Les Cahiers d'André Walter was published anonymously, at Gide's expense, first in February 1891 in an edition of seventy copies which the author soon afterwards destroyed; but a new edition appeared in April. In one copy of the first edition the heroine's name is given as Madeleine. The book was a complete failure. Nevertheless, although it did not please the public, it opened to its author the doors of Mallarmé's Tuesday evenings in the Rue de Rome, where he was introduced by Pierre Louÿs. Inspired by this Cénacle he produced, in little more than a week, the *Poésies d'André Walter,* which was published, anonymously, as a posthumous work in 1892. Gide was later to claim that these poems were too good for a silly fool like André Walter, but to most of his admirers the *Cahiers* is a vastly more interesting and fruitful work, for he was not a natural poet.

Les Cahiers d'André Walter did not however have on Madeleine the effect Gide had hoped, for it seems to have frightened her. He proposed marriage to her but she refused him on the plea that she did not yet feel prepared to marry anyone. Had she accepted him his later life—and hers too—might well have been vastly different.

At the end of 1890, while *Les Cahiers d'André Walter* was printing, Gide went to Montpelier to see Paul Valéry to whom he had a letter of introduction from Pierre Louÿs. Gide's conversation with the poet inspired his next work, *Le Traité du Narcisse,* which he published under his own name. In the public gardens of Montpelier there stands a monument dedicated to the memory of the daughter of the poet Young, inscribed 'Placandis Narcissae Manibus'—'For the peace of the shade of Narcissa'. The name 'Narcissa' recalled to the two young men the name of Narcissus and they each wrote a work inspired by him—Valéry his poem *Narcisse parle,* and Gide his treatise on Symbolism, *Traité du Narcisse.* The latter relates how Narcissus, in a desire to know himself, contemplates his own reflection in the river of Time, and dreams of lost perfection. The river flows back to the past, to the Garden of Eden where Adam, reigning alone in a state of perfect bliss, in a moment of idleness breaks a twig from the tree Ygdrasil. Immediately time is born and imperfection. The tree is blasted and Adam is split in two, and left forever longing to rejoin his other half. Henceforth man has a nostalgic yearning for perfection which is unattainable. Narcissus, trying in vain to embrace his image in the stream, decides that truth and perfection cannot be possessed but only perceived, by intuition, through their symbols. The treatise contains an excellent definition of the doctrine of the Symbolist Movement in France. Gide's treatise was published in January 1891 in a review, and so it is in fact his first published work, though bibliographers do not seem to have noticed this fact.

Gide had thought that by writing *Les Cahiers d'André Walter* he would purge himself of anxiety and distress, but he found that he could not escape. He threw himself into frivolity and pleasure because Madeleine would have nothing to do with him or his book; yet none of this satisfied him and, at the end of the year, he returned to God for help, thinking that he had strayed too far. The thought of his cousin still followed him and he wrote in his *Journal*: 'I thank thee Lord, that the only feminine influence on my delighted soul, which wished for no other, is the influence of Em. I take joy in thinking that if she were to return to me I should have no secrets from her.' She had broken off her correspondence with him after she had refused him.

In November 1892 Gide was called up for his military service, but he was soon invalided out of the army on the score of a predisposition to tuberculosis.

His next work, a novel called *Voyage d'Urien,* was

published in 1893, but its final chapter was printed separately in December 1892 under the title *Voyage à Spitzbergen*. When he showed this in manuscript to Mallarmé he noticed an expression of perplexity on the face of the Master, and later learned the reason. 'You gave me a fright', said the poet, as he returned him his script, 'I really thought you had been there'. He imagined that he had been given a travel-book to read but he, the poet of absence and non-fulfilment, was delighted with a journey its author had never taken. *Le Voyage d'Urien* is the first of Gide's works in which irony and satire are found, which will be marked characteristics of some of his later works. In this new mood we may perhaps discern the influence of Oscar Wilde, whom he first met in 1891 and then saw fairly continuously for some time. This was at the height of Wilde's fame and prosperity, many years before his downfall. His influence was to wean Gide from preoccupation with purely ethical values.

In 1893 Gide composed *La Tentative Amoureuse* in which he deliberately dissociated love, which is a spiritual affection, from desire, which is a physical pleasure. The hero longed for love but was afraid of physical possession; the heroine, however, insisted on giving herself to him and all the summer they experienced the increasing boredom which comes from love's pleasures too lightly snatched, and finally, in the autumn, they parted.

All through 1893 Gide was restless and chafing against restrictions; he was longing to escape, to find new Gods, and to enjoy life without always wondering whether what he was doing was right or wrong. He wanted particularly to experience the joys of the flesh and to escape from the puritan chastity of his up-bringing. 'I lived until the age of twenty-three completely virgin', he wrote, 'and utterly depraved; crazed to such a point that eventually I came to seek everywhere some piece of flesh on which to press my lips'.

In October 1893 emancipation came when Paul-Albert Laurens, the son of the painter, invited him to accompany him to North Africa. Gide set off, as he says in his autobiography, as if in search of the Golden Fleece, which was sexual experience, and he hoped thereafter to find classical balance and harmony. He felt that this journey was an important step forward in his life, and to mark its significance, he left his Bible, from which he had not been parted for a single day for many years, at home. It had been his source of strength, his daily bread, but precisely because he had relied on it so much, he intended now to wean himself from it. It was however not without a painful wrench.

2

THE FRUITS
OF THE EARTH

Gide spent the summer holidays of 1893 at Yport with
the family of Paul-Albert Laurens who had been his
schoolmate at the École Alsacienne and had now won
a travelling scholarship in painting. He chose to visit
Algeria and invited Gide to accompany him. This was
the first of Gide's many visits to North Africa.

The trip unfortunately started badly. At Toulon,
where they spent the night, Gide, who had caught a
chill, was beginning to feel very ill. He did not mention
this to his friend, but thought for a moment that it
might be wise to abandon the trip altogether; yet he
went on, meaning to turn back if he got any worse.
They had a fine crossing and as they entered Tunis
harbour Gide had the impression of coming into the
land of the Arabian Nights, of which he had dreamed
in his childhood. The golden flying fish and array of
camels on the quayside all seemed to him romantic and
mysterious. They first turned towards the south, through
the desert, but the weather was bad, and when they
reached Susa Gide seemed very ill. Laurens called in a
doctor who took a serious view of his state of health
and dissuaded them from going any further through the
desert. They spent six days at Susa and there occurred
an episode which was to be significant for Gide's future

development. Laurens used to go out painting every day and Gide, when he felt well enough, accompanied him. One day, after he had allowed his friend to outdistance him, he tells us—or rather hints—that he discovered his true nature, his homosexual leanings. It was the little Arab boy, who accompanied him to carry his rug, and guessing more about him than he knew himself, who initiated him. When he met Laurens again he did not tell him of his experience, but buried it in his heart, not willing to face it yet.

Since the two young men could not continue their journey through the desert, they decided to spend the winter at Biskra, and while Laurens used to sally forth with easel and paints, to make pictures, Gide would sit in the warmth of the hotel terrace and try to regain his health.

Then Laurens decided that it was time that they carried out the plan which had been one of their main reasons for going to Africa, for he was as anxious as his friend to find sexual experience. Gide was now however less interested than formerly, but thought that with normal experience he might forget his unnatural cravings. Laurens, who had met an Arab girl and fallen in love with her, now suggested that they should share her, and that she should come to their lodgings since Gide was not yet strong enough to go to hers. The experience was not however successful as far as Gide was concerned, for in her arms he thought only of the Arab boy at Susa.

Gide's health did not improve very quickly and when one day he had a haemorrhage, Laurens became so alarmed that he mentioned it in a letter to his parents who thought it only right to inform Gide's mother. She came post-haste to Biskra to nurse him, bringing with her the old family servant Marie. One morning, when she had awakened early and was seated at her window, she saw the Arab girl creeping out of Laurens' room at dawn; she questioned her son about this and he, not wishing his friend alone to bear the blame, confessed to her that he too had shared Merriem. His mother wept, he wept with her, and the result was that they ceased asking the girl to their house, but went to hers instead.

By the spring Gide was better and he felt an upsurging love of life, a longing to enjoy it to the full. It was then that he composed his *Ronde de la Grenade* which he later incorporated in *Les Nourritures Terrestres*.

Seeing him now so much better his mother returned to France, and Gide and Laurens left Africa to travel in Sicily and Italy, visiting Rome and other cities, and finally reaching Florence where they encountered Oscar Wilde. After that they separated, and Gide went to Geneva to consult a doctor recommended by his uncle, who informed him that there was nothing wrong with his lungs but that his nerves were overstrung. Gide then returned to Paris feeling like a man reprieved, for he had been much afraid of having contracted tuberculosis. In Paris, however, he felt as Lazarus must have felt when he came back from the dead, that no one understood him. He returned to the stifling atmosphere of the Paris salons where, as he says, 'the agitation of each one stirred up the stench of death'. He went on to say that it would have brought him to the brink of suicide had it not been for the escape he found in describing it ironically in his next work, *Paludes*. This is the story of a young man who is writing a book, also called *Paludes*. It tells of the life of the animals who live in dark caves and lose their sight through not using it. It is one of Gide's most brilliantly written works and, when he had finished it, he felt that he had liberated himself from all that had previously made him suffer. He believed that he could now safely return to North Africa.

He felt Blidah bitterly cold with the icy wind blowing, and moreover could find no satisfactory lodgings; he was just on the point of leaving the hotel when he saw written on a slate in the office the names of Oscar Wilde and Lord Alfred Douglas. When he had met Wilde previously he had known nothing of his reputation, except as a man of letters, but since then rumours of his habits had reached him; and now, fearful for his own reputation, he erased his name from the slate, paid his bill, and went off to the station. Then, with characteristic Gidian scruples, he became ashamed of his cowardice and returned to the hotel. When he met Wilde later in the evening with Lord Alfred he found him much changed, more vulgar and blatant in flaunting his homosexual habits, for it was as if the presence of his friend urged him on to greater daring. Lord Alfred took it for granted that Gide was of the same persuasion for he said to him: 'These guides are stupid, they will insist on taking one to cafés full of women. I hope that you are like me, I have a horror of women and like only boys!' Wilde also, to his surprise for he had never mentioned the subject to him, assumed the same attitude and one evening, after his friend had left, took him to a certain café and procured a boy for him. Gide wrote subsequently that he had found with the youth a joy and serenity which he had never yet experienced. This time he had no pangs of conscience and was at peace with himself, now that he had openly admitted his leanings. In this state of bliss he conceived *Les Nourritures Terrestres* and wrote several passages of it; although it was not finished then it belongs to this moment of happiness and freedom. The work springs primarily from his discovery of the liberation which came through sexual experience. It is an answer to the problem of *Paludes*.

In writing *Les Nourritures Terrestres* Gide intended to preach evasion from the shackles of convention and usage. 'One must act', he says, 'without pausing to consider whether the action is good or evil; love without troubling whether it is good or evil'. And again: 'Commandments of God, you have made my soul ill, you have surrounded with walls the only springs to quench my thirst'.

Those who disapproved of the work—and there were many—saw in it the glorification of sensuality, the destruction of discipline and authority. These strictures were to annoy Gide, for he knew that his intentions had been pure; and indeed, the pleasures that he advocates are innocent, and not devoid of idealism. The spiritual joys are for him the supreme joys, but he longs for them to be less puritanical and less connected with mortification of the flesh.

In *Les Nourritures Terrestres* Gide addresses the young through Nathanael, who is the symbol of youth; that is why he exercised so great an influence in the nineteen-twenties. He draws them aside when they are weary from reading many books, and from finding nothing in them on which their souls may feed. He tells them that he writes for them alone. Then, having spoken to them, in the hours of sadness and loneliness, he advises them, after finishing his book, to cast it away, to emancipate themselves from it. 'Do not think that your truth can be found by anyone save you. Throw away my book and say to yourself that here is only one of the possible gestures in front of life. Find your own. What someone else could have done as well as you, do not do. Cultivate in yourself only what you feel is nowhere else, and create the most irreplaceable of beings.'

Each youth in the nineteen-twenties, reading these lines, felt that they had been written for him alone, and many were turned into rebels. It is a work calculated to appeal to the young, with its lyrical expression of joy. Those, however, who have reached maturity and who have read Gide's later writings in a classical style of austere beauty, will sometimes find the ecstatic lyricism of *Les Nourritures Terrestres* somewhat too lush, too reminiscent of Walter Pater, and, in spite of its obvious sincerity, it will strike them as somewhat too studied and artificial.

In the midst of composing *Les Nourritures Terrestres* in Biskra Gide was interrupted in March 1895 by his mother, whose letters recalled him because she had been anxious lest he should be becoming too independent, and feared also that he might be enjoying an illicit relationship like the one she had uncovered the previous year. He returned to France and spent some happy weeks with her, amongst the happiest of his life; their only topic of disagreement was the title of his book, which she thought suggested licence. He was serene and contented and looking forward to spending the summer with her at La Roque, where he hoped that Madeleine might join them and that she might now consent to marry him. He was staying with friends while his mother went ahead with Marie to open up the house, when a telegram reached him from the maid telling him that the old lady had had a stroke. He hurried to her but found her dying, and he was not even certain that she still recognised him. She died some days later, in May 1895, not in July as he states in his autobiography.

Gide's grief shattered his recent joy, and he turned to religion once more for comfort, living in an exalted state when all he prayed for was the possibility of sacrificing himself. Then he abandoned the unfinished *Nour-ritures Terrestres* since it no longer reflected his mood, and conceived his play *Saul* which takes the diametrically opposite view.

Gide was always irritated later when critics praised *Les Nourritures Terrestres* at the expense of his other works, and he himself deplored its influence in the twenties, for by that time he had written many books with other views. In a Preface to an edition in 1927 he declared that it had been the work of a convalescent, and that through it he had regained his health, but that nevertheless it was not his only book and that he refused to be judged by it alone. He declared that the dangers of the doctrine had been so apparent to him that immediately, as an antidote, he had conceived his play *Saul*, the subject of which is precisely the ruin of the soul and the extinction of the personality, the inevitable results of non-resistance to temptation.

All Gide's thoughts at this time were centred on his cousin Madeleine, and he clung to her as to his only hope and ideal. She seemed to him everything that he most admired and needed; she believed in him and in his higher possibilities, whereas he was always uncertain of himself and obsessed by a feeling of guilt. He proposed marriage to her and this time she accepted him.

Gide was subsequently severely criticised for having married her, since by then he was aware of his homosexual leanings; but he did not take the step lightly, and consulted a doctor who assured him that since he loved her, all would be well, and told him that his aberrations were like those of a starving man who had tried to feed on nothing but pickles.

It was not solely on his own account that Gide had wished to marry Madeleine. He hoped that he could now devote his whole life to her and make up to her for the suffering of her girlhood; he longed to give her happiness and to share with her the bliss that he had enjoyed himself for so short a time. But you cannot give happiness, your own form of happiness, to another; it can only grow through fusion, and that did not happen. Their life together did not turn out as Gide had hoped and there was, as will be related later, strife and struggle between them. But she remained the great love of his life, his only really deep emotion. Had he never married her, had he remained single, his work would certainly have been different. It would probably have been the poorer, for it might have lacked its spiritual polarisation.

Gide and Madeleine were married in October 1895 by the same protestant clergyman who had married his parents thirty-two years before. He was twenty-six and she twenty-eight. They set out for a long honeymoon lasting almost six months. They spent the autumn in Switzerland, the early winter in Italy when they visited Florence, Rome and Naples; then they moved south to North Africa which, in spite of his other travels, still beckoned to Gide.

They returned to La Roque in May 1896 and Gide was immediately elected mayor of the commune by an overwhelming majority—the youngest mayor of France. He said later that those who claimed that he was indifferent to the public weal did not realise how much civic zeal he had brought to his arduous duties. He took them very seriously. He joined couples in holy matrimony, frightened hardened alcoholics into reforming, and had cases retried when he thought that there had been a miscarriage of justice.

He spent some of the year also at Cuverville, and there he finished *Les Nourritures Terrestres*, which appeared in April 1897. It fell completely flat, and in ten years only five hundred copies were sold. George Painter relates a joke which he says was current in the offices of his publisher; they used to beg visitors to take away a few of the 'Fruits', saying that they were a glut on the market and would not keep much longer. Gide, however, had his revenge twenty-five years later, when the book became his most popular and influential work.

In the mean time he was also working on *Saul* and on *Le Prométhée mal enchaîné*. They were both finished in 1898; the second was published in 1899, although the first did not appear until 1903.

3

PROMETHEUS MISBOUND

After his return from his honeymoon Gide was occupied in finishing *Les Nourritures Terrestres*, but he did not seem able to recapture the mood of total joy he had experienced in North Africa. He sought diversion and change in composing *El Hadj*, the treatise of the false prophet, on which he worked in 1896. It relates how a Prince leads his people, with the promise of spiritual joys, to the salt marshes of the Eternal City. On their journey thither he does not permit them to enjoy even the pleasures of the oases in which they rest by night, for fear that they might be turned away from their high purpose. As they reach the borders of the promised land the leader dies and his people are left without a guide. They are led back again to their earthly city by El Hadj who would have them enjoy the pleasures of this world. They are glad of his leadership and are convinced that he is a prophet, but he knows that he is only a false one. Gide here doubts the spiritual as well as the material solution for the problems of life, since both prove disappointing. *El Hadj* was published in 1899, in the same year as *Le Prométhée mal enchaîné*.

Having completed these works Gide took up *Saul* again and finished it in a mood of deep pessimism in 1898. When he had begun *Les Nourritures Terrestres* he had wandered through pleasant paths and by-ways, but he thought now that they had led him only to destruction. He now wanted to prove that those who do not resist temptations will end by being destroyed by them, as well as those who set themselves up as sole judges of their own deeds. All the desires to which, at the time of *Les Nourritures Terrestres*, it had seemed wholesome to yield now came to destroy Saul, and amongst them the one to which Gide had surrendered with such a sense of liberation. Saul was tempted by his dawning passion for David, and he slew his wife because she had discovered his guilty secret. David, however, had also guessed it and then turned against him whom he had previously considered as his Master, and joined forces with his enemies.

After finishing *Saul* Gide grew weary of dwelling on the inevitable retribution which follows sin. There was, as was usual with him, the swing of the pendulum to the other extreme. It was as if he felt that he had been too severe on Saul, who had really been the victim of a cruel and unjust God. He then composed *Le Pro- méthée mal enchaîné* as an antidote, and it is inspired by the same vein of irony as *Voyage d'Urien* and *Pa- ludes*. Here occurs the first of the 'actes gratuits' of which so much has been written. An 'acte gratuit' is an apparently motiveless action, the freest of all actions, Gide says, the one which separates the man from the beast, for it is performed for no personal—hence limit- ing—motive. It is the act which man performs with the whole of his personality, with all his characteristics. The most famous one is that in *Les Caves du Vatican* where the hero, without any motive, murders a perfect stranger in a train by hurling him out of the carriage door. Although such an action might, at first sight, appear to be gratuitous, it seems so only because the motive is deeply hidden even from the perpetrator of the deed.

Gide was to reach this conclusion later, when he was a member of a jury and had to make decisions on questions of behaviour. He writes of one of these in *L'Affaire Redureau*, the case of a young man who had killed, without apparent motive, seven people. Gide then believed that if the personality had been fully aware of itself, fully co-ordinated, then the crimes would never have been committed; if the personality had been free from the obsessions and inhibitions which had caused psychological maladjustment, then violence might well have never occurred.

The Greek Prometheus has been chained to a mountain by Zeus as a punishment for having tried to increase the freedom of man, and an eagle is sent daily to feed on his liver. Gide's Prometheus, finding his chains, which symbolise his scruples and conventions, irksome, casts them off and descends into the city of modern life, but he does not know where to go. He sits in a café to find out. People pass and the waiter tells him that they are men in search of their personalities. He has with him his eagle which gives him a certain distinction. He has affection for it and feeds it on his flesh so that it grows sleek and beautiful. He does not love man any more, but only the eagle that devours him, that is the special passion that torments him. The eagle also symbolises man's conscience and he must make his peace with it and finally conquer it. Prometheus ends by killing his eagle and eating it. It is with one of its feathers that the author has written his tale.

In spite of its satire and the gaiety of its style, *Le Prométhée mal enchaîné* is serious in intention. It is a further restatement of the thesis of *Les Nourritures Terrestres,* the quest for individual values which were discarded in *Saul.* Here Gide symbolises God as a corpulent and unreasonable banker who performs stupid 'actes

163

gratuits' to the discomfiture of man, handing out meaningless retribution and unfair torture. Prometheus, standing for man, is wiser and stronger than he.

With *Le Prométhée mal enchaîné* we come to the end of Gide's discussion of man's solitary destiny, the conquest of personal liberty. Hereafter, for the next twenty years, the problem that will occupy him is the one dealing with his relationship with his wife. He examines then the dangers which beset and threaten the liberty gained. During all these years, in spite of his great love for her and hers for him, he lived in a state of conflict and distress. The problem is not an easy one to clarify for much of it is shrouded in mystery, but everything we read leaves behind it an impression of tragedy and misunderstanding which rouses compassion for these two unhappy beings who loved one another deeply and yet were driven to bring each other much unhappiness and distress. The works that Gide composed from now until the end of the First World War all reflect, from differing angles, the same problem. He worked it out in every aspect, giving it different possibilities and solutions. How was he to reconcile his need for complete individual freedom with his duty to his wife—nay, his deep love for her and anxiety to please her? How reconcile her austerity, even puritanism, with his longing for every kind of experience? The Prodigal son in his tale does return home, but very reluctantly and with the impression of having failed in his purpose by yielding so soon, but he encourages his young brother to escape and warns him not to follow his example.

Every facet of Gide's relationship with his wife is to be found somewhere in his work during these twenty years. He wrote of nothing else. But, since he was a great artist, the scenes and episodes are transfigured

164

and transposed, and the characters become real beings in their own right. They are not wholly himself nor his wife, for he said that what was lacking in each of the characters that he carved from his own flesh was that modicum of common-sense which prevented him from carrying their follies as far as they did. He worked out the problem of his married life as a theorem in each book that he wrote. He studied it from different angles and drew out all the different aspects of that long and painful struggle, particularly in *L'Immoraliste, La Porte Étroite* and *La Symphonie Pastorale*. The different contrasting aspects are seen particularly in the first of these works. *L'Immoraliste* is the story of a man who destroys his own and his wife's happiness through his egoistical conception of personal liberty. *La Porte Étroite* tells of a girl who destroys her own happiness and that of the man she loves but never marries, through a false conception of virtue.

There was between him and his wife incessant struggle which was never really resolved. In that conflict what he most feared was to become an unconscious hypocrite. It was to crystallise that terror that he conceived *La Symphonie Pastorale*. Here the 'pasteur', though a good man and frequently actuated by genuine Christian ideals, brings about disaster through his self-deception. Hypocrisy, unconscious or otherwise, was a problem that fascinated Gide and it is the human failing which he attacked most fiercely.

The forty-three years of Gide's married life were years of lack of understanding and intimacy. Roger Martin du Gard describes his first visit to Cuverville, and the distant politeness of the pair to one another, the courtesy of casual acquaintances. Neither could draw near the other, and Gide complains several times that nothing was ever brought out in the full daylight, and that there never was between them a frank discussion on anything. Yet every line he ever wrote reflects his longing for sympathy and understanding. He said that every work until *Les Faux Monnayeurs* was written as an appeal to her, but she would never read any for she knew beforehand that she would disapprove. Although she never reproached him openly, her life with him was a long silent reproach for his being as he was, and she did not give him the warmth of understanding which would soften disapproval and make it light to bear. All through his married life he did not cease from longing for that intimacy; it was an open wound which nothing would heal.

In spite of her goodness there was some hard streak in her, as when she deliberately wounded him by giving away a carefully chosen gift. It was as if she would not allow herself to enjoy anything he had given her, nor let him guess her pleasure. She also made it patently clear to him that she did not read his writings by leaving the pages of his contributions uncut in periodicals in which she had read the other articles.

It is not certain whether she ever realised his homosexual tendencies. In his letters to Claudel in 1912 he declares that she is ignorant of the fact and that, as he loves her more than his life, he is always afraid she may learn of it. Yet, when he writes of his honeymoon it would seem impossible that she should still have been in ignorance, as he describes how he neglected her for young artists' models in Italy and how, through the carriage window on the train, he tried to attract the attention of some youths next door. These passages, written after her death in a moment of self-flagellation, do not however ring true.

One has the impression that she lived beside him for more than forty years in silent disapproval which she never openly expressed, loving him deeply, yet always wishing him to be different. There was no doubt that she loved him to the end, although her love was mingled with grief. She said to him once, very much later: 'I owe my greatest joy to you, but also my greatest sadness—the best and the most bitter'.

On several occasions in letters and Journal, Gide declared that he felt no physical desire for her, or for any other woman; but he did not say this at the time of his marriage, only very much later. At first he certainly imagined that women do not feel sexual desire as men do. In his dreams his wife appeared to him as a will o' the wisp always eluding his grasp, and the dream became a nightmare. It is possible to believe that had she been able to break down his reserves they might have reached full happiness. She was the older and he had, all through his childhood and youth, deferred to her and waited on her command, so that later he found it impossible to take the virile lead which marriage requires, and then took refuge in the excuse of his homosexuality. He suggests, though he does not say so specifically, that the marriage was never consummated, and he takes the full blame for this, attributing it to a definite resolve on his part. He may have preferred this reputation to the one of incapacity—Jerome in *La Porte Étroite,* who is a reflection of Gide himself, gives the impression of impotence. His wife was no help to him. She had her own obsessions and inhibitions. She had a fear of physical passion, wounded as she had been as a girl by her discovery of the change wrought in her own mother through passionate love; and so Gide, afraid of hurting or disgusting her, did not persevere. He tells us that she would have liked a child but was too reserved to let him know this, and so, in unconscious vengeance against him for not having sufficiently loved her—as it must have seemed to her, doubting her charm for him —she did everything she could to destroy the image he once had of her and the things he had loved. She allowed her physical beauty to vanish and no longer cultivated her mind. All he could do was look on in impotent despair. She destroyed her gifts as Alissa did in *La Porte Étroite*. Whenever her shadow passes through the *Journal* we are conscious of anxiety and distress.

Yet she remained for Gide his idol and his ideal of woman, and probably inspired him more than if she had given him peace and contentment. Thinking of her he strove always to be better than he was by nature. These two beings lived side by side for almost half a century, loving one another deeply yet each laying waste the heart of the other.

With this problem we reach a new Gide, preoccupied with psychological more than with lyrical and personal problems. Now, with the opening of the twentieth century, we have, until *Les Faux Monnayeurs* in 1925, his greatest and richest period as a creative artist.

4

STRAIT IS THE GATE

With the new century we reach a fresh phase in Gide's work, a nobler phase than hitherto, where he shows greater mastery as a writer, and greater psychological awareness. He is no longer the artist struggling alone against fate, but a man concerned with the problem of living together with another individual, with whom he must find harmony. There is a corresponding sobering of his lyric style and a pruning away of all previous lusciousness. Now, for the first time, we find André Gide the creator of faultless prose.

Here begins also his period of psychological distress and 'angst', when he floundered in doubts and scruples, and was pulled hither and thither, never knowing whether what he was doing was right or wrong; when the opinions of others had power to wound him deeply.

It is the time also when—as we learn from the *Journal*—to escape from the restrictions, imagined or real, of the conjugal home, he used to wander solitary through the streets of Paris at night, toying, it seems mostly in imagination, with the temptation of furtive homosexual experience. These encounters, if indeed they ever became real, never developed into relationships.

It is at this time that he began to be widely known— and also ostracised.

This period of twenty-five years could be subdivided

into two fairly even parts, separated by *Les Caves du Vatican* of 1914.

In the first part Gide was preoccupied with the problem of his marriage and his study of it in his writings. It contains *L'Immoraliste, L'Enfant Prodigue, La Porte Étroite, Isabelle* and the initial conception of *La Symphonie Pastorale* which, by inspiration, belongs to it. Gide declared later that each of his books was a work of criticism. *L'Immoraliste* criticizes a form of individualism; *La Porte Étroite* a mystical and religious tendency; *Isabelle* a kind of romanticism; while *La Symphonie Pastorale* is an indictment of self-deception. He studies the problem of his marriage in all its aspects and purges himself of much perplexity in the process of writing.

L'Immoraliste is the first of these works. Unfortunately, there are no entries in his *Journal* for the time of composition, and we do not know whether they were ever written or whether they were destroyed, and so we have no clue to his state of mind. But, from subsequent entries, and from the testimony of letters, we gather that he became, after his honeymoon, increasingly troubled, and that he suffered a great deal nervously.

L'Immoraliste is written, as are nearly all Gide's works, in the first person. This enabled him to give greater verisimilitude to his writing. The story is not, however, wholly his and many of the episodes which actually did happen in his life have their chronology and emphasis altered. He created his characters from his own flesh and blood, but they are never wholly himself, though, as he admits, he would become them so entirely as he wrote that they seemed to be himself. Then he allowed himself to be carried away to where he would not have gone on his own. He said later that people always insisted on seeing personal declarations of faith and beliefs in the utterances of each of his characters however diverse and contradictory they might be.

In *Les Nourritures Terrestres* Gide had sung lyrically of the necessity for self-realisation and the joys that came therefrom; but in *L'Immoraliste,* on the contrary, he shows these no longer in imagination but in real life, as a problem to wrestle with and solve, and to fit into the frame-work of human relations. His aim now was to study psychologically the effect of these beliefs on human beings. Is it possible, he asks by implication, especially in married life, to live according to the philosophy of *Les Nourritures Terrestres*? The answer to this question is *L'Immoraliste.*

In this tale Gide retraces the stresses and strains of his life with Madeleine. The hero Michel has the same paralysis of the will before his wife. He tries to escape from his bonds but can only do so by hurting, indeed eventually killing, Marceleine. It is emotionally necessary for Gide that she should die, as she symbolises all the restraints against which he had been chafing. But, after she is dead, he is left with guilt and despair.

L'Immoraliste is the first of Gide's works written in limpid and pure prose which does not fall far short of his greatest works; and it is far in advance of any of his previous compositions.

Gide's next works, two short ones, are in the nature of an interlude in his personal problems. They were written as a tribute to Oscar Wilde who had died in 1900 and whose funeral he had been unable to attend on account of absence abroad. They are *In Memoriam* and *De Profundis,* slight essays which study Wilde's personality rather than his writings; but there exists no truer picture of the conversationalist, and that was how Gide chiefly saw him at this time, though later he regretted not having treated his writings more seriously.

It was Gide who asked Wilde why his books were not better considering his gifts, and was then answered that he had put his genius into his life and only his talent into his works.

Gide would have liked to write immediately the companion book to *L'Immoraliste,* the reverse of the same medal, *La Porte Étroite,* but he was inhibited for many years. It has usually been argued that the lack of success of the earlier book had discouraged him, but it is more likely that his inhibition was due to that paralysis which always overcame him when he wanted to portray his wife. In *La Porte Étroite* he was obliged to deal with matters which deeply touched his emotions, and the problem was now to show how in the failure of the couple the woman, as well as the man, shared in the blame. He would also, in the portrait of Alissa, have liked to please his wife—or at least not to hurt her. Few of us, however, are satisfied with our portraits by others—even when they are flattering—for they do not correspond to that secret picture we hide in the depths of our heart; we feel that we have not been understood, and to be understood is what, in our blindness, we imagine that we most want. There were scenes which meant much to him and which he could not achieve to his satisfaction, particularly the one where Jerome comes on Alissa weeping over her mother's infidelity, kneeling by her bedside. He wrote the scene again and again without success. In desperation he went to North Africa to seek inspiration, ostensibly to write a travel book, but secretly with the hope of recapturing the joy of *Les Nourritures Terrestres.* It was, however, a book of sadness rather than of joy that he brought back: *Amyntas,* a renunciation of travel.

After this he was drawn back to Cuverville which was now his home until his wife's death, since, after finishing *L'Immoraliste,* he had sold his own property. He set to work on *La Porte Étroite,* and after several years he wrote that he was beginning it again for the fourth time, and he considered giving it up altogether. So difficult did he find it to finish that he interrupted it for a time in 1907 to write, in a few weeks, *Le Retour de l'Enfant Prodigue.* Here the prodigal, after his return, doubts his wisdom and urges his young brother to leave and never to come back. Gide was indeed a prodigal who often, despite his deep love for his wife, felt the pressing need to break away from home. He describes himself as creeping out of Cuverville at dawn, after a sleepless night due to his sorrow at the thought of paining Madeleine, but, at the same time, full of joy at the anticipation of freedom. 'Even at the moment when you were leaving her, you could not hide your joy from her. Why then were you almost irritated that she could not hide her tears from you?'

Gide finally finished *La Porte Étroite* in October 1908. When he had completed it he said that it was like a piece of nougat in which the almonds were good—that is the letters and Alissa's diary—but that the mass which held them together was of poor quality. That is not the opinion generally held, for it is considered to be one of his most perfect works, in style and content.

La Porte Étroite had been conceived many years before, at the same time as *L'Immoraliste,* and he always claimed that they should be taken together. He called them twins and said that they were two facets of the same problem and that, had he been able physically to write them at the same moment, he would have done so. *L'Immoraliste* had shown how one form of egoism, if allowed full license, would destroy everything. Now he wanted to demonstrate that it is not the egoist alone who is guilty, but that some of the blame must also go

173

to the allegedly virtuous party. In a letter to Claudel he declared that his intention had been to show the error of that heady form of superior infatuation and of contempt for all pleasures of this world. This could, naturally, be mingled with true nobility and greatness.

La Porte Étroite is the most moving personal of all Gide's work. It mirrors the mystic orientation of his life and his dedication to his cousin. It reflects also his consciousness of failure with her. In real life he may have married her, but he remained, nevertheless, as shut out as the hero of the tale, by the strait gate. Alissa's reluctance to accept Jerome is complex. It was not only that she wished to make a sacrifice of her love to God: there were other obstacles as well. Through the shock she had received as a girl, when she had discovered her mother's infidelity, she had kept a neurotic fear of love as a force that brought destruction. There was also puzzled amazement at, perhaps even contempt of, a love that seemed rooted in impotence. Her religion was her escape and also her excuse, but to see her altering little by little, to see her sacrifice all her gifts of beauty, taste, and intellect in a mistaken idea of virtue, Jerome suffered as Gide declared that he had suffered at a similar diminution in his wife.

Finally, in a scene of great literary and psychological beauty, Alissa says farewell to Jerome, at a little gate leading into the garden, symbolical surely of the strait gate through which he can no longer accompany her. She enters it alone and bids him not try to follow her.

There is a similar little gate at Cuverville, and Gide could never look at it without emotion, for he had lived so intensely these moments with Alissa and Jerome that tears would run down his face as he showed it to visitors. 'I walk here like a ghost', he said, 'in a past that is dead'.

La Porte Étroite is Gide's most exquisitely planned and written work. It has a harmony of style and a unity of action which are truly classical. The psychology too is more sure and subtle than in any of his former novels, and it is not only the two main characters who are drawn with such skill but also the host of different minor ones who make up the complex family circle; all are portrayed with sympathetic understanding and placed in their own correct setting. The tale has only one fault of construction. It would have been truer and more artistic to have ended it with Jerome reading the last entry of Alissa's diary, that she left him in her will, instead of adding the more conventional Epilogue, where he visits her sister ten years afterwards and sees in her room the furniture he had known so well in Alissa's. They talk of bygone days and he realises that he will never forget the past.

To the surprise of everyone the novel sold, and it was the first of Gide's works to reach a wide public. His publishers, thinking that a thousand copies would be ample, had destroyed the type—they could not imagine that a book which quoted the Bible could be a success—but in less than a month the whole edition was sold out and a new one demanded. Although criticism did not cease, Gide had become overnight an author who sold.

Except for *La Symphonie Pastorale,* conceived at the same time as *La Porte Étroite,* though only finished nine years later, and which he then called his last tribute to the past, Gide had finished expounding the problem of his married life. He wished now to emancipate himself from previous preoccupations, and he began to write *Corydon,* to set forth the problem of his homosexuality; by 1910 he had finished two dialogues of this apology— justification rather—of homosexuality, and even went so far as to have them privately printed, but he allowed himself to be dissuaded by his brother-in-law from publishing them. Instead he wrote *Isabelle,* which is the least personal of all his works and contains nothing of himself or of anyone closely connected with him, though it does take place in landscapes that he knew near his property La Roque. It is not an important work, though it shows mastery and skill, and some fine descriptive writing. It is a tale of mystery and murder, of shots in the dark, of adultery and an illegitimate crippled child. It is the subject of the 'roman noir', but with a Gidian twist that gives it originality. Isabelle, as she is on the point of eloping with her lover, is seized with panic at the thought of freedom, and she sends an old servant to intercept him and to prevent him reaching her; he is overzealous and kills him. Through refusing to yield to temptation—a very Gidian conception—and through fear of liberty, Isabelle lost her chance of fulfilment and all in vain, for she later became no better than a whore. The story might have been the conventional one of a young girl seduced by her lover, but prevented from eloping with him by a faithful retainer, and then bearing a crippled child through her efforts to disguise her condition. That hers should be the real guilt adds spice to the story.

Isabelle closes the first part of Gide's main creative phase. In this period he began to write literary criticism, in which he is far from negligible. *Prétextes* was published in 1903 and was followed by *Nouveaux Prétextes* in 1911. Then too he began to collect a host of followers somewhat younger than himself, not the large number of the nineteen-twenties, but nevertheless a goodly number, most of whom counted in literature before the First World War. Amongst them were Ghéon, Copeau,

Schlumberger, Rivière and many others. With some of them he founded *La Nouvelle Revue Française* in 1908, which continued until the Second World War to unite and to publish the most progressive writers in France.

5

IF IT DIE

Les Caves du Vatican marks the transition between the first and second parts of Gide's main creative period, and it indicates the break with the past. It was begun in October 1911 and finished in June 1913. In construction it is similar to the later work *Les Faux Monnayeurs*; in both novels the various plots are skilfully interwoven at different points to form a pattern of great complexity. In *Les Caves du Vatican* the points of intersection are formed by the fact that the main characters in this devious story, with all its plots and ramifications, are members of the same family, either by birth or marriage.

Gide calls it not a novel but a 'sotie' which, by dictionary definition, is a work in which everyone is mad or foolish. He wishes to show all the ways in which men are fools. Fools are those who live in a certain system of beliefs in order to attack those who live in another; fools are the 'bien pensants' with their bigoted faith; fools too the free-thinkers just as bigoted in their atheism; fools too the ambitious pursuing vain honours. All of them are fools afraid of life. Amongst them stands out the hero, Lafcadio, the free individual, a bastard bound by no ties to the past. He is a young man somewhat like the David in Gide's play *Saul*, but even more like Julien Sorel in Stendhal's novel *Le Rouge et le*

Noir. He is a youth handsome and strong in body and determination who, whenever he considers that he has betrayed his real feelings, punishes himself by plunging a knife into his thigh. It is he who has the courage and daring to perform the 'acte gratuit' when he kills a complete stranger, one of the fools of the 'sotie' and a born victim.

Les Caves du Vatican ends on the question of whether or no Lafcadio is going to give himself up to the police for his crime. Gide liked this uncertain ending and was to use it again in *Les Faux Monnayeurs*. We must assume that Lafcadio did not die, since he was to be the hero of the later novel which was to be composed of his private diary. He was eventually to become Bernard in the finished work.

Les Caves du Vatican is an amusing and brilliantly written book the irony of which is more subtle than that of *Paludes* or *Le Prométhée mal enchaîné*. There are some critics who consider it as Gide's greatest and most accomplished work, though not all would agree with this opinion. There are many, on the contrary, who feel that he reaches greater heights when his work is inspired by deep human emotion, contained in and restrained by perfect language.

The work brought him much criticism from Catholics on account of its flippancy and anti-clericalism, and it made Gide's relations with Paul Claudel very strained. One of the reasons which inspired him to write it may well have been irritation against his friend who had been trying, since they met in 1905, not always tactfully, to convert him to Catholicism. The quarrel over *Les Caves du Vatican* virtually put an end to their friendship. Gide had borrowed a line from Claudel's play, *L'Annonce faite à Marie,* as a heading to the section dealing with the papal conspiracy, which said: 'Of what

King speak you and of what Pope? For there are two and no one knows which is the true one'. Claudel was naturally referring to the fourteenth-century, when there were two claimants to the papacy, and he requested Gide to remove this line from his work as he did not wish to be connected with it in any way, both on account of its attitude to Catholicism and its very dubious moral tone.

There now occurred a psychological crisis in Gide's life which lasted for some years and from which he emerged a very different person. The crisis had started before he began *Les Caves du Vatican,* and as a result he went through years of deep mental suffering and turmoil. We can reconstruct the general lines from his correspondence with Claudel. It was an emotional as well as religious crisis—or rather it was an emotional conflict which gave rise to a religious one. Gide always needed some conflict in order to obtain the energy for composition. He wanted now to study the problem of his homosexuality. He felt that it should be eradicated or else accepted, not furtively, but openly. This problem had begun to trouble him after he had finished *La Porte Étroite* and it continued all through the writing of *Les Caves du Vatican.* He wished to complete his *Corydon* and to make full confession, in total sincerity. The conflict came to a head when Claudel requested Gide to remove the offending quotation from his book and then went on to say that he considered it dangerous for Gide from every point of view. He warned him that he ought to realise that after *Saul* and *L'Immoraliste* he should be very careful, and not place weapons in the hands of his opponents. He asked him how he could have written certain passages in the book and then said: 'Must we then believe, what I have never wished to, that you are yourself a participant in these hideous practices? Answer me you must! If you are not a homosexual, then why this strange predilection for that sort of subject? If you are one, then unfortunate man get treated and don't publish these abominations.'

This started a long and acrimonious argument. Gide answered heatedly demanding by what right his friend asked such questions in such a manner. He said that he made no mystery of his leanings and went on, in the strictest confidence, to confide in him his secret conflict, begging him not to reveal it to anyone. 'If I were alone', he said, 'I could make little of the contempt of the world, but I am a married man. As for the harm which you say my books are doing, I cannot believe it since I have come to realise the number of people whom the hypocrisy of our morals stifles as it does me . . . I can-not believe that religion casts out those who are like me. Through what cowardice, since God calls on me to speak, can I burke the question in my books? I have not chosen to be thus. I can struggle against my desires, I can overcome them, but I cannot choose the object of these desires nor invent others by imitation.' Then he confessed to him, as to a priest whose duty it was to keep his secret. 'I have never felt any desire towards a woman, and the great tragedy of my life is that the most constant and deep love is not, in my case, accompanied by what usually precedes it. It seems as if, on the contrary, love in me prevented desire.' He renewed his request for discretion: 'I implore you then to consider only this, that I love my wife more than my life, and that I could never forgive you if any act of yours touched her hap-piness'. He begged for his help and said: 'I do not know how to solve the problem which God has inscribed in my flesh'.

Claudel answered saying that God has not allowed anyone the right to use his own judgment to decide between right and wrong, that the law is written in black and white for all to follow. And moreover he considered that cynicism is worse than hypocrisy, that to sin and then to do penance is preferable to trying afterwards to find excuses and justifications. 'I repeat you are destroying yourself, putting yourself outside the pale, amongst those who are outside the pale, outside humanity. Public opinion in Paris hides itself better, but it is every bit as merciless as in London. You won't count any more.' He said that if Gide would remove the offensive paragraphs, little by little all would be forgotten. This was the most unbearable cut of all to Gide. 'Shall I confess that your striking phrase "little by little all will be forgotten" seems to me shameful', he answered. 'No! I do not want whitewash or compromise.'

In a desperate effort to obtain help in his struggle Gide now turned, for a time, towards the Catholic faith; and it was then that his friends hoped most for his conversion.

In the meantime the First Great War had broken out. In July 1914 Gide had been on the point of going to England; he had even bought his ticket and was about to embark at Dieppe when he bought a paper and suddenly realised that war was inevitable. He hurried back to Cuverville to look after his wife. When war finally came he went to Paris to find some work to help in the war effort. He thought at first that during a war a writer's duty was to abstain from writing. He worked in the early days for the Red Cross, and next in a convalescent home for soldiers. Then, with the German advance on Paris, he feared for the safety of his wife, and returned to Cuverville to arrange for the evacuation of the women and children of the village. He stood at his own door, waiting for the arrival of the enemy. Then came the Battle of the Marne, and the thrust towards the Channel ports was averted. In October 1914 he became assistant director of a Foyer Franco-Belge, to give food and shelter to the refugees. He remained there for nearly eighteen months and then, through some cabal, he was deposed from office and returned to Cuverville. He took up again his pre-war preoccupations and began once more to write and think.

His thoughts were much taken up with religious speculations, especially when a close friend was killed at the front; he was a recent convert to Catholicism and the moving letters which he wrote to his wife, and which Gide had read, broke down much of his lack of faith. There was also the conversion of Ghéon, in January 1916, which moved him greatly. The day after he heard of it he read the opening verses from the fifteenth chapter of Saint John, and they assumed for him an added meaning. 'If a man abide not in me, he is cast forth as a branch and is withered; and men gather them and cast them into the fire; and they are burnt.' He felt suddenly that he himself had been cast into the fire, the fire of abominable desires. He suddenly saw that everything in him needed reforming and that he must conquer his sensuality. Seeking help in his struggle, he thought he might find it in religion. All through 1916 he dwelt in darkness and distress of soul. In February he began to keep two diaries, the usual one in which he recorded his daily life, and another, published later under the title *Numquid et tu,* in which he related his anguished search for God.

George Painter, in his recent biography, sees the conflict differently. He explains it as due merely to a conventional emotional triangle when, according to him, Gide fell in love with the daughter of his eldest woman friend, a girl young enough to be his daughter, and sought help from this in religion. He does not give his evidence for this statement, and Gide's *Journal* and letters do not support it. Moreover Gide assured Claudel that he had never felt desire for any woman, and in his posthumous work, *Nunc manet in Te,* he declared that he was capable of sexual power only when his emotions were not involved.

There was, however, certainly some serious difference between Gide and his wife during 1916, for he did not write in his *Journal* for three months and said afterwards: 'I take up this *Journal* again which I dropped last June. I had torn up all the last pages for they reflected a terrible crisis in which Em was involved, or more exactly of which she was the cause.' Since these pages had been written for her he destroyed them as soon as she had read them, if not exactly at her request, because he knew that that was what she would have wished. However, he later regretted them bitterly because he said that they were amongst the most heart-felt he had ever written.

This new love for another woman—if love there really was—remains mysterious, for Gide does not speak of it, and it did not in any way impair his deep devotion for his wife. In October 1916 there was some plan that he should spend the winter with old friends in the south of France, but when he spoke of it to Madeleine, he saw such resigned sadness on her face that he abandoned all thought of the visit. He gave it up, he said, as well as many other projects, because anything which he would have purchased at the expense of her happiness would no longer have brought him pleasure.

La Symphonie Pastorale was finished after the mental tribulations of this year. Painter believes that what he calls the love affair with the young woman coloured his view of the novel (which had been conceived in 1910) and altered it.

La Symphonie Pastorale is a return to the novel in the first person, and it consists of the diary kept by a Swiss Protestant minister who is, as was Michel in *L'Immoraliste,* what Gide feared that he might become if he gave way to certain of his tendencies. Although he shares many of the minister's characteristics he is not wholly like him, and he was much annoyed when people tried to identify him with him. It is, as are most of Gide's books, a work of criticism. He criticizes the materialistic attitude to religion of the wife, but also the way in which the minister manages to deceive himself and to twist the Gospels to suit his own ends. It is Gide's most despairing work, and evil seems to be triumphant all along the line. Although it has certain faults of construction, especially a very faulty ending, it is a work of great beauty and purity. The style is more effortless than even in *La Porte Étroite,* and more stripped of lyricism and imagery; it is Racinian in its telling economy, which matches the purity of the landscape and the religious nature of the subject. All the characters are well drawn and the minister is one of Gide's most masterly creations, one of the best portraits of the hypocrite, or rather self-deceiver, in French literature.

After the book was published Gide tells us that he received a letter expressing surprise that he could have written such a work after *Les Caves du Vatican* and that he answered that it was a debt to the past which he had not settled and which was now liquidated. He means that it belonged to the individual problems which he had treated in *L'Immoraliste* and *La Porte Étroite.* He had now finished with that phase of his life forever.

When Gide started his religious Journal, *Numquid et tu,* in which he set down his anguished search for belief, he was willing to sacrifice his personal liberty for the comfort and support of complete faith. However, no matter how long and how earnestly he prayed, grace did not descend on him; his spiritual pride was too great and he did not recover the heart of a child as he had hoped. When the conflict was over he left revealed religion behind him forever, though he never lost his longing for God. 'Catholicism is inadmissible', he said, 'protestantism is intolerable; and I feel profoundly Christian'.

1916 had been a year of great distress and perplexity for him, but when it ended he reached calmer waters. He solved to his satisfaction the problem of his homosexuality. Its solution was helped by his relationship with Marc, which began in 1917. In spite of all that has been written about Gide's homosexuality this is the only known relationship of this kind, the only one that was more than a furtive encounter.

Then Gide decided to turn his back on his past and to be moral in his own way. He cast aside self-torture, hair-splitting about motives and guilt, and became what he thought was finally himself. 'I allow the contradictions to live in me.'

Then, wishing to liquidate the past and to start afresh, he planned his autobiography, *Si le Grain ne meurt,* meaning to indicate by the title that except the seed die it cannot bring forth fruit. The seeds that will bring forth much fruit in the harvest to come will be the seeds of his dead past, all the distress and 'angst' of his earlier years. He wanted them to die now so that he could begin a new life of freedom and serenity. He began writing it in 1916, though the greater part of it was written after the war. It was first privately printed in 1920 and 1921, but the commercial edition appeared only in 1926. It is an account of his life from his birth to his marriage. Here is again recorded his love for his cousin, the 'mystic orientation' of his life. It ranks amongst the great autobiographies of the world, though it is nearer in form to confessions. It has not the abundance of Rousseau's *Confessions,* nor their lyric sweep, but it has a classic restraint that makes it worthy of the great masters of French prose in the seventeenth century. It contains passages of Gide's finest writing, although it has frequently been severely attacked for its frankness and its discussion of homosexuality.

In May 1917 Gide began his long and deep attachment for Marc, the son of an old friend. It was the friendship in his life which brought him most joy, for a number of years at all events, and was the main reason for his recovery at the end of the War. He adopted him as a son and took him over to England when he went there in June 1918. This overt action of Gide's wounded his wife more deeply than anything she had yet endured with him. We do not know what she said to him—it was not her habit to say much—but he wrote in his *Journal*: 'I leave France in an indescribable state of anguish. It seems to me that I am saying farewell to the whole of my past.'

When he returned home again he had occasion to ask to see the letters he had written to Madeleine since his boyhood—perhaps he needed some material for his autobiography. Then she confessed to him that after he had gone to England she had burnt them. He was shattered at this unexpected blow from her who had always been so gentle, that she should do this to him. He knew that he had always put the best of himself in his letters to her, and it was as if she had killed their child, his and hers, when she had destroyed them. He wept for over a week, from morning till night, near the fireside, in the living-room with her, and at night alone in his room, hoping against hope that she would come to him, that she would make some sign. That was the bitterest

187

blow of all, her indifference. She went about the little daily jobs, never looking his way. He felt that he had lost her, that everything was shattered in him, the past, the present and the future. He hoped for days that she would yield and come, but she went about the daily round passing beside him as if she did not see him. He did not recover his confidence in life until many years had passed and he felt that he had regained once more her esteem. Seven years later he wrote: 'Since then I have lived only, as it were, a kind of posthumous life, on the fringe of real life.'

The second part of *Si le Grain ne meurt* was written after the destruction of the letters.

She too, poor woman, must have suffered deeply when she found herself alone in the great house, after he had gone to England with Marc; and then, in a panic of despair, she destroyed the letters. Yet they were, she once admitted, her most precious possession; but seeing him have so little regard for her, in her humility, she doubted his love for her and would keep nothing of him, no reminder.

For almost twenty years she lived estranged from him, making all efforts to detach herself, to destroy everything that might still attach him. She now gave to God what she had once given to him, and he was jealous of this rival who was stealing everything that he longed to have. In *Nunc manet in te* he expresses his distress as he sees her turning more and more not to the protestantism of her upbringing but to the Catholicism of her forbears. One of her friends has said, since her death, that it was only loyalty to Gide that prevented her final conversion.

Yet, in spite of everything, Gide knew that he loved her more deeply and more desperately than ever. In 1925, when he was leaving for Africa, he begged a friend to tell her, should he not return, that she had always remained his dearest and most precious treasure, and that it was because he loved her more than life itself, that, since she had withdrawn from him, life seemed to him of so small price.

6

THE COUNTERFEITERS

A great change came over Gide as he emerged from the crisis of the War years. He grew less anxious and his face began to assume the expression which surprised those who knew him first in the nineteen-twenties. In 1928 he wrote to Charles du Bos: 'It is true that I have ceased to love "angst". I think it is good to have known it, but that it is wrong to remain in it and to love it for itself. That is why Pascal touches me nowadays less than Goethe.'

He next finished *Corydon,* which had been hanging fire for so many years that he had feared lest someone should forestall him, for he considered it a topic of such urgent interest that anyone might wish to treat it. He finished it in June 1918 but, restrained by his friends, he still hesitated to publish it.

In the meantime his next published work was one dealing with Dostoevsky, composed of talks which he gave at the Vieux Colombier in 1922 to celebrate the centenary of Dostoevsky's birth. It marks an important stage in Gide's development as a writer, for it reflects the moment when he was emerging from the state of the tormented introvert whom we knew in the early works, and becoming the serene philosopher of the later years. Here, for the first time, he suggests that happiness may well come from renunciation, and that the individual may triumph by sacrificing his individualism; or, as he was later to say: 'the triumph of the individual is in renouncing individualism'. Dostoevsky showed him that he who lives cherishing his own life shall lose it, and that he who surrenders it shall earn life eternal. Gide was now moving towards altruism and forgetfulness of self. He saw in Dostoevsky the reconciliation of extremes, a man who accepted his inconsistencies and proved that the imploring cry of anguished humanity could never rise from the righteous who are sure of their own salvation. Gide contrasts his psychological portrayal with that of Corneille, who depicts characters trying to conform with an ideal which makes them different from what nature intended them to be if they yielded to their natural impulses.

Although, in these lectures, Gide was trying to be objective, it was still himself that he was unconsciously seeking; and he discovered in Dostoevsky only what was like himself, what would be useful to himself.

Eventually, in 1924, Gide determined to publish *Corydon*. It was probably Proust's sorry picture of inversion in *Sodome et Gomorrhe,* published in 1923, that finally urged him to action. He was disgusted that Proust had exemplified only the ugly and decrepit aspect of homosexuality, and had never shown it young and fair. He stigmatised his attitude as hypocritical and cowardly, for Proust had admitted to him that the fairer aspects had been used to embellish heterosexual love in *A l'Ombre des Jeunes Filles en Fleur.*

To the end of his life Gide considered *Corydon* as one of his most important works, but most readers find its special pleading unconvincing. It takes the form of Socratic dialogues. The narrator is a militant heterosexual who has been much perturbed by certain homosexual scandals. He calls on Corydon, a doctor of medicine and also a well-known homosexual, to discuss the matter with him so that he can arrive at an unprejudiced opinion. Corydon argues with his friend, and proves to his complete satisfaction, by zoology first, that homosexuality is not contrary to nature; next by sociology that the only reason why heterosexuality prevails is that it is favoured by convention and training; and finally he goes to history to establish that the epochs when homosexuality was most rife—in classical Greece and during the Renaissance—were epochs of rich artistic, intellectual and spiritual achievement, and that, on the contrary, the prevalence of heterosexual love is a symptom of decadence.

The result is a cold and logical argument the premises of which cannot be accepted, and this alienates sympathy. This was a deliberate purpose as Gide explains, saying that he had avoided all arguments which would touch the heart as he wanted to appeal only to the head.

The publishing of *Corydon* was disastrous to Gide in every way. He was violently attacked on all sides, even by close friends, many of whom he lost. His wife was very much distressed by the unsavoury publicity it aroused and she wrote to him: 'What disturbs me is the evil campaign which has been started against you. Ah! if you were invulnerable I shouldn't be so much afraid. But you are vulnerable and you know it and I know it.' She defied him to find a single honest person who approved of the book; but then, as Gide remarked, she would not consider anyone who did approve of it an honest man.

Gide was startled and amazed at what he considered an unforeseen betrayal. He sold his house in Paris and all his books—even those inscribed to him by writers who were his friends. In the Preface to the catalogue of the sale he wrote: 'Since he [that is himself] is planning a long absence, he has decided to part with his books amongst which are those which had remained very dear to him so long as they awakened only memories of friendship'.

Gide was to leave Paris as soon as he had finished *Les Faux Monnayeurs* on which he was working. He completed it in June 1925, and then set out for French Equatorial Africa whence he was to return only a year later.

In *Les Faux Monnayeurs* we have something different from Gide's previous works. He calls it his only novel, meaning to indicate that the canvas is larger than in his previous tales, where the characters are limited almost to the main protagonists. It is true that the frame-work of *Les Caves du Vatican* is almost as large, but that is a 'sotie' and not a novel.

In *Les Faux Monnayeurs* he would have liked to have been able to dispense with a plot—the ambition of all those who study man's nature deeply—and to include everything without limitation. Although there are some elements of himself in the novelist Edouard, the main character, he did not intend him to be a selfportrait; he makes it clear in *Le Journal des Faux Monnayeurs* that Edouard would never have been capable of achieving what he himself had done. He is, he claims, an amateur, a failure, a 'raté'. As there are so few elements of self-portrayal *Les Faux Monnayeurs* is the least subjective of his works, the most impersonal. It is a very deliberate composition, and he tells us that he aimed at achieving what Bach had done in *The Art of Fugue,* and that he did not see why what is possible in music should be impossible in literature. It is indeed a musical work in which the themes appear and disappear as in a fugue, and all the plots are interwoven with subtle musical skill. It is also a very complicated work, not easy to take in at a first reading; but if persevered with it becomes rewarding. The reader must visualise each character as belonging to several groups, sometimes playing a part in several actions at once. The main character, the novelist, is involved in all the actions and he is, musically speaking, the main subject, the main theme. It is he who draws all the subsidiary characters together. These, more complicated, subtle and tortuous than any hitherto in Gide's work, are all metaphorically counterfeiters—though only Strouvilhou and his associates are counterfeiters in the real sense—for each of them, as soon as he is with other people, even the children, acts a part and ceases to be himself. They all use the false coin of ready-made feelings. Only Bernard tries to find out what he is and to be simply and courageously himself. He is a further reincarnation of Lafcadio from *Les Caves du Vatican,* but Lafcadio grown noble and serious. Gide had first intended *Les Faux Monnayeurs* to be a continuation of *Les Caves du Vatican,* a further chapter in the history of its hero; and in the earliest drafts the character which eventually becomes Bernard was called Lafcadio. However, as Gide wrote, the characters developed out of his control and Bernard became a deeper and more interesting person than ever Lafcadio could have been. He, the finest character in the novel, wrestles with the angel who is also at times the devil, and comes out victorious. He decides on his future conduct, taking his formula from the novelist: 'One must follow one's bent, so long as it is upwards'. He should really have been the hero of the novel, but Gide grew to like Olivier so much that he could not bear to make another young man the hero, and so brought in the novelist to be the main character. Edouard, like Gide, is writing a novel which he is also going to call *Les Faux Monnayeurs.* We hear much of the difficulties he encounters, and this helps the reader to an understanding of Gide's problems of composition and his manner of solving them.

All Gide's well-known themes appear in *Les Faux Monnayeurs*: The conflict between youth and age; the struggle against conventions; the folly of those who live by too rigid principles; the urgent necessity of discovering one's true self; and so forth.

We find here too, for the first time, that altruism and wide sweeping human compassion which will be characteristic of Gide's next phase. The angel, with whom Bernard had struggled, leads him first to the grand Boulevards frequented by the rich full of self-confidence and unconscious of anyone but themselves, yet full of heavy cares. 'Is this happiness?' Bernard asks and feels his heart full of tears. The angel then leads him to the poorer quarters of the city and night begins to fall. They wander through the sordid streets where prostitution, crime, hunger and want lurk. Then Bernard grasps the hand of the angel who turns his face away to weep. The angel symbolises devotion to something beyond oneself.

Les Faux Monnayeurs is a *tour de force* in a very difficult and complicated technique, and it does not quite come off. This is largely because the separate themes are treated more slightly than is necessary, though to treat them fully would have required a novel of unprecedented length. Roger Martin du Gard felt the inadequacy of treatment, and he kept urging Gide to elaborate more fully. He tells us that there were to have been further chapters at the end, but that Gide, somewhat appalled at the thought of the work still needed to complete the novel, was very much relieved and proud when the idea occurred to end it on an interrogation which had no finality. Edouard says: 'I am curious to get to know Caloub'. Caloub is Bernard's young brother who has played no part in the novel, and we imagine it beginning all over again from a different angle; but Edouard has not finished his own *Faux Monnayeurs,* and we know that he will never complete it however many instalments he were given.

Gide himself does not seem to have thought that his novel was an unqualified success as it stood, for he published separately, under the title *Journal des Faux Monnayeurs,* the diary which he had kept while writing the book, and this is of immense interest and elucidates much that is not clear in the novel itself.

Les Faux Monnayeurs is an interesting and subtle work which has influenced the form of the novel all over the world, but it is not without serious faults of construction. The intervention of the author himself, such as occurs in the chapter entitled *The Author judges his Characters,* is out of place in a novel in the first person. There is in any case, without this aside, sufficient objective analysis of the characters. Indeed there is too much *Journal* altogether, and it seems too easy a way out of the difficulties of construction. Gide keeps a *Journal* while writing a novel; his hero is a novelist who also keeps a Journal while writing his own novel about a novelist who keeps a *Journal* while writing a further novel. It is as if one were looking at oneself in a mirror reflected in another mirror and so on to infinity.

When Gide set off for Africa in July 1925, Claudel thought that it was in defeat, with the deliberate intention of not returning—just as in old-fashioned English novels the jilted hero goes East to shoot big game. Then, with the tactlessness which was characteristic of him, he wrote to Madeleine Gide with the purpose of meeting her to discuss the problem of her husband, the outcast: 'Madame', he wrote, 'the impression obsesses me that perhaps you would like to discuss with me a being who is dear to you, whose thought has preoccupied me for twenty-five years, and whose key God has placed in your hands. If I am mistaken please forgive me. If not I should be happy to meet you where and when you like, either in Paris or Cuverville.' Her answer too is characteristic, characteristic of the woman whom Gide had loved so long and so devotedly. 'Dear Monsieur Claudel', she answered, 'your letter is for me a further pledge of the faithful friendship in God which you cherish for my husband. This friendship has always deeply touched me. I have felt, it is true, much anxiety concerning this long and distant visit to darkest Africa which he has wished —but if I had more faith, then I would not be so troubled. All those who love André Gide as that very noble soul deserves to be loved, must pray for him, I do it every day—and you also, don't you? It is thus, I think, that for his greatest good, we can best meet. Dear Monsieur, may I express to the friend that you are all my gratitude, and to the author my admiration.'

Gide, however, did not set out for Africa in any spirit of defeat, or to die there. He now emerged from distress and despair. The birth of his daughter in February 1923 gave him further reasons for hope in the future. She, like his favourite characters, was illegitimate, and he did not openly recognise her until the death of his wife in 1938. He hoped that his wife did not guess the truth, and he told Claude Mauriac that he had suffered much on that score, as he was never sure whether she knew or not. Although she may not have known the girl's paternity, she did express disapproval of her illegitimate birth, and said that it was all due to the fact that her mother had been brought up without any religious principles. Painter says that in 1922 the love-affair of 1916 was resumed, but Gide's novel *Geneviève* would suggest the possibility of another interpretation. What is certain is that he was extremely proud of having produced a child, and was always delighted in pointing out to friends how like him she was, and how unmistakably his offspring. It was as if it were a constant marvel to him, to have fathered a child.

Gide set off for equatorial Africa with his young friend Marc, now a young man of twenty-three, who, on the journey, began to show his talent as a photographer by making an excellent film of the scenery and native life of Africa. In the thirties he was to produce exquisite films like *Lac aux Dames*.

Gide brought back from his travels two books, *Voyage au Congo* and *Retour du Tchad*. They are composed of the *Journal* that he kept during the trip, and contain descriptions of scenery, village dances, receptions by native chiefs. The amazed enchantment he had enjoyed when he was young returned to him and he forgot his age and the distress of his estrangement from his wife; he became young again. There are passages which might have come from *Les Nourritures Terrestres,* and foreshadow *Les Nouvelles Nourritures Terrestres* which was to appear ten years later. There is a moving little story which he extracted from the books and printed separately under the title *Dindiki,* the account of the death of his pet potto sloth who rode for hundreds of miles on his shoulder. The poor little beast suffered from some form of persistent constipation for which Gide tried every kind of cure, every kind of diet, in an endeavour to save it, and when it finally died he declared that he knew the sorrows of a bereaved parent.

7

THE GOD THAT FAILED

The journey to Africa cured Gide; and with his liberation from personal conflict he now felt free from his
obsession of self, and had energy to spare for objective
considerations, not merely for the problem of personal
guilt and salvation. Freedom from the problem of self
kindled in him a sense of social injustice which was to
dominate his life for more than a decade. When he returned from Africa he wrote: 'Henceforth an immense
lamentation dwells in me!' Then he said to Charles du
Bos: 'I would like not only to reach happiness myself,
but to make others reach it as well. I consider that it is
in renouncing oneself. That is why to be happy is nothing; happiness is to make others happy.' He now became
the champion of under-dogs and victims—criminal of-
fenders for whom he demanded more sympathetic
treatment; women, for whom he asked equality—especially spiritual equality; and the colonial natives whose
cause he pleaded in the two books he wrote on his return from Africa; and finally the socially under-privi-
leged—it was then he took up Communism and went to
Russia.

Gide's books about Africa created some sensation and
there were even questions asked in parliament concerning the conditions which he described, but the
Minister for the Colonies, in the usual manner of minis-

ters, answered that everything would be put right in time.

The next works which he wrote were three novels forming a trilogy—*L'École des Femmes, Robert* and *Geneviève*—and they were undertaken to ask the question of what woman can expect in a modern world. The narrator of the first is Eveline, a woman who is in the period of 'décristallisation', as Stendhal might say. She had once loved her husband but has become disillusioned. He is an unconscious hypocrite who deceives himself about his true feelings and motives. *Robert* is the answer, in the first person, by the husband, and very cleverly Gide makes him convict himself out of his own mouth. Here the portrait of the hypocrite is deepened. Six months after finishing *Robert* Gide began the third volume of the trilogy, *Geneviève,* which was to tell the story from the point of view of the younger generation, the daughter of Eveline, the modern girl of the nineteen-twenties, but he was to find it impossible to finish for many years. At first he intended his heroine to reach salvation through Communism, but after he had worked on the novel for a couple of years, he saw the artistic mistake of using a character in a creative work as a vehicle for his personal opinions. He thought then of writing an abstract work on Communism; this was however never written, as he became disillusioned before he could do so; and he purged *Geneviève* of political theorising. The novel was rewritten several times during the next few years, and finally, despairing of ever finding a satisfactory solution, he published the two parts which were already written, and never wrote any more.

Gide felt that the problem he had chosen was incapable of solution, that Nature had weighted the scales too heavily against woman, not on the physical plane alone which is the only aspect usually considered, but on the spiritual and emotional plane as well. The real enslaver of woman is her own temperament. Geneviève says to her mother: 'I cannot admit to give myself entirely to someone', and Eveline replies: 'You speak as someone who has never loved'.

The trilogy is written in Gide's most austere style, when he had stripped it of all ornamentation and metaphor, in an effort, as he said, to reach the classicism of Racine's art without sacrificing any of the poetry. He declared that ornamentation served merely to conceal faults and blemishes, and that only a thought which was not sufficiently beautiful need fear complete nakedness. Some readers, however, have found the style of the trilogy too stark and unrelieved, and indeed it does not always avoid aridity and monotony; but, at its best, it has a deceptive simplicity and austerity which only a supreme artist could achieve.

There now emerges a new shade in Gide's conception of liberty. In his play *Oedipe,* of 1931, the hero exemplifies the final and utter destruction which comes to the individual when he accepts nothing as greater than himself, and values his personal liberty above all else. Yet Oedipus starts out with all the advantages which Gide thinks necessary for a free individual, but is finally defeated by trying to be completely self-sufficient.

Oedipus, King of Thebes, discovers that the man he has killed in self-defence is his father, and the woman he has married is his mother. He blinds himself in retribution and goes into exile. It is a punishment for his past egoism and spiritual blindness, and he now accepts a new discipline. He becomes convinced that man without God is doomed to defeat and despair unless he substitutes another idea for that of God. Oedipus rejects the God he has once adored, and chooses man; Gide took up Communism. He now thought that liberty was not sufficient in itself, that it destroyed itself if it was not linked to some ideal beyond mere egoistic self-expression—to some duty even. In 1931 he wrote in a preface to *Vol de Nuit,* by Antoine de Saint Exupéry: 'I am particularly grateful to him for having thrown light on that paradoxical truth, which is of paramount importance, that the happiness of man does not lie in liberty but in the acceptance of some duty'. He now talked of 'l'individualisme serviable mais non servile'. This is a new departure from the individualistic and personal sense of liberty expressed thirty years before. Looking then for some duty, some sense of obligation and responsibility, he turned to Communism. He thought that he would find there, with its ideal of service, with its discipline, the complete affirmation of the individual. 'The triumph of the individual', he wrote then, 'is in renouncing individualism'. He declared that for a long time, for too long a time, he had been without a *credo,* but that he had finally found faith, and that was in the belief in the future of the Soviet Union. Hitherto he had had the reputation of being a man who would not commit himself, but now he committed himself wholeheartedly and uncompromisingly to the Communist solution for the ills of the world, and it was a kind of religious conversion. In 1931 he wrote: 'I would like to cry aloud my sympathy for the Soviet Union, and hope that my cry might be heard and have effect. I would like to live long enough to witness the triumph of that tremendous effort, which I hope from the bottom of my heart will succeed, and for which I would like to work.' Although he was ready to sacrifice some of the sanctity of his individuality, he did not think that this should be necessary, or that there was any reason why there should be a clash between individualism and Communism.

It was not through Marx but through the Gospels that Gide reached Communism, and in 1932 he wrote: 'My conversion is like a faith. My whole being is bent towards one single goal, all my thoughts—even involuntary—lead me back to it. In the deplorable state of distress of the modern world, the plan of the Soviet Union seems to me to point to salvation. Everything persuades me of this. And if my life were necessary to assure the success of the Soviet Union, I would gladly give it immediately. I write this with a cool and calm head, in full sincerity, through great need to leave at least this testimony, in case death should intervene before I have time to express myself better.'

In 1935 Gide produced the only major work which appeared during his Communistic period, *Les Nouvelles Nourritures Terrestres,* addressed to the same Nathanael as the first *Nourritures Terrestres.* He had already published a fragment of it in 1921, composed just after he had emerged from his Season in Hell, and when he was in the early days of his relationship with Marc. The greater part of Book One was written in an ecstasy of joy in life. But soon there came the tragic contrast in a series of passages entitled *Rencontres,* describing Baudelairean characters—outcasts and failures—encountered in the streets of Paris. Nathanael asks him the reason for these tales of sadness in a book dedicated to joy, and he answers that he does not want happiness that springs from another's sorrow, and that, in order to be happy himself, he needs the happiness of others. He adds that there are in the world such immensities of poverty, distress and grief that a man of integrity cannot be happy, for he sees them. He declares that his reason cannot hold him back on the slope of Communism which seems to him to lead upwards, but, on the contrary, has joined his heart there. He now addresses Nathanael as 'comrade' and says that progress is only possible by thrusting aside the past; he cites the example of Lot's wife who was turned into a pillar of salt, a pillar of frozen tears, because she had looked behind.

During a meeting in Paris of *L'Union pour la Vérité* in 1935, when Gide was asked to defend his opinions, he answered: 'I consider that on account of its compromises Christianity is bankrupt. I have written, and I firmly believe, that if Christianity had really prevailed, and if it had fulfilled the teaching of Christ, there would today be no question of Communism, there would indeed be no social problem at all.' He added later, during the general discussion: 'If I have felt no contradiction between the community and its individual position, it is precisely because that contradiction is only theoretical and artificial. It is not Marx who brought me to Communism—I have made the most strenuous efforts to read him, but in vain. I persevere, but it is certainly not his theory that won me over. What brought me to Communism, with my whole heart, was the fact of the privileged position which I personally enjoy—that seemed to me preposterous and intolerable.' He had become ashamed of being a man of independent means, of never having been obliged to earn his bread in the sweat of his brow.

Many people, however, amongst them his colleagues of the *Nouvelle Revue Française,* thought that he was speaking without sufficient experience or knowledge of the Soviet Union, and Jean Schlumberger, in a leading article, advised him that he ought to go there and see it all at first hand. So, in June 1936, Gide took up the challenge, and went to Russia, with three other writers, all as guests of the Soviet Government.

He went to Russia hoping that the Soviet Union would be able to produce the finest flowers of civilization without enslaving the mind, or reducing to serfdom a single class, or denying the benefits of civilization to anyone. He went to Russia fully realising that a new world might entail sacrifice of much that was good in itself; he knew that some artistic standards might have to be lowered for a time, for the sake of social and material gain. He agreed that men could not be improved morally and intellectually until the social abuses had been removed, and the social system altered. He was eventually to consider that the price it entailed was too high. He could then discover no difference between what he saw in huge letters on the walls of Italy and what he observed in Russia. There were the same slogans, 'Believe, obey and fight,' identical in both creeds. The Communist spirit had ceased to be contrary to the fascist spirit, or even differing from it.

Gide reached Communism through the Gospels, but he found little of that spirit in Russia itself. He was fêted everywhere, for he was a glorious gain, the greatest living European writer and a man known for his integrity and fairness of mind. He had showered on him all the privileges of a decadent civilization; but he did not need incense, for he was singularly free from personal vanity. He saw everywhere the gulf which separates the privileged from the underprivileged; the same enslavement of the mind against which he had protested elsewhere. He had gone to the Soviet Union to find criticism allied to discipline, a new conception of life and liberty. 'No culture is possible without criticism', he said; but in Russia he found no possibility of doubt or criticism.

Gide had set out for Russia in June 1936 full of hopes; his subsequent disillusionment is expressed in the two books which he wrote on his return, *Retour de l'U.R.S.S.* and *Retouches à mon Retour de l'U.R.S.S.* One cannot claim that these books are amongst Gide's most satisfactory, intellectually or artistically, but much of what was considered prejudice in 1936 is seen now as sound judgment.

When Gide had finished these books he said that they were the final payment in the long sacrifice that he had made of his art to social preoccupations. 'Since these began to encumber my head and my heart', he said, 'I have written nothing of value'. That is true, and the thirties are Gide's leanest years as far as literary productions are concerned. During the Second World War, looking back on that period, he said: 'Slowly I came to convince myself that when I thought I was a Communist, I was in fact a Christian'.

Between the entries for April and August 1938 a thick black line is ruled across the pages of Gide's *Journal*. This symbol of mourning marks the death of Madeleine Gide. He was, sadly, not with her when she died. A telegram from Cuverville recalled him from where he was staying. He was, as he says, with a woman of his acquaintance, but he does not give her name. The prodigal arrived too late on this final occasion. He had left his wife a few days earlier in a 'precarious state of health', but not in an alarming one, so that he departed without fear. 'She was not only what I loved most in the world', he wrote at her death-bed, on his return, 'but it even seemed to me that it was in relation to her that I lived'. As he gazed on her, lying ready for burial, he reflected that there was now in her face none of that smiling amenity which, in life, had always tempered her gravity. She seemed like Alissa from *La Porte Étroite* who, likewise, had died alone. She resembled one of the Jansenists painted by Philippe de Champagne.

Happily, at the end, after their estrangement of almost twenty years, they drew near one another again. It was when she feared for his safety during his ill-fated visit to Russia. This new closeness *in extremis* was amongst the sweetest experiences that he had known with her. She allowed him then to do things for her permitted to no one else; to dress the ulcers on her legs, abandoning herself gratefully to his care, and was nearer to him then than at any other time since their marriage; so that old and infirm as she was he felt that he loved her more than ever. After fifty years the mystic orientation of his life remained the same.

It was of her that he had written, five years before she died, when she was sixty-six: 'Each time that I see her again I feel anew that I have never really loved but her; and it even seems to me that I love her more than ever'.

The pages of his *Journal* in which after her death he records his distress and despair, so that, as he says, another in similar circumstances may on reading feel less alone, are amongst the most poignant that he ever wrote.

He was now free, free as he had never been before, he thought ironically, but it was only the freedom of a kite when the string is cut. He spent the summer of 1938 at Cuverville, where Em had always lived, and to which the prodigal had so often returned, trying to find reasons for continuing to live. 'Since she is there no more', he wrote, 'I have only pretended to live, without taking any interest in anything, or in myself; without appetite, without taste, with neither curiosity nor desire, and in a disillusioned universe; with hope for nothing else save to leave it'.

He realised, however, that if he did not find serenity, then his life would have been in vain. 'If I do not manage to reach serenity then my whole philosophy is bankrupt'.

The last line in the collected volume of his *Journal*, before the War, is an adaptation of the final words from *Le Cimetière Marin* by Paul Valéry: 'Il faut tenter de vivre'. Gide says: 'Here am I free, as I have been before; terribly free. Shall I still have power to "tenter de vivre"?'

8

THE TESTAMENT
OF THESEUS

Gide was almost seventy when the Second World War
broke out. His first reaction was one of horror—not
only for France, but for the whole of civilization which
might perish. It was when it was threatened that he began to realise fully the greatness of the works it had produced. It was then that he began to see the value of
tradition and to appreciate the past. During the winter
of the 'phony war' it was classical authors that he read,
as if to cling to them before they were carried away by
the hurricane of war—Racine and La Fontaine—passages of which he learned by heart so that they could
never be taken from him. La Fontaine especially kept
his thoughts from dwelling on the disasters of war. 'Ah!
how, with him, we are far from the war', he wrote.

Then came the defeat of 1940, which he accepted, refusing all excuses—it was as if it were a personal defeat
which he acknowledged, and for which he took full
blame. He was enraged by the articles of explanation
and excuses which the newspapers published. He agreed
with Pétain when, in his first speech, just before the
Armistice, he said: 'Since the victory [that is of 1918] the
spirit of enjoyment has conquered the spirit of sacrifice.
They wanted to economise effort and today they are
reaping disaster.' A few days later he heard with stupour

the Marshal's second address when he denounced the Free French and England. Gide imagined, in exculpation, that his speech might have been dictated to him by the Germans. 'Is it not enough that France should be vanquished, must she also be dishonoured?' That dishonour he thought the cruellest of France's defeats.

In August 1940 he wrote that the philosophic acceptance of fate—the *Amor Fati* of Nietzsche—did not go as far as the acceptance of the disaster. This explains the horror that he felt in 1941 when he received Chardonne's book, *Chronique Privée de l'An 1940*. Yet Chardonne had been a writer whom he had formerly admired and encouraged; but he could not accept, from a Frenchman, his idealisation of the German defeat of France, nor the plea, pretending to come from the French point of view, in favour of German domination in Europe. Chardonne declared that he wished to view the present with the impartiality of a future historian. He said that historic events are always obscure for those who are living through them, and generally horrible. Only very much later will they be fully explained and then they will prove to have been beneficial. In this manner he was able to make out a good case for the disaster which had overwhelmed France—it was an event of history, like the defeat of the Roman Empire.

During 1941 and 1942 Gide published in *Le Figaro* a series of imaginary interviews, in which he showed that he had completely regained the verve and irony which he had temporarily lost since the death of his wife. It is the same style of brilliant satire which he had used in *Paludes,* but inspired now by the serenity and courage of an old man who had been able to encompass events intellectually. His sword had not lost its sleight nor his tongue its cunning. The interviews were supposed to deal with innocent literary topics—grammar, prosody, the novel and the future of poetry. But there is some brilliant *double entendre* when dealing subtly with the contrast between the genuine French spirit and the cowardly treachery of Vichy. The values which Gide postulates are those which we have met frequently before in his work—indeed he says that he must resign himself to repeat himself if he is not to talk arrant nonsense.

In these interviews a further development in Gide's conception of individuality and liberty becomes apparent, a new departure from the total and irresponsible liberty of his youth, and also from the 'liberté serviable' of his middle years. Now he believes that absolute liberty destroys the individual, and also society, unless it be closely linked with tradition and discipline. He declares that if civilization depended solely on those who initiated the revolutionary theories, then it would perish, since culture needs, for its survival, a continuous and developing tradition. Yet he had claimed earlier that the world could only advance on the dead bodies of those who went before, on the dead ideas of those who had preceded us. Now he believes in preserving our heritage, our Graeco-Roman heritage based on Christian principles—Gide never strayed far from the Gospels.

For two years after the fall of France Gide remained in the south of France with his daughter, either with his friends Madame Van Rysselberghe and her daughter, or else with Simon and Dorothy Bussy. Finally, in May 1942, he sailed for North Africa and there he spent the rest of the War. When it was liberated he could have gone over to England—a plane was ready to take him—but he preferred to remain with his own people. He founded a new literary magazine, *L'Arche,* the title of which explains itself, to take the place of *La Nouvelle*

Revue Française which had collaborated with the Germans.

There, in North Africa, in the clear white light of Tunis, he thought again of the myth which had followed him through most of his life, the myth of Theseus, the builder of Athens. There it came to life and he began to write it. It was published in 1946 and it is his last great work, his literary testament.

The theme of Theseus had dwelt with him now for almost half a century. It is interesting to see how it has developed and altered during these years. At first he saw the thread which bound Theseus to Ariadne as a hindrance, dragging him back to whence he had come, to woman, who will always be a brake on man's desire for progress. This was the time when the bonds of marriage gave weight to this interpretation. Later he imagined Theseus as entering the Maze assured only by the thread of an inner fidelity. And finally, in the finished work, he shows that Theseus had returned only because he had never broken with his past, because he had clung to the thread of tradition. This is the time when Gide had learnt, through the dangers of war, of the value of the past and of tradition. In his tale he follows, step by step, the path traced by the old legend, drawing his material from Euripides, Plutarch and Racine. Theseus is the last of his heroes—the last also of his bastards, since he was supposed to have been the son not of his reputed father, Aegeus, but of the sea god, Poseidon. Gide tells the well-known story in such a way as to symbolise his own preoccupations and those of humanity. He has even succeeded in rationalising the supernatural events, so that there remains nothing in the tale to strain the belief of even the most materialistic of readers. What is new here, and not in the Greek legend, is Gide's conception of the dangers of the labyrinth; he sees those who venture in as over-come by the fumes, as if of drugs and wine, which make them reluctant to leave it.

New also in Gide's tale is the last meeting between Oedipus and Theseus, when the latter recognises that although he has been successful everywhere, he must acknowledge the former as his equal. Indeed he was at first inclined to think that his own victories were small things in comparison with what Oedipus had accomplished, he who had dared, in the name of man, to throw down a challenge to the Gods. Why then, Theseus asks himself, did he accept defeat? Why indeed, by putting out his eyes, did he contribute to that defeat? That was something Theseus could not understand and, on this meeting, he asked him the question. Oedipus answered that he could turn his anger on no one but himself, and had put out his eyes to punish them for not having seen what they should have seen. But there was something more, Oedipus added; darkness had suddenly become for him another light, and he realised that the world invisible to our senses is the real one; all the rest is only illusion which obscures our contemplation of the divine, and one must cease to see the world in order to see God. Theseus did not deny the importance of the spiritual world, but did not see why it should exclude the material one in which we live and have our being. Oedipus interrupted to say that it is only in suffering that man can accomplish a heroic destiny, that when he falls a victim he forces recognition from Heaven, and disarms the vengeance of the Gods.

Theseus is not convinced and when he is alone he formulates his own *credo*, and we feel that it is Gide himself who is speaking and leaving his own testament to the world. He declares that he remains a child of this

213

old world of ours and that man must play with the cards he holds, that he has nothing else. He says: 'I have built my town. After me my thought will be able to inhabit it eternally. It is consenting that I draw near my solitary death. I have enjoyed the benefits of the earth. It is pleasant for me to think that, after me, and thanks to me, men will find themselves happier, better and freer. For the good of future humanity I have lived.'

For more than five years Gide waited for his own 'solitary death', and, although he wrote nothing new of value, these years were filled in adding further details to his portrait of the grand old man of French literature. He spent his time in preparing his work for publication, writing the final pages of his *Journal*, gleaning the last sheaves from the rich harvest. He spent time also in lectures and travel, preaching a message of hope and courage to the weary and disillusioned post-war young. For Gide, in personal and public matters, defeat is not total tragedy; it is an impulse to continue the struggle for a deeper life. We do not find in his last works the blank despair, albeit noble despair, of a Camus for whom life is an absurd and meaningless farce towards which the only attitude is one of stoic resignation, what he calls sainthood without God.

A young student wrote to Gide after the War telling him that the chief thing he had learnt from his work was that despair is the only dignity left to man. Gide was horrified and much distressed at this travesty of his ideas, and he answered him publicly, saying that absence of faith is pernicious, for there is a meaning in the world, and that it depended on man, that man was responsible for God. He returned to a similar conception in the Bryce Memorial Lecture which he gave in Oxford in June 1947. He took as his text the lines from Vergil where Aeneas is described as fleeing from burning Troy with his aged father on his back. Gide said that these lines should be interpreted symbolically, that Aeneas was not merely bearing his father on his shoulders but the whole weight of his past. In the same way we were fleeing from the burning city of our civilization based on the sanctity of each human soul, and it was our duty to see that it did not perish. Though the city of European culture might be burning we could still preserve its most precious essence.

Unfortunately this lecture exists now only in the memories of those who heard it, for Gide, as soon as it was delivered, destroyed the script because his old friend and adviser, Roger Martin du Gard, had told him it was 'médiocre et insuffisant'.

In June 1947 Gide received his first honour, although he was seventy-eight at the time: the degree of Doctor of Letters, *Honoris Causa*, at the University of Oxford. In November of the same year he was awarded the Nobel Prize for literature.

After *Thésée* there was no further major work, but Gide did not remain idle. He published a prose translation of *Hamlet* which was performed with considerable success in France and abroad; also a stage version of *The Trial* by Kafka which was produced by Jean-Louis Barrault in 1947. In 1949 came a book of essays entitled *Feuillets d'Automne*—a pun on Victor Hugo's *Feuilles d'Automne*—also an anthology of French poetry, with a long introduction on the nature of poetry. During the last two years of his life he took an active part in filming *Isabelle*, and in dramatising *Les Caves du Vatican* which was produced at the Comédie Française; he also appeared in person in a film called *La Vie commence demain*; in January 1950, a year before he died, he read the final passage from *Thésée* on the Radio, which was, as it were, his testament and farewell to life. And finally, also in 1950, he published the last volume of his *Journal*, taking the account up to his eightieth birthday. He did not intend to write any more however long he lived. A born writer however dies hard, and he kept a note-book in which he recorded, without dates or order, the random thoughts that occurred to him. This was published posthumously under the title, *Ainsi soit-il, ou les Jeux sont faits*.

The key-note of the last volume of the *Journal* is serenity, but mingled with sadness; for he knew that he was taking his leave, and that death had slipped in between himself and things, so that the union could no longer be effected. He noticed this without bitterness but only with a certain melancholy.

He was in failing health for the last few years of his life, but did not, even then, lose interest in the problems of the world; for a month before he died, he answered a Japanese scholar, one of the atom-bomb victims of Nagasaki, who had written to ask what attitude man should take on the eve of the conquest of the world by the union of conformism and machines. Gide answered in a long and full letter in which he said that, in spite of everything which had happened, it was to individualism that he clung, it was in individualism that he saw the only hope. The individual, with his hatred of falsehood, offered a solid foundation, a sort of rampart on which to meet and come to an agreement. There lay the only possibility of salvation. 'We are like unto one', said Gide, 'who, to light his way, follows a torch that he himself is carrying'.

At the end of his life Gide reached the complete serenity without which he would have considered it a failure, and he waited with calm for death to come, surrounded by his family of daughter, son-in-law and grand-children whom he loved dearly. In *Feuillets d'Automne*, his last work, he had written: 'Take things as they are, play with the cards one has; insist on being what one is, which does not prevent one from struggling against all the falsehoods, falsifications, that man has imposed on a natural state of affairs against which it is vain to revolt. The acceptance of what can be modified is not contained in the *Amor Fati*, which does not prevent one from expecting from oneself the best, after one has recognised it for such. One does not make oneself more like oneself by giving full expression to the least good.'

Death finally came for him on February 19th, 1951, after a few days of illness. He was buried on February 22nd, in the little country cemetery at Cuverville where his beloved wife lay. He had wished to be buried without religious ceremony, but the protestant rites were read at his grave-side.

Gide did not believe in personal immortality, but even in his own life-time he had become immortal through his works. He had already taken on that shape, as Mallarmé said of Poe, 'tel qu'en lui-même enfin l'éternité ne change'.

CONCLUSION

Gide was a man who found his own harmony and movement in a duality of polarisation. He needed this perpetual motion to obtain power for creation, just as some writers need to sin to gain the dynamic force of remorse. He had aspirations towards spirituality, asceticism and puritanism; but also leanings towards sensuality, self-indulgence and sin. It was not the contrast and clash between *Spleen* and *Idéal*, which we find in Baudelaire, man's longing for purity and beauty in conflict with his inevitable proclivity towards sin and vice. That was not Gide's problem; his was one of equilibrium and balance. It was necessary for him to find that one point between both poles where he could freely balance, like a see-saw, from one to the other, backwards and forwards, with equal attraction to each, refusing the necessity for blame or remorse when he came down on the side of what is called vice. Yet, at the same time, he desperately needed sanction and approval, and to feel always that he was right. When composing *Corydon* he was not content with merely gaining freedom and immunity for his own instincts, he needed as well the sanction and support of science and history. In the same way, when he had finally accepted atheism, he claimed confirmation for his lack of faith in the Bible itself. This curious twist of his nature was the cause of the accusation of intellectual dishonesty which has so often, unjustly, been made against him. But it came rather from the deep uncertainty in him which no amount of success, no amount of experience, could cure. He needed intellectual sanction to feel that he was right, and to be right was what he wanted more than anything else. But he would not compromise in order to achieve it, and this led him into the contradictory state of desire for martyrdom, which is, in fact, an inverted way of being right. Unable to believe in himself without assurance, he was forced into that vacillation and twisting which are the most characteristic aspect of the Gidian personality. In the same way he had a longing to be loved which no amount of affection could satisfy. When he was young he wrote: 'My constant question—and it becomes an unhealthy obsession—could anyone love me?' And at the end of his life he wrote: 'An extraordinary, an insatiable need to be loved; I believe this is what dominated my life and urged me to write'.

Yet he did not achieve the perfect relationship where love might have blossomed, and in that failure he was not himself without blame. He was always so morbidly afraid that he might be vanquished by woman, by his wife, as he had been in youth by his mother, that he tore himself away, destroying the delicate tendrils which encircled him, before they could bind him. His behaviour to his wife, incomprehensible at times, was an effort to escape intact.

His own affection and sympathy went out to humble, pitiable and unsure beings, to those unfavoured by life. There were the beggar children in Normandy amongst whom he used to sit, reading them the Fables of La Fontaine. They considered him their friend, running to meet him when they saw him in the distance striding along, his full pilgrim's cloak billowing in the wind. He never felt disgust though he had often, when he got home, to shake their vermin from his clothes.

That same sympathy he showed also to unfortunate dumb animals. He used to pick up injured and sick birds in the woods to nurse them back to health in his bedroom, feeding them on drops of milk as if they were delicate babies, and tending them through long nights of crisis; one of these died, and he wrote to a friend: 'He died this morning, the night had been too cold. This little sorrow has made me very gloomy'.

Although Gide was particularly interested in his own problem as an individual, he was passionately interested as well in the larger problem of individualism in the world today. This brought him many of his readers in all parts of the world, those who seek a remedy to our present discontents. The problem of our time, as Gide sees it—the real crisis of our age—is how to reconcile the inalienable right of the individual to self-development, and the urgent necessity for the diminution of the misery of the masses. In these days of collectivity and mass-thinking, when security from the womb to the tomb is the goal, there is the danger that the individual may be strangled in the ever-increasing coils of bureaucratic red tape. For Gide there was no contradiction between belief in the individual and belief in the community—he had hoped to find the reconciliation in Communism—but he would not sacrifice the sanctity of each individual human soul, since he believed that only by being truly himself could man be of service or value to others. He had a horror of the slow ruminating of the herd, pedigree or otherwise, chewing over the same cud of ideas. He preferred to wander and be lost rather than follow the well mapped-out paths. He had the pride of the one lost sheep, safe in the knowledge that the Eternal Shepherd will scour the hillsides to look for him, and that there will be more rejoicing in Heaven at his being brought safely back to the fold, than for the ninety-nine which never strayed.

In his sixty years as a writer there had been a constant evolution in Gide's style of the same order as the transformation which occurred in his thought. At first he was a poet, preoccupied with himself, using language to express personal lyric feelings—there are some who regret the disappearance of this personal artist—and eventually he became a moralist with a style of pure and sober classicism. In his early writings he adopted the musical manner of the Symbolists and favoured 'la chanson grise', which gave full freedom to his imagination. By the end of the First World War, however, he had banished all extraneous ornamentation from his style. One need only compare *La Symphonie Pastorale* with the early works to realise the difference. The complete simplicity of the language now matches the dazzling whiteness of the snow. Later his language became still more stripped and bare as he perfected the art of Racine, of expressing most by saying least, a strict form containing and restraining deep emotion.

Although all through his life Gide went out with eager anticipation towards the future, he remained, after he reached maturity, classical and universal in the truest meaning of the expression, and became a repository of the past, to protect it against destruction. European civilization for him, in spite of Christianity, grew from Graeco-Roman roots; and, although he was interested in foreign literatures, reading and absorbing much from such writers as Dostoevsky, Shakespeare, Blake and Nietzsche, he nevertheless felt deep down that it was in French classical culture that it had reached its most perfect flowering.

After an examination of sixty years and eighty odd

volumes of Gide's writings the impression remains that he is a moralist, psychologist and stylist rather than a pure novelist or dramatist. Each of his novels is an attitude which he adopts for the sake of argument, of speculation—he tells us so himself—and that makes him less of a novelist than a moralist; less of a novelist than an investigator. He does not concern himself with creating complex characters giving the illusion of life; he is less interested in *men* than in *man*, in the classical sense. 'Man is more interesting than men', he says, 'it is he whom God has made in his own image'. He is less anxious to make an amalgam of contradictions than to isolate some special characteristic. He is a chemist who isolates certain substances to obtain their purest essence. Each of his works is a chemical experiment in purifying some particular quality or vice which he pursues to its logical conclusion.

La Porte Étroite is probably Gide's most perfect and moving book, but his *Journal* is perhaps his most characteristic and original. It is a work unique in French literature—indeed in any literature; a treasure-house of discussion on every artistic and intellectual movement, on every moral problem, of more than sixty years. As a whole it may lack form and unity—indeed how could it be otherwise, with its million words dealing with so many topics and phases of life; but individual passages are amongst his finest writing. He has written few pages of greater beauty, simplicity and poignancy, than his description of the death of the writer Charles-Louis Philippe, and his funeral amongst the simple peasants who were his family.

Little by little, as we read the *Journal*, a picture of its writer begins to take shape in our minds; not the full-length psychological and critical portrait which, one day, will have to be attempted, but the series of impressions we receive from those whom we frequent with pleasure and sympathy; a picture of a man of rare delicacy, sensitivity and perception; a man more at home with simple and unpretentious people than with the learned or sophisticated; a man of great humility, and singularly lacking in vanity who, until the end of his life, remained shy and unsure of himself and surprised when people thought highly of him. At a lunch given in Oxford in his honour he had to wipe the tears away from his eyes as he replied to the speech of welcome, and he said it was the first honour he had ever received: 'Regardez', he added, 'je n'ai pas de rouge à ma boutonnière'. Of all those who came into close contact with him, although there might be many who, at times, were exasperated and infuriated by him, there were few who did not love him, for he was an eminently lovable man. Only those who knew little of him disliked him.

Gide declared that the whole of his work up to *Les Faux Monnayeurs* was written as a plea to Madeleine; the *Journal* might have been written as a plea to posterity for understanding, not in a cold and detached way, but with sympathy and lack of condemnation. This explains why he did not seek the bitter self-knowledge of a Baudelaire. It was not hypocrisy which led to whatever suppressions there are in the *Journal*. Indeed he feared the accusation of hypocrisy more than any other, and this led him to confess things which others, not necessarily through hypocrisy but often through a sense of human dignity and decency, keep hidden in their hearts. There is no humility in Gide's frankness, but pride, pride that he is able to admit what others do not reveal. That was his special pride.

In spite of all the movements which have come and gone since Gide began to write, in spite of the great changes which world upheavals have wrought, his influence has not ceased to prevail. He relates, in the last volume of the *Journal*, how a young man of twenty-two wrote to him for help, saying that he had struggled for five years against his influence, trying to do what he had advised his readers to do in *Les Nourritures Terrestres*, that is to throw his book away and to leave him behind; but he had to admit: 'I still live with everything you taught me. But I am thirsty. All young people are thirsty with me. You can do something. A glimmer from you might indicate the direction to take—if there is a direction.' Gide answered him that the world would be saved, if indeed it can be saved, only by the unsubmissive. 'Without them it will be all up with our civilization, the culture which we love and which gave a justification to our life on earth. The unsubmissive are the salt of the earth and responsible for God.' Thus the old man of seventy-seven wrote to the youth of twenty-two.

Gide's influence has spread even to the East, witness the letter from the atom-bomb victim of Nagasaki, which has been previously mentioned. All those who sought Gide out hoped that they would find in him help in their distress. There has even been founded a new review by a group of young writers, called *Prétexte*, to express their admiration for him. He would have asked for no better fate than, from beyond the grave, to be able still to speak to the youth of the day.

The tangled skein that is Gide will one day have to be unravelled. There is in everyone, however many the contradictions, one main thread which runs through everything, outlining the individual pattern and making it clear. In Gide it will be found to be a spiritual thread. All through his life, in spite of lapses—even in these lapses—it has been spiritual values that he has always sought, albeit sometimes in the byways. Proust had called his own work, the work of his life-time, *A la Recherche du Temps Perdu*; Gide might have called his *A la Recherche d'une Âme*. 'All our thoughts which have not God for object', he said, 'are of the realm of death.'

Gide's ultimate fate will be to be considered as a moralist in the great French seventeenth-century tradition—the tradition of La Rochefoucauld and Pascal—whose integrity and nobility of thought, whose purity and harmony of style, give him an immortal place amongst the great masters of French literature.

BIOGRAPHICAL NOTES

1869 Gide born in Paris, on the 22nd November, at 19 rue de Médicis.

1880 Death of André Gide's father, at the age of forty-eight.

1889 Gide passes his *Baccalauréat*.

1891 Gide becomes a member of Mallarmé's 'Tuesdays'. Meets Valéry at Montpelier.

1893 Gide's first visit to North Africa. He falls ill there and returns to Paris.

1894 Gide's second visit to North Africa.

1895 Death of Gide's mother. He marries his cousin, Madeleine Rondeaux.

1896 Gide elected Mayor of La Roque.

1908 With Jacques Copeau, Jean Schlumberger, André Ruyters and Gaston Gallimard, Gide founds *La Nouvelle Revue Française*.

1914–1915 Gide works at the *Foyer Franco-Belge*, in aid of Belgian refugees.

1918 Gide visits England with Marc.

1922 Gide lectures on Dostoevsky at the Vieux Colombier.

1923 Birth of Catherine, Gide's only child.

1925 Gide's journey to French equatorial Africa.

1936 Gide visits the Soviet Union.

1938 Gide travels to Greece, Egypt and the Senegal. Death of Madeleine Gide.

1939–1942 Gide lives in the south of France.

1942 Gide goes to North Africa.

1944 Gide founds the review *L'Arche.*

1945 Gide returns to Paris.

1945–1946 Gide travels in the Near East.

1947 Gide is given the degree of Doctor of Letters, *Honoris Causa,* by the University of Oxford. He is awarded the Nobel Prize for literature.

1950 *Les Caves du Vatican* is produced at the *Comédie Française.*

1951 Gide dies in Paris on the 19th February. He is buried at Cuverville on the 22nd February.

BIBLIOGRAPHICAL NOTES

A. LIST OF GIDE'S WORKS (Those published in English translation are marked with an asterisk.)

1891 *Les Cahiers d'André Walter.*
     Le Traité du Narcisse.
     Notes d'un Voyage en Bretagne.

1892 *Les Poésies d'André Walter.*

1893 *Voyage d'Urien.*
     La Tentative Amoureuse.

1895 *Paludes.* The Marshlands.*

1897 *Réflexions sur quelques points de littérature et de morale.*
     Les Nourritures Terrestres.* Fruits of the Earth.

1899 *El Hadj.*
     Le Prométhée mal enchaîné.* Prometheus Misbound.
     Philoctète.
     Feuilles de Route.

1900 *Lettres à Angèle.*
     De l'Influence en Littérature.

1901 *Le Roi Candaule.*
     Les Limites de l'Art.

1902 *L'Immoraliste.* The Immoralist.*

1903 *Saül.*
     Prétextes.
     Oscar Wilde.
     De l'Importance du Public.

1904 *De l'Évolution du Théâtre.*

1906 *Amyntas.* Amyntas.*

1907 *Retour de l'Enfant Prodigue.*

1908 *Dostoevsky d'après sa Correspondance.*

1909 *La Porte Étroite.* Strait is the Gate.*

1911 *Nouveaux Prétextes.*
Charles-Louis Philippe.
Isabelle.* Isabella.

1912 *Bethsabé.*

1914 *Souvenirs de la Cour d'Assises.* Recollections of the Assize Court.*
Les Caves du Vatican.* The Vatican Swindle.

1919 *La Symphonie Pastorale.* Pastoral Symphony.*

1923 *Dostoevsky.* Dostoevsky.*

1924 *Corydon.* Corydon.*
Incidences.

1926 *Les Faux Monnayeurs.* Coiners.*
Le Journal des Faux Monnayeurs.* The Logbook of the Coiners.
Numquid et tu.
Si le Grain ne meurt.* If it die.

1927 *Voyage au Congo.* Travels in the Congo.*
Retour du Tchad.* Return from Lake Chad.

1929 *L'École des Femmes.* The School for Wives.*
Suivant Montaigne.
Essai sur Montaigne.
Un Esprit non prévenu.

1930 *Robert.*
L'Affaire Redureau.
La Séquestrée de Poitiers.

1931 *Oedipe.* Oedipus.*

1932 *Goethe.*

1934 *Perséphone.*
Pages de Journal, 1929–1932.

1935 *Les Nouvelles Nourritures Terrestres.* New Fruits of the Earth.*

1936 *Nouvelles Pages de Journal, 1932–1935.*
Geneviève.
Retour de l'U.R.S.S.* Back from U.S.S.R.

1937 *Retouches à mon Retour de l'U.R.S.S.* Afterthoughts on the U.S.S.R.*

1938 *Notes sur Chopin.*

1939 *Journal, 1889–1939.** *The Journals of André Gide, Vols. I-III.*

1941 *Découvrons Henri Michaux.*

1942 *Le Treizième Arbre.*

1943 *Interviews Imaginaires.*
Attendu que.

1944 *Pages de Journal.** *The Journals of André Gide, Vol. IV.*

1946 *Thésée.** *Theseus.*
Le Retour.

1947 *Paul Valéry.*
Le Procès.* *The Trial.* (A stage version of Kafka's novel.)

1948 *Correspondance, Francis Jammes et André Gide.*
Préfaces.
Rencontres.

1949 *Robert ou de l'Intérêt Général.*
Feuillets d'Automne.
Anthologie de la Poésie Française.
Correspondance, Paul Claudel et André Gide.* *Correspondence, Paul Claudel and André Gide.*

1950 *Journal, 1942–1949.** *The Journals of André Gide, Vol. IV.*
Littérature Engagée.
Lettres de Charles du Bos et Réponses d'André Gide.

1951 *Et nunc manet in te (Suivi de Journal Intime.)** *Et nunc manet in te.*

1952 *Ainsi-soit-il ou Les Jeux sont faits.*

B. SELECT LIST OF WORKS DEALING WITH ANDRÉ GIDE

R. M. Albérès: *L'Odyssée d' André Gide,* 1951.

Paul Archambault: *Humanité d'André Gide,* 1946.

Yvonne Davet: *Autour des Nourritures Terrestres,* 1948.

François Derais et Henri Rambaud: *L'Envers du Journal d'André Gide,* 1951.

Charles du Bos: *Le Dialogue avec André Gide,* 1929.

Ramon Fernandez: *André Gide,* 1931.

Albert Guerard: *André Gide,* 1951.

Jean Hytier: *André Gide,* 1938.

Renée Lang: *André Gide et la Pensée Allemande,* 1949.

Klaus Mann: *André Gide and the Crisis of Modern Thought,*
   1948.
Harold Marsh: *André Gide and the Hound of Heaven,* 1952.
Roger Martin du Gard: *Notes sur André Gide,* 1951.
Claude Mauriac: *Conversations avec André Gide,* 1951.
Henri Mondor: *Premiers Temps d'une Amitié,* 1947.
George Painter: *André Gide,* 1951.
Léon Pierre-Quint: *André Gide,* 1932 and 1952.
Paul Souday: *André Gide,* 1927.
D. L. Thomas: *André Gide, the Ethic of the Artist,* 1950.

François Mauriac

For Wladimir Weidlé

PREFACE

A short study such as the following must be selective. Writing for an English audience I have been governed to some extent by two assumptions: that my readers will be largely ignorant of those works of M. Mauriac that have appeared so far only in French, but that they will have ready access to the novels that have been translated into English. If I have sometimes given the former more attention than is their due, it is to fill in an otherwise incomplete picture.

I have used where available to me the excellent translations of the novels by Mr. Gerard Hopkins. Their merit is patent to all. Thanks are due to Messrs Eyre & Spottiswoode for permission to quote them.

Two debts of gratitude in particular I must pay: to Dr. T. V. Benn, of the French Department in the University of Leeds, for information about the loan of books, and Mr. Graham Clarke, of the Anglo-French Literary Services Ltd, London, for constant help and advice.

1

BACKGROUND

Newman believed that if the fields and the sky give us the impression they do of purity and innocence, it is because nature was created before man the sinner, and took no part in Adam's crime. But from the time that man first lives on the earth, lies down to sleep or to cry, to the time he sinks and returns to dust, nature has become human. She is made of the ash of man's sin and has no resemblance to what she was when she was born in the thought of God . . . We cannot imagine the world as it was before man appeared . . . I doubt whether desert islands and uninhabited lands sing the glory of God as clearly as our old countryside proclaims the struggles and the sufferings of man.[1]

Biography is never literary criticism; and in the case of François Mauriac it could never even attempt to be. What does one need to know, apart from his works, about the uneventful life of this novelist, critic, editor and (dare we say?) tyrant of letters? Born in 1885; made a member of the Académie française in 1933; a denouncer of the Franco régime in the Spanish war; on the side of the Resistance during the occupation—he even wrote a *Cahier Noir* for the secret periodical *Edi-*

1. *Journal* (1932–39), p. 32.

tions de Minuit, and in 1943 some signed articles of his appeared in the Swiss, Portuguese and Balkans press, of which one was quoted by Général de Gaulle in a radio talk to the French before the liberation; but he refused to take part in the purges after the war;[2] now a powerful influence in the direction of the literary organs *Figaro, Figaro Littéraire,* and *La Table Ronde.* Here are the bare bones—and they tell us little. What is far more important, to prepare us for and even to explain the strength and the limitations of his work, is the picture of his home and childhood. No subtleties of Freudian analysis are required to show us the permanent influence upon him of the Landes (the marsh-and-pine country round Bordeaux) and the people it breeds. A people with small minds, tight fists and deep roots; with a loyalty difficult to distinguish from tenaciousness. And their roots go so deep into the soil that they are entangled with all the other roots that snuggle there: hence the frequent identification of man with his crops. Sometimes, indeed, man even takes on the less important role of the two: 'Why was it that the heath villages never caught fire?', mused Thérèse Desqueyroux, during a time of scorching weather. 'It seemed to her unjust that it should always be the trees that the flames chose, never the human beings.'[3]

The worst horror is that with the coming of the storm will come the hail, and smash the vine-harvest:

> The Bishop had ordered public prayers for rain: personally I'd rather have drawn up a pact with the drought. With us the ground is firm enough for the vines to be able to do without water for months; they stand up like strapping fellows right

2. North, pp. 64–5.
3. *Thérèse,* p. 70.

in the furnace and in the midst of sweltering summers they sing the Song of the Three Children . . .
For it's a miracle if rain comes without a storm,
and the storm brings hail . . . In the thickets of
the sky these snarling beasts come rushing out in
packs, like wolves: they invade us on all sides.
If you hope to escape the one that comes from the
west, you won't get away without the one that lies
in ambush behind the hornbeam trees in the south,
the monster with its lowering forehead. Sometimes
it hesitates, seems to draw away—as happened last
September 8th; and then suddenly it changed its
mind: a furious icy wind hurled the hail-storm
against us. In the tumult we thought we heard the
trees crying in terror.[4]

Small wonder that the union of man and harvest in a
wedding of empathy should give birth to an obstinate,
sturdy peasantry and a close, cautious bourgeoisie:

A prudent, circumspect, canny race, whose insur-
ance policies are paid up for time and eternity.[5]

'And eternity'; for here eternity is still assumed, however casually, and before the midnight mass at Christ-
mas the servants watched over the masters' reserved
seats up till 11 o'clock at night.[6] Nor is it purely formal.
There are occasional outbursts even of a demonic sort
of paganism which testify to a stormy past history.
Félicité Cazenave, for instance,

believed in nothing that she could not touch.
She had been born in the days when only a few
sandy tracks linked the Landes with the outside

4. *Journal*, p. 36.
5. *Commencements*, p. 102.
6. Ibid., p. 102.

world. The 'Terror' had driven the priests away. Her own mother had not made her First Communion till the day she was married. At the beginning of the previous century the children of the Landes had had but one religion, that of the implacable and fiery sun; had known but one Almighty, the blaze that burned the pines—a swift-moving, unapproachable God who left in the wake of his progress a host of smoking torches.[7]

While on the other hand, from the midst of the pious mechanical murmur of self-protective devotion, there arises from time to time a genuine anguished cry of beseeching. Mauriac remembers his grandfather's last visit from Langon, the day before his death—Mauriac himself was five at the time.

He sat down heavily in an armchair and looked at the photographs of the deceased, among whom were some of his own relations. 'What a cemetery!' he sighed. The next day he went to revisit all the places he loved, his property at Malagar, the alms-house he administered; then after dinner he went round to some old friends where he used to make up a hand at 'boston' every evening. And it was here that the supernatural intervened. 'M. Mauriac', asked the old lady, one of the two friends, 'I'm going to Benediction; will you come with me?' My grandfather had been a strong anti-clerical all his life, and a declared enemy of the Marist fathers of Verdelais. Though he had softened (under the influence of my mother, of whom he was very fond) he hadn't set a foot inside Church for years. To the surprise of everyone, he agreed to go with the old lady, and appeared to be very recollected right till

7. *Genetrix*, p. 155f.

the end of Adoration. On the way back, in the road, in front of the Misses Merlet, he stumbled, and collapsed. They carried him as far as his bed. He had time to reply to a friend who was begging him to pray: 'It is faith that saves us', and he joined his hands.[8]

It is worth remembering this authentic incident, coming as it did at the boy's most impressionable age, when we come to consider the 'death-bed conversions' in Mauriac's novels. Indeed, I have not seen it pointed out that these very words, 'la foi nous sauve', are put into the mouth of Numa Cazenave, the husband of old Félicité Cazenave, who died while his wife was away with their son, Fernand. In fact, the whole scene of Cazenave's death is taken almost verbatim from Mauriac's account of his childhood.[9]

So many critics have objected to these conversions on the threshold of death—of Gabriel Gradère,[10] of Louis, the rapacious, jealous grandfather,[11] of Irène de Blénauge,[12] of Fabien Dézaymeries (though here it is a mortal sickness from which in fact he recovers),[13] as well as that of old Numa Cazenave just mentioned. They have contended that such conversions are false, artificial and unconvincing. So it is only fair to remember the closeness of their resemblance to actual historical instances of the same kind of thing. Of course, the critics may go on to say that even such genuine instances may lack conviction within the novel, because of some failure of presentation or technique, and that it is with the novels

8. *Commencements*, p. 12f.
9. *Genetrix*, p. 178.
10. *Angels*.
11. *Knot*.
12. *Lost*.
13. *Enemy*.

that they as critics are concerned. Sometimes this is true, as we shall see in our third chapter. But one suspects that this is not always the real objection, that this judgement by these critics would be passed equally severely on the cases in real life, and that behind the judgement there lies an irritable (and understandable) resistance to the whole reign of what might be called 'conversion melodrama' in early twentieth-century literary France.

That it was a reign, we cannot doubt. Journals and correspondence are as much under its domination as novels, and the Claudel-Gide letters have been a sort of *atelier* in which lesser artists have been unfortunately trained. One of the striking flaws in what is otherwise among the most impressive of Mauriac's novels, *The Knot of Vipers*, occurs when Louis suddenly notes in his diary-cum-confession-cum-autobiography:

> After my death, among my papers you [Isa, his wife, to whom the diary is directed] will find a statement of my last wishes. They date from the months immediately following Marie's [their daughter's] death. . . You will find, too, my profession of faith. It runs something like this: 'Should I agree, at the moment of my death, to accept the ministrations of a priest, I herewith, while my mind remains clear, protest against the advantage that will have been taken of my weakening powers —physical as well as mental—to extort from me what my reason rejects'.[14]

But many years before this had appeared M. Roger Martin du Gard's novel, *Jean Barois* (1913); and the central theme of this novel is precisely this: should such a vow (given in almost identical terms), solemnly taken by a freethinker, be simply brushed aside when evi-

14. *Knot*, p. 111.

dence of a genuine and quite conscious conversion later occurs at his death? (In fact, it is brushed aside.) Mauriac produces the same dilemma again, as a sort of anti-clerical's stock-in-trade; but he leaves it lying on the page, never refers to it again, and later appears to have forgotten all about it.

However, there is perhaps a special reason why Mauriac may be allowed a little more liberty than others in treating of these themes: that he is not, in the usual sense, a 'convert'. No doubt as a child at home, and then under the Marist fathers, he developed an excessive scrupulosity. But the regular *examen* and weekly confession gave the novelist an insight into the self which (to say the least) would be effectively turned outward later.

> My first communion remained the event which dominated my life. During the months of preparation for it I had acquired a taste for perfection. M. Maysonnave, the senior curate, had sent me a book, sumptuously bound, which was a moral account book: each day I had to mark down the number of victories I'd won over my besetting sin, all my prayers, and all the merits I'd acquired by them. During the retreat I had three days of agony. I tortured myself with thoughts of death and eternity, with my general confession and with sins vaguely specified.[15]

This is a reminiscence of Jacques, the hero of Mauriac's second novel, which appeared in 1914; but there is no doubt that it is a piece of the author's autobiography. However, we must be clear that this pious childhood was not all gloom.

15. *Robe*, p. 21f.

Why was I a sad child? It would be silly to blame religion for it: it gave me more joy than pain in those days. What was it but the scruples with which I tormented myself to pay back for the emotional delights of the great Feasts . . . Far from religion casting a shadow over my childhood, it enriched it with a pathetic joy. It is not because of it, but in spite of it, that I was a sad child, for I loved Christ, and He consoled me.[16]

Later, it is true, Mauriac tended to condemn this sweet-toothed piety of his youth. In 1927 he wrote a preface to a new edition of his collection of early verse, *Les Mains Jointes:*

The truth is that what I dislike in this little book is not its technique but above all its spirit. This cowardly, terrified adolescence, turned in on itself—I repudiate it now. Not that I deny my faith at that period, any more than I deny my poetry; but my manner of believing was worth about as much as my manner of verse-writing; oh, the facility of it! A child who is scared of everything sniffs incense, gets an emotion from the sacraments and enjoyment from the ritual. . .[17]

This was the point in his career when Mauriac was re-examining the relationship between his faith and his vocation as a writer, and the next year saw what has sometimes been described as his 'conversion'. By this is meant an act of deference to his Catholic critics, and, resulting from that, a more conscious and specific use of his talent in the cause of the Faith. But it should not be exaggerated. He may have written his *Bonheur du Chré-tien* in answer to those who said that the earlier *Souf-*

16. *Commencements*, pp. 22–4.
17. Quoted in du Bos, p. 46.

frances du Chrétien was too negative; but it was his journalistic and critical work rather than his novels that were immediately affected.[18] As Mr. North says,

> The man had taken a great step forward in the knowledge of his faith. The writer, however, changes but little. The same bitter version of the world persists in his writing, and though he avoids certain subjects now, it would be difficult to see him as an apologist for the faith, an author convinced of the goodness of man. This very real aspect of his thought will find its expression in his essays on religious subjects, in his newspaper comments, but hardly in his novels.[19]

And perhaps even his condemnation of his youthful piety has to be modified slightly in view of a still later, indeed quite recent, pronouncement. In July 1951 he spoke at the prize-giving in his old school, Grand-Lebrun, and said that he owed it a great debt:

> The poetic state which is the state of childhood is most often contaminated, soiled by real life, by the horrible and hard life of grown-ups. I don't think badly of the education which French boys get in the *lycées*. I even think highly of it . . . But a pupil of Grand-Lebrun, at least in my time, was marvellously shielded, protected from the corrupt and criminal world: a catholic college like Grand-Lebrun, behind its high walls, under the trees of its enchanted gardens, in the silence of its chapel, preserves this pure water of childhood which collects there as in a very deep well. This well, on which I have never ceased to draw during my life

18. See North, p. 63.
19. North, p. 77.

as a writer, has not yet dried up after so many years.[20]

There is another aspect of Mauriac's general development that should be mentioned at this stage, since it belongs only incidentally to a criticism of his own work as a novelist, but is none the less revealing: his appreciation of and reaction to other writers. I think he is making no false boast when he says of himself, writing in 1938:

> I feel myself to be less unjust to-day towards the living and the dead than I used to be at twenty . . . I feel that I am now a long way from the simplicity of my youth which made me damn people with lightheartedness . . . The mystery of the judgements of God on each one of us in particular is the very mystery of pity.[21]

He is actually speaking of Renan, on whom he now passes a gentler verdict than earlier; but it would apply to his judgement on others too. Even of Gide he sometimes writes in a way which suggests genuine disinterested appreciation rather than (as, alas, seems the case at other times) a forced attempt to be fair growing out of professional Christian charity. What is more surprising is his apparently warm and sincere admiration for D. H. Lawrence. It is true that he does not show very much understanding of Lawrence. And Gide was rightly annoyed by his musings about *Lady Chatterley's Lover*:

> In twenty years, or thirty [wrote Mauriac], what will Lady Chatterley do with her game-keeper? Will they continue the same gesture till death? When satiety comes, in their old age, they will seek elsewhere for a means of nourishing a lust which

20. Speech printed in *La Table Ronde*, Aug. 1951.
21. *Journal*, pp. 348–50.

they have always exercised so skilfully that it is bound to go on dominating them even in their final decrepitude. I think of that terrible book: *The Old Age of Lady Chatterley*.[22]

Gide expostulates: 'If I have any remorse today, it is indeed for not having taken better advantage of my youth'.[23] Neither he nor Mauriac, of course, was aware that Lawrence himself foresaw this sort of objection ('Old people can have a lovely quiescent sort of sex, like apples.')[24] Still, it is interesting to find Mauriac writing a preface to a French translation of Lawrence's *Boy in the Bush*[25] (what a choice!) and to find him noting in his diary:

> Dear Lawrence, with Catherine Mansfield, my best English friends! I don't understand or love the English till they are dead . . . This Lawrence: I swear that I met him one day at Daniel Halévy's . . . I remember death visibly written on his drawn face, from which one averted one's eyes out of delicacy . . . Was it him? . . . It's so sad to think that I could have said to him: 'We are as far away from each other as two writers of the same age could possibly be. And yet, dear Lawrence, I admire you, I know all about you, I love you.' [26]

On the other hand—and it will already be clear from the above—Mauriac is, like so many French critics, extremely personal in his literary judgements. It is true that he sees clearly, at least in theory, that writers like Racine, Corneille, and so on, should be judged on their works—by contrast with those like Rousseau, Voltaire, Chateaubriand, whose works we forget, but remember

22. *Journal*, p. 110.
23. Gide: *Journal* (E.T., vol. iii, p. 359), 9th Aug. 1937.
24. Lawrence: *Letters*, ed. Huxley, p. 773.
25. Pref. to *Jack dans la brousse*, tr. Lilian Brach (Gallimard, 1938).
26. *Journal*, pp. 152–4.

the man.[27] But in practice Mauriac's criticism is of the kind that can be suitably given such titles as *Mes Grands Hommes,* 'Writers in my life' . . . etc. And the result is inevitably that, in spite of occasional and almost accidental moments of genuine detached critical insight, we are mostly conscious of arbitrary and unrelated judgements; sometimes indeed, we must think, of sheer misjudgements. In a little (and little-known) book on the Catholic novelist and biographer, René Bazin,[28] Mauriac can be seen defending a second-rate writer because, one suspects, his critical theory demands that he be considered first-rate:

> Bazin has always shown himself compassionate towards the humble heroes of his books. It is certain that no trace remains in this novelist of the implacability characteristic of the French naturalists of the last century, who despise the human being—the human beast, as they call him—and who only pause from hating man when they want to mock him . . . M. René Bazin has contrived to see what greater men have not: the action of Grace in the world. He has been in a sense more naturalistic than Flaubert, Maupassant and Zola, because he has gone below the surface of beings. For him the drama of the creature is not confined to the conflict of instincts . . . Let us above all admire the way he introduces God into the most human drama. Whereas so many have failed to see this perilous enterprise through, and find themselves daily accused of scandalously mixing up the divine with the fleshly, the author of *Donatienne* and *Le Roi des Archers* brings off this *tour de force* in each of his books, perhaps with too great ease.[29]

27. *Journal*, p. 430f.
28. *René Bazin* (ed. 'Les Quarante', Alcan, 1931).
29. Op. cit., p. 10f.

But the qualification in this last phrase comes too late to save the passage. We shall have to bear it in mind when, in our third chapter, we discuss Mauriac's own attempts to 'introduce God into the human drama'. Meanwhile, one cannot but feel that this is not so much objective literary criticism as self-defence. Whatever may be said theoretically in favour of the theological type of criticism here implied, a serious critic could not speak in the same paragraph about Flaubert and the author of *Oberlé*. And the self-defence comes out even more crudely in Mauriac's concluding remarks on Bazin:

> His reward today lies in the certainty he can have that he has never upset a single one of these little ones who believe in Christ, that he has not to give an account of a single scandal, but that on the contrary he has helped a great number towards salvation. What joy and peace an artist must experience in the evening of his life, when he possesses the assurance that no soul has ever been wounded by him! [30]

How Mauriac comes by criteria such as this for assessing the work of an artist can partly be seen in the background we have tried to sketch. How his own works come out of an assessment of the same nature we shall not directly discuss (though it will be implied in later chapters) since we do not accept the validity of these criteria. But already we can see that the permanent problem of Mauriac's own literary career, as well as the general problem of relating literary to theological (or, worse, to homiletic) assessment, lies behind this naïve paragraph.

30. *René Bazin*, p. 30.

2

SCOPE AND LIMITS

Scope

In a brief study it is impossible to outline or analyse all the novels (still less the plays as well); nor is it necessary, since most of the important novels are easily accessible in English. But a delineation of the breadth of Mauriac's canvas is worth keeping in mind as the background to an analysis of some representative works. If we dwell longer upon the early works than they really merit, it is because they have not been, and are not likely to be, translated into English, and they do confirm what the more famous novels suggest about Mauriac's particular gifts and preoccupations.

The first novel of all, *L'Enfant Chargé de Chaînes*, gives us the education of a young Mauriac; Jean-Paul Johannet is brought up at a pious school, becomes interested in the young Catholic Social movement, and tries to put social theory into practise by befriending, in a self-conscious and ungainly way, a working-class boy called Georges Élie; the experiment fails, and the novel ends desultorily with Jean-Paul's first love-affair. There is nothing much in the book, but there are hints of a power to create 'atmosphere' which will be stronger as time goes on. There are also embarrassing apostrophes to the characters, or to God, in which the author intrudes blunderingly upon the scene—a weakness which, as we shall see, he never outgrows. Here, for instance, is his encouraging chat to the heroine, Marthe Balzon, who has fallen in love with Jean-Paul—they are the closing words of the novel:

> At this very same hour you, Martha, were sitting on your bed in a large room in the country . . . On the mantelpiece, in the light of the lamp, you had left Jean-Paul's last letters lying, too. Their tender and passionate words had awoken in you the joy that you expected no longer. You are smiling bravely, Martha, at all his possible betrayals: you absolve them all in advance; your meticulous love foresees, as its future revenge, a redoubling of tenderness—and the serenity of silent acts of forgiveness.[1]

Next appears *La Robe Prétexte,* which does not carry us much further, but does introduce us to the devout bourgeoisie (the governess, the nun-companion, the diplomatic, tea-drinking Abbé) and to the stock contrasts in worldly men (the would-be-rakish uncle and the father, an artist now dead) all of which will reappear in later novels. The clandestine correspondence, too, between the hero, Jacques, and Camille, a girl at a convent school, which is intercepted and stopped by the interfering Mme de Vatémesnil, is merely a foreshadowing of the similar attempt by Jean de Mirbel to communicate with Michèle, successfully foiled by Brigitte Pian.[2] *La Chair et le Sang* can equally be ignored; and *Le Fleuve de Feu* merely pursues once more the stream of first passion: this time in a girl, Gisèle de Plailly, who escapes from her guardian and follows the young man—and the grand romantic tradition—to 'the banal décor

1. *L'Enfant,* pp. 273–5.
2. *Pharisees.*

of a hotel bedroom in the Pyrenees'[3]; she is last seen praying in the church of a little village where she had taken refuge. There are also three little tales which follow soon after, and which begin to be characteristic of Mauriac's bitter vision. They appear collected together as *Trois Récits* in 1929: *Coups de Couteau, Un Homme de Lettres,* and *Le Démon de la Connaissance*; but the first was actually written three years earlier. Here we have a husband who knows his wife so well that he can, in bed, ask her advice about a failing love-affair he has with another woman—and who retains his wife's affection, or at least her pity, precisely by being made to suffer by this lover! We have the artist who is so stifled by his wife's admiration that he goes off and lives in dirt and discomfort with a woman who has two sickly and noisy brats—but later returns, having tried this experiment only to get 'copy'. Finally we have the boy who loses his faith in God, and therefore in creatures too. The second of these three tales is worth pausing over, since it gives us a character who does not occur in any other of the novels (and perhaps not in life, either), and who evidently represents a problem, cast in fictional form, for the author. Jérome is a writer who pours so much of his experience into his books that he has no sincerely personal life left. He had boasted that he had left his wife Gabrielle because

> the love which a woman has for us is not a wall behind which to take shelter; it's an obstacle to be overcome . . . And then, to create, we must have some semblance of solitude. Bertha, occupied with her children, often forgets me altogether. I was the whole of life for Gabrielle. However hard she tried to efface herself beside me, I heard her

3. Hourdin, pp. 44-5.

thinking of me. I have only written a single poem during the fifteen years of our liaison.[4]

But he soon belies this by leaving Bertha, and she declares that all along he was only using her as fodder for literature. Even at the supreme moment of passion he is taking notes for a novel:

> I will bury this booty [he says to himself] as a dog does a bone; I shall find it again one day, but so mingled with my own creatures that I shan't even recognise it.[5]

And when the 'I' of the story tells Jérome what he is really like, Jérome merely seizes this analysis of his own character with avidity, remarking:

> That'll be a beautiful conclusion to my obituary.

It is an interesting statement, and not wholly unconvincing, of the personal problem of the compatibility of a writer's belief and behaviour with his métier.

Meanwhile by now Mauriac had begun on the well-known novels; indeed, the first, *A Kiss for the Leper*, appeared as early as 1922. From then on we have a steady succession of tales, giving us the lives of provincial folk, broken marriages, possessive mothers, sordid love-affairs, analyses of most of the possible human motives, and occasional flashes of grace. Frequent satire there is, occasional near-cynicism, but never humour. The range is evidently narrow, and when Mauriac tries to widen it by describing the fast town set, the lovers and gigolos and painted beauties that he sometimes seems to find necessary to his plots, he always and obviously fails. When, for instance, Fanny unexpectedly

4. *Récits*, p. 117.
5. Ibid., p. 129.

meets Fabien in Venice—she in company with the un-convincing ballet dancer Cyrus Bergues and his Swedish impresario, Donald Larsen—we are told:

> She raised her face to his, careless of the danger she ran in thus displaying its mask of paint and powder in the harsh light of the hotel hall. But tears had seamed the mask and broken its surface.[6]

Or here is Denis Revolou, on the subject of his sister Rose:

> He was devoured with impatience to have a look at Rose's dress . . . It would, he supposed, be like all dance-frocks—frankly immodest . . . In less than an hour's time she would be standing in a drawing-room doorway, offering to the common gaze the spectacle of her throat and shoulders, of her back, and even of those childish breasts that were set a shade too high. She would allow herself to be clasped, thus stripped, in the arms of the first man who might care to ask her for a dance.[7]

Are not these (and they are not merely early writings: they were written in 1924 and 1939 respectively) the stock pictures, the reactions of one for whom the town can never be anything but a mystery, superficially ob-served and then described in clichés? The same must be said of Mauriac's attempts to present other areas of life which he only knows from a distance and at a surface level. Here, for instance, is a psychiatrist's wife on the subject of her husband, Elis. She has been eavesdrop-ping, and has heard part of a patient's (Thérèse's) long, rambling, incoherent confession, through the door of

6. *Enemy*, p. 203.
7. *Sea*, p. 3f.

her husband's consulting-room. She is half sorry for Thérèse, for, she muses:

> Elis was quite incapable of understanding her, even of feeling compassion for her. All he would do, as he had done with other victims, was to urge her to find relief—to free her emotions through the gratification of the body. That was what his method amounted to. The same filthy key served him whether it was heroism, crime, sanctity or renunciation he had to interpret.[8]

And we cannot say that this is merely subtle 'thinking in character', for it is the sheerest caricature, not merely of the work of a psychiatrist, but of a possible judgement from a psychiatrist's wife; and unfortunately the style shows us that it is Mauriac's own view sneaking in.

As if half-aware that, with the failure of these attempts to widen its scope, his repertoire was beginning to run out, Mauriac in 1938 turned to the stage. This is not, admittedly, his own account of the experiment. What he says is:

> An author is often accused of never renewing himself. I believe on the contrary that his first duty is to remain himself, to accept his limitations. It is excellent for a novelist to submit himself to constraints which he has not known before. I don't believe in the incompatibility that is so often alleged between the gifts of a novelist and those of a dramatist. There is no reason why the characters we create should not be able to assume a body and a voice . . This same desire to discover a new mode of expression inclines me to reserve the fu-

8. *Thérèse*, p. 134.

ture for matters concerned with the cinema . . .
[But] the exacting technique of the theatre, exacting
because of the multiple problems it poses, the
obstacles which it ranges in front of one, seems to
me to be a better school for the artist than that of
the screen.[9]

Mauriac has on the whole shown great skill in adapting
himself to this theatrical technique. But skill is one
thing, dramatic success another. The unreal figure, for
instance, of Blaise Coutûre in *Asmodée* seems to me a
melodramatic projection of what Mauriac imagines a
priest *manqué* ought to turn out like in the circumstances of a country family house: he is the product of
a formula. Could any speech be less convincing than
this of Coutûre's:

> Of all the creatures upon whom I have acted
> there isn't one whom I haven't first of all inspired
> with aversion. Emmanuèle? But I only ask you for
> three days in which to make her see only through
> my eyes, make no gesture that isn't inspired by me,
> and in which my will may be substituted for hers
> and command even the beating of her heart.[10]

Of course no man, even if he were like that in fact,
would speak like that of himself. Clearly it is the author
speaking from the wings while he twitches the strings
of the marionette. We shall see the extent to which this
also happens in the novels; but in a play it is even more
fatal, for a flaw of this sort cannot on the stage be
concealed behind a curtain of descriptive prose. And
the plays that have followed since, though again skilful
in their way, cannot be said to have enabled Mauriac

9. *Journal*, pp. 369–371.
10. *Asmodée*, p. 177f.

to bring precision to his particular talent, still less to enlarge his range. Indeed, perhaps they have helped to reveal a weakness that is native to him. He has recognised himself that his novels are successful in part 'thanks to a certain gift of atmosphere'.[11] And there is no doubt that the effectiveness of most of his scenes is due, as we shall see in the last chapter, to the atmospheric background against which they are played—the sighing of the pines, the morose silence of the marshes, the croaking of frogs. Deprived of this, his dramatic experiments have had to rely on the naked interplay of character and motive, and the author is too easily tempted to supplement this bareness by working into them the comment which either should never be made from outside at all, or at least be reserved for the narrator and not tacked on to the dialogue within the play.

And if, finally, we are to some extent to judge Mauriac's range by bringing the examination of his works as nearly up to date as possible, it cannot be said, unfortunately, that the long-short stories to which he has returned recently show us that his excursion into the theatre has effected a renewal of creativity. In *The Little Misery* there is a touching enough picture of the snotty, wizened little *sagouin*, a picture which shows, perhaps, something more of pity and less of disgust than, for instance, Mauriac's earlier picture of the young Jean Péloueyre with his 'ferrety face', his 'miserable undeveloped body, untouched by the normal miracle of puberty'.[12] And we can add that the slight sketch of the pleasant, kindly marxist schoolmaster is unusually objective. But the melodramatic conclusion—the suicide of father and son in the millrace—is arbitrary and unconvincing. *Galigaï*, too, repeats several old formulae,

11. *Journal*, p. 218.
12. *Leper*, p. 15.

though the central character, Mme Agatha ('Galigaï') who loses young Nicolas Plassac and gains instead the old widower, Armand Dubernet, is well presented. It is significant that the author seems to see the story as the education of Nicolas, whereas I think the average reader will find Nicolas shadowy and uninteresting and Galigaï herself the real centre; significant, because Mauriac constantly misjudges his own operations, and the misjudgement reveals a fundamental uncertainty in the writer which can be detected in the handling of the novels themselves. It is, of course, within the creation that the creator's weaknesses are seen. To that creation, in more detail, we therefore now turn.

Limits

(i) The most obvious, though not the most important, indications of a writer's limitations are to be found in his repetitions. There is a repetition that makes for strength—the spiral development which like a fugue uses repetition precisely to build up. But there is also a repetition that is mere tautology. Sometimes Mauriac's repetitions are spiral, as when he tries out a character like Mme de Blénauge,[13] and then realises her more fully in a Brigitte Pian;[14] or an Yves Frontenac[15] whom he expands (though also with some loss of freshness) into Pierre Costadot[16]—Pierre is allowed to quote the poetry which Yves merely wrote. But often there are similarities between characters which suggest that Mauriac is merely falling back on a convenient pattern, e.g. the unknown priest to whom Mme de Blénauge confesses, the young Abbé Alain Forcas, to whom Ma-

13. *Lost.*
14. *Pharisees.*
15. *Frontenac.*
16. *Sea.*

thilde Desbats (and later Gabriel Gradère) confess,[17] the Jesuit to whom Lucienne Revolou makes an unsatisfactory confession before her last illness,[18] the young priest whose solitude Thérèse understands and sympathises with,[19] and finally, of course the Abbé Calou who brings peace to the soul of Brigitte Pian. And if it is replied that the very impersonality of the priest rightly makes the appearance of a standard repetitive pattern inevitable, we can point to other types—to the stagey villains who appear at the right moments to provide appropriate temptations (usually sexual); to the faithful peasant retainers who hover at the foot of stairs; to the weak, bewildered, often asthmatic or dyscardiac fathers-in-law whose vegetable existence occasionally stirs into violent eruption. Apart from close verbal echoes (like the account of the children's game of making whistles from apricot stones, which appears almost word-for-word in *Le Mystère Frontenac*[20] and *Woman of the Pharisees*[21]) there are some striking repetitions which M. Joseph Majault has listed for us.[22] In *Woman of the Pharisees, Le Mystère Frontenac* and *Desert of Love* a man, affected by congestion of the lungs, dies beside his mistress. In *Dark Angels, Le Mystère Frontenac* and *Thérèse* there are identical descriptions of a station with saw-mills and resinous planks stacked nearby. In *L'Enfant Chargé de Chaînes* and *La Chair et le Sang* occurs the same sentence: 'un peu de valenciennes paraît dans l'entrebâillement du corsage'. All little girls in the novels appear to have sturdy legs and low, broad

17. *Angels.*
18. *Sea.*
19. *Thérèse,* p. 67.
20. P. 43.
21. P. 7.
22. Majault, pp. 108–10, and cf. pp. 153–4.

rumps; many of the women have bilious-looking faces, but broad, often enormous, foreheads.

(ii) Such careless echoes would not matter, if there did not go with them an uneasiness in the actual handling. We have suggested that Mauriac too often helps himself out by importing, from outside his own experience, stock incidents or characters which can get him round the next corner of his plot. Let us examine some examples. The young doctor in *A Kiss for the Leper* is obviously injected into the book merely to test Noémie's loyalty to Jean Péloueyre's memory; what we are told of him is totally unconvincing:

> He had elongated eyes like an Andalusian mule, and he turned them boldly on Noémie, tracing the lines of her body with a lingering thoroughness . . . The medical talk came strangely from lips better suited to dispense kisses than scientific comments.[23]

> His mind was busy with Noémie. There she was, within reach of his hand, yet he never touched her. 'All the same', said the sportsman in him, 'I've winged her: she's wounded'. He knew instinctively when a female victim had been brought to bay and was begging for mercy. He had heard the cry of her young body. He had possessed many women —some, forbidden fruit; some, the wives of men and not discarded bits of rubbish like that wretched Péloueyre. Winged now, and less capable of resistance than most, was she to be his only failure? [24]

If it be said that this piece of novelettish villainy belongs after all to a fairly early work (1922), then we

23. P. 74f.
24. P. 85.

must set beside it another from *Woman of the Pharisees,* written nearly twenty years later. It describes how a pious schoolmistress, who was under the Abbé Calou's care, gets under the evil influence of one Hortense Voyod.

> a type of amazon not wholly unknown, contrary to general opinion, in country districts. There are people who set their toils and are prepared to go hungry for a very long while before any prey lets itself be caught. The patience of vice is infinite. One single victim will content such people, and a brief moment of contact will ensure them long years of happy repletion.[25]

Two things have gone wrong here. First, the whole incident, even the existence of the otherwise irrelevant, and never clearly visualised, schoolmistress, is only introduced to show the Abbé Calou's sanctity, and resulting unpopularity: it has, therefore, the unreality of a chess-move. And second, the author having failed to get a clear picture of the villainess in his mind, has tried the dodge of putting her over for us by means of a long-drawn-out and hazy entomological metaphor. But what we are left with is no precise conception of her, but only the vague evocation of a 'spider-and-fly' cliché.

Unfortunately this kind of unreality tends even to invade the central characters. Since *Woman of the Pharisees* has been widely proclaimed as Mauriac's masterpiece, let us take Brigitte Pian herself. As I hope to show later, the conversion or transformation of Brigitte seems to me excellently done. But it is at a cost: the cost of an over-drawn, sometimes even incredible, picture of the earlier Brigitte. When the boy who tells the story, Louis, discovers the love-affair between Octavia

25. *Pharisees*, p. 153f.

Tronche and M. Puybaraud, and is longing to reveal it to his step-mother, Brigitte, this conversation occurs:

> 'Mother', I said, 'there's something I want to tell you. But'— I added with a touch of hypocrisy— 'I'm not sure whether I ought.'
>
> 'My dear child' [replies Brigitte], 'I have no idea what you have to say. But there is one rule which you would do well to follow blindly, and that is, never to keep anything from your second mother. For on her has devolved the duty of bringing you up.'
>
> 'Even when it is a secret involving others?'
>
> 'If it involves others that is all the more reason why you should tell me', she replied sharply.[26]

I frankly do not believe Brigitte would have found that in her books of piety and moral theology; still less would she state it thus bluntly. Later, having pursued and persecuted poor M. Puybaraud and Octavia, now his wife, Brigitte is shown to us bewailing their ingratitude and speaking, again to her step-son, these unlikely words:

> I sometimes wonder, dear child, whether I don't give too much of myself when I work for the salvation of my neighbours. Oh, I know that the least among them is of infinite worth. I would give my life that one might be saved. But there are moments when I am frightened to think how much time I have wasted (at least, it *seems* wasted, but of that God alone is judge) over insignificant, nay, evil persons. It is the cross laid upon the great-hearted that they shall exhaust themselves in darkness and

26. Op. cit., p. 17.

uncertainty on behalf of the spiritually mean and inferior.[27]

Finally, when she has got Puybaraud and Octavia into her financial clutches, and the defenceless Octavia is threatened with a miscarriage, if not with worse, Brigitte with an unbelievable complacency excuses herself for endangering her life by revealing the worst to the unsuspecting pregnant woman, thus:

> She might [she said of herself] have been weak enough to yield to his [Puybaraud's] representations [that she should spare Octavia by concealing bad news from her] had she been dealing with one of those worldly persons . . . who know nothing of the ways of God. But she had decided that a Christian like Octavia ought not to remain ignorant of the consequences of her acts, that she ought to face the trials which Providence had seen fit to lay upon her. 'Since it was already part of the Divine plan that you should live on the charity of a devoted friend, and that M. Puybaraud should be unable to find suitable employment in the workaday world, I felt that I had no right to spare you the effects of so salutary a lesson.[28]

What one feels about all these three passages is that they have been simply 'cooked'; that for the sake of the enlightenment that is to come to Brigitte, movingly, at the end of the book, we must be allowed to see her in an arbitrarily imposed blackness beforehand. And the reason this carries no conviction is that a woman as subtly cruel and self-satisfied as she is thus supposed to be would be too intelligent to reveal her arrogance by

27. Op. cit., p. 58.
28. P. 126f.

talking, especially talking to a boy, as Brigitte is here made to do. One more instance of this sheer failure in imagination comes from what I believe to be in many ways his best novel, *Le Mystère Frontenac*. Yves is talking to his girl-friend, his 'pick-up', in Paris, soon after he has had the bitter experience of the death of the Frontenac children's 'Uncle Xavier'—the experience that ultimately jolts Yves out of the life he is living at this moment.

> While he was talking, she powdered and rouged her face. When he told her about the death of Uncle Xavier, she asked distractedly whether he was an uncle who had anything to leave.
>
> 'He had given us practically all he had' [replies Yves], 'while he was still alive.'
>
> 'Oh well; then his death is no longer of much interest.' [29]

Now, this would be all very well in a novel by Miss Ivy Compton-Burnett, where the whole technique (and the whole fun) consists in making characters improbably say exactly what they are thinking. But in Mauriac's semi-realistic technique it is really a shocking misjudgement.

(iii) I have used the phrase 'semi-realistic technique'; and I think as a matter of fact that a further weakness in Mauriac's novels lies in his uncertainty what technique to adopt. He himself admired James Joyce's and Virginia Woolf's use of the 'interior monologue', which, he says, is so suitable for expressing 'this immense, tangled world, always changing, always motionless, which we call a single human consciousness'.[30] And Mauriac often uses this monologue to considerable ef-

29. *Frontenac*, p. 268.
30. *Le Romancier et ses personnages*, p. 117f., quot. Majault, p. 243.

fect. But sometimes he mixes it with other elements that do not marry. At one point he is even so jejune as to raise the difficulty and defend himself within the novel itself. The narrator, Louis, in *Woman of the Pharisees,* says:

> Someone will be sure to ask: 'But how do you know so much about events of which you were not a witness? What right have you to reproduce conversations which you cannot have heard?' Well, if the truth must be told, I have outlived most of my characters, several of whom played an important part in my life. Besides, I am the sort of man who keeps old papers, and I have at my disposal not only a private diary [Monsieur Puybaraud's], but various notes made by Monsieur Calou which Mirbel found after the priest's death.[31]

Mauriac would have done better never to raise the question. As it is he has now to make the unconvincing attempt to adjust the rest of the narrative to the availability of the evidence—though fortunately for the tale he does not always remember to do so.

Another flaw in technique is I think the overlapping, so to speak, of two time-sequences. This is particularly marked when Mauriac gives us a sudden 'flash-forward' into the future. We have quoted an example already— the end of his first novel, *L'Enfant Chargé de Chaînes.*[32]

32. Vide sup., p. 19.

A clearer, and really more disturbing instance occurs, twice over, in *Le Mystère Frontenac.* José, the 'bad boy' of the family, has been very obstinate towards Blanche Frontenac, the mother of the family; and it has taken Jean-Louis, the older brother, to bring him to his senses:

31. Op. cit., p. 33.

The two brothers came towards her.

'He'll be sensible now, Mother, [says Jean-Louis], 'he's promised me.'

She drew José towards her, to kiss him, poor unhappy child.

'Darling, you won't ever put on that expression again, will you?'

He would put it on again once more, this terrible expression, several years later, on the evening of a lovely clear, warm day, towards the end of August 1915, at Mourmelon, between two bivouac camps. No one would pay any attention to it, not even his companion, who was just reassuring him: 'It looks as if there's going to be a thundering great artillery preparation—they'll all be laid flat; we'll have nothing to do but advance with slung rifles, our hands in our pockets . . .' José Frontenac would look at him with the same expression, empty of all hope—but which on this day will frighten nobody.[33]

And the same flash-forward happens again later. Yves has just heard from Joséfa, Uncle Xavier's mistress, that old Xavier is very ill with angina. When she has gone, he throws himself on the couch, and thinks back to his family days.

'Mother!' he sobbed, 'Mother . . .'

The tears came. He was the first of the Frontenac children to call on their dead mother as if she was still alive. Eighteen months later, it would be José's turn to do it, his stomach gashed open, for a whole interminable night in September, between two trenches.[34]

33. Op. cit., p. 172f.
34. Ibid., p. 243.

This way of settling the fate of a character in a few lines by prophetic prediction is always dangerous in the novel, but more so when it represents the superimposition of one technique upon another.

Sometimes Mauriac's uncertainty is less obtrusive; it is betrayed by a clumsy arrangement of unlikely coincidence, which is always the sign of a failure to make a genuine *internal* relation between events. For instance, after Gabriel Gradère has dropped every conceivable melodramatic hint of his intending murder of someone (either Symphorien Desbats or his mistress, Aline) he goes to intercept Aline when she arrives by train, with intent to lead her off into the waste ground and there do away with her. At this moment Alain Forcas, the priest, is praying in his room, with Gradère's confessional note-book open before him.

> The rain fell harder. He told himself that it was rustling with just the same sound on the roof of the chateau of Liogats, where in one of the rooms the poor soul who had covered these pages with scrawled writing was lying asleep . . . At that moment, he had an almost physical sense of the coherence of human souls, of that mysterious union in which we are all of us involved alike by sin and grace. He wept for very love of sinners. The whistle of a train came to his ears through the darkness. The wheels of a long line of trucks rumbled over the rails. The noise of escaping steam filled the air. He thought: 'That must be the nine-o'clock just running into the station.' Why should the arrival of that particular train have any meaning for him? Suddenly a load of sadness descended upon his spirit with so crushing a weight that he leaned his

267

head upon the table. His forehead touched the thin blue book.[35]

This seems to me admirably to illustrate Mauriac's strength and weakness: the strength in the conveyance of spiritual oppression, the weakness in the artificial arrangement of the situation. Who, in fact, says the words: 'Why should the arrival of that particular train have any meaning for him?' If it is the priest's own premonition of trouble, it is too far-fetched. But if not, then it can only be Mauriac's own question, inserted *ab extra:* and this at once disturbs the flow of the novel.

Another exhibition of uncertainty of handling occurs when Mauriac requires an incident or experience to happen to one of his characters, but, in default of clear visualisation of it, tries to hint at a vast expanse in a hazy paragraph. Roger North considers that the end of *Woman of the Pharisees* is a failure because the doctor, Gellis, with whom Brigitte falls in love at a late age and who teaches her the meaning of human affection, is only introduced hurriedly in the last seven pages. He considers that if Mauriac had ended with the death, sad but triumphant, of the Abbé Calou, and with Brigitte's humiliation, it would have been more plausible and more effective.[36] There is truth in this, though I do not find the failure of technique so serious here as elsewhere, because it is redeemed by the last pages of the book. A better example of this brusque skating-over a difficult passage occurs at the end of *The Unknown Sea*. After Pierre Costadot ('Pierrot') has been nearly involved in the sudden death of the family's former lawyer, Landin, he 'goes wild' in Paris:

> The only way [thought Pierrot] to make a beginning was to come to grips with fallen human nature

35. *Angels,* p. 285.
36. North, p. 89.

and its morbid growths. But this wretchedness of man's estate, this wound in the soul which might once have prompted his religious instincts to find a solution in the mysteries of faith, worked now in an opposite direction . . .

He takes a mistress; but this phase of life is indicated in the vaguest of generalisations and moralisations:

> He could never get rid of the feeling that virtue was going out of him. Argue as he might, he could not but be convinced that all his satisfactions led to death. The filthy sewage of the world was in his eyes and nose, his ears and mouth. He lived in a constant state of spiritual agony, unable to endure the very pleasures which had become more necessary to him than bread and wine.[37]

And so on. The whole episode is over in three pages, and is brought to an end by Pierre reading a book recently published by Renan's grandson, and also Péguy's *Mystère de la Charité de Jeanne d'Arc.* This is very edifying, no doubt; but it is not novel-writing.

If we look closer I think we shall find that the trouble in all these passages lies in a failure of *attention.* When we hear a singer falter and her notes become uncertain and forced, we know that she has forgotten the song itself and is thinking of her diaphragm or breath-control. Sometimes this kind of self-consciousness comes out into the open in Mauriac. The well-known preface to *The End of the Night,* in which he explains that he had originally written the description of Thérèse's death-bed reconciliation, but had destroyed it because he could not visualise the priest who would hear her confession—this we must respect for its transparent honesty. And perhaps even the charming preface to *Trois Récits,* which con-

37. Op. cit., pp. 187, 189.

tains a similar self-exculpation, is too ingenuous for anyone to quarrel with:

> 'To offer oneself, by means of humiliations, to the coming of inspirations': the most beautiful tale of this collection, and the one which ought to have this *Pensée* of Pascal's as its *exergum,* is the fourth, the one the author has not written, has not yet deserved to write.[38]

But too often we are conscious within the novel itself of the reflex attention of the author upon the process of writing. Louis, the 'I' of *Woman of the Pharisees,* occasionally exclaims: 'If I were writing a novel, I should . . .' —a well-known novelists' dodge. And once Louis claims to be suppressing some evidence he has—the correspondence between Puybaraud and Octavia:

> Not because it does not deserve publication, but because I doubt whether there are many readers capable of appreciating the charm of true humility, of that particular manifestation of humility which takes no heed of itself and seems completely ignorant of its effect on others.[39]

This is a somewhat artless attempt to divert critical attention from the author's inability to present this humility, by directing it against the pretended imperceptiveness of the public. But the crudest example of 'author's technique' called to the rescue in a difficult literary situation is the conclusion of one of Mauriac's least successful stories of passion, *The Enemy.* Fabien Dézaymeries, after a protracted love-affair with Fanny, spends a restless night wandering by the river, as a result of which he not unnaturally gets pleurisy. He nearly dies, and in

38. *Récits,* p. xxxif.
39. Op. cit., p. 53.

that condition he is reconciled to the Church. When he recovers, he makes the break with Fanny, and, to his pious mother's delight, destroys a letter from her unopened. There follows the conclusion of the story:

> In order that his mistress should be saved he had refused to open his heart to the call of human happiness, and already he was dead to the world. But for all his resolution the claims of the body could not be altogether stilled. For long months it had been gorged: how then, when it had once more woken to life, could it be kept from craving satisfaction? The real story of Fabien Dézaymeries should, properly speaking, begin at this point, for all that had gone before was in the nature of a prologue. But how is one to describe the secret drama of a man who struggles to subdue his earthy heritage, that drama which finds expression neither in words nor gestures? Where is the artist who may dare to imagine the processes and shifts of that great protagonist—Grace? It is the mark of our slavery and of our wretchedness that we can, without lying, paint a faithful portrait only of the passions.[40]

When a creative writer starts to justify himself for what he cannot do, we begin to doubt the effectiveness of even what he can, as the public orator who begins to anticipate possible heckling will forget the very speech he has come to deliver in his anxiety to keep the bad eggs at bay.

40. Op. cit., p. 279.

3

THE APOLOGETIC
NOVELIST

To consider the familiar problem of the 'Catholic novelist' would require a separate treatise. Here we shall
submit this aspect of Mauriac's work to a criticism similar to that in the last chapter, that is, a criticism of it *as
writing*. This is not to subscribe to a dogma of art as
'pure form'; it is merely to say that theological or metaphysical weakness betrays itself even in style and organi-
sation.

(i) Mauriac, especially since his 'conversion' in 1928 to
1929,[1] has found it incumbent upon him to indulge in
apologetic. From the Christian point of view this is com-
mendable, of course. We do not, for instance, forget the
courageous letter he wrote to the philosopher Gabriel
Marcel in 1929 ('Mais enfin, M. Marcel, pourquoi n'êtes-
vous pas des nôtres?'[2]), with what the Christian must
consider its important and fruitful consequences. And
when he turns, as in his excellent little book *La Pierre
d'Achoppement*,[3] to a serious and responsible scrutiny
of the world of popular Catholic devotion and practice,
he performs a most valuable task for us. But two disad-

1. Vide sup. 13, for the sense in which we use this word of him.
2. Vide G. Marcel, *Être et Avoir*, p. 29f.; R. Troisfontaines, *Existen-
tialisme et Pensée Chrétienne* (1948), p. 33.
3. Pub. 1951.

vantages have accompanied this development: apologetic has frequently been replaced by apologizing; and much of the apology has had to be directed towards his own people. This latter disadvantage has been serious, in that it has induced that nervousness about his reception, that self-exculpatory anxiety, which has harmed even his creative writing. In his preface to *Trois Récits,* already cited, he tries to meet his Catholic critics:

> And so I pride myself on painting a world in revolt against the Tribunal of conscience, a miserable world, devoid of Grace, and so, without rejecting any of my freedom as a writer, to reach an indirect apology for Christianity. It is quite impossible, I said to myself, to reproduce the modern world as it exists, without displaying the violation of a holy law.[4]

As he puts it later in *Dark Angels* (it is actually Gradère, writing his confession in his diary), 'The way into the supernatural often starts from the depths'.[5] And Mauriac's own comment in the same novel, preparing us for Gradère's conversion, is:

> Did the wretched man, who had poured into this child's exercise-book all the abomination of his life, know of what good he was capable? Those who seem dedicated to evil may, perhaps, be chosen above their fellows: the very depth of their fall gives a measure of the vocation that they have betrayed. None would be blessed had they not been given the power to damn themselves. Perhaps only those are damned who might have been saints.[6]

4. Op. cit., p. xiv.
5. *Angels,* p. 155.
6. Ibid., p. 284.

In 1937 Mauriac heard a sermon from the Bishop of Mans in the church of Saint-Roch, Paris, declaiming against writers who

> on the pretext of freedom of inspiration, actually claim to be able to reconcile audacious descriptions and paintings with the practice of the sacraments . . . These men pride themselves on being pious while they trouble and pervert others.[7]

Mauriac is relieved to learn later that he was not meant to be included in this condemnation—that, indeed, Monsignor Grente enjoyed his novels. But it drove him to a further attempt to defend the Catholic novelist.[8] He manages, by great self-control, even to accept the action of a Catholic review for *bien-pensants,* which listed his play *Asmodée* under the heading: 'For informed adults who for certain reasons (e.g. for a family party) cannot in a particular circumstance refuse to go to the theatre'. In this defence Mauriac repeats the old theme, that a writer's works 'can have no other essence than corrupted nature, since they take their origin from there and since even the least impure of them are always born of this corruption'.[9] And finally, as recently as December 1951, Mauriac found himself still having to meet the same criticism from within the fold.

> At the moment of publishing *Galigaï* I experience the same disquiet as thirty years ago when one of my books was born; the fear not, admittedly, of scandalizing, but of disconcerting those of my readers who have religious preoccupations in common with me. The misunderstanding is shown,

7. *Journal,* p. 375.
8. Ibid., p. 375f.; and in expanded form in a volume of essays, *L'Homme et le Péché,* ed. Présences (Plon, 1938).
9. *L'Homme et le Péché,* p. 218.

besides, in other circumstance than the publication of a novel. Thus, a man of religion writes to me that he has been deceived in *La Table Ronde*: my sole presence at the head of the Editorial Board had incited him to read it, and no doubt to recommend it to his young people. This Father considered it strange that I should devote time to so *useless* a periodical. There is the misunderstanding: for a man of religion, and even for a simple layman, if he is devout, to write means first of all to serve. That the artist has no other concern than to paint well and to clarify his painting, as Gide set himself to do—this is what an 'apostle' has the utmost difficulty in conceiving.[10]

And Mauriac goes on to make some interesting observations on his own works. Re-reading them for a complete edition, he says:

I see in many places Grace cropping up—but, it seems to me, a bit less so the older I have grown. It still emerges in a niggardly way in the last pages of *The Little Misery*. In *Galigaï*, to guess that the destiny of one of my characters points towards God you have to wait for the very last sentence, the last word.

What a black picture! This deformed humanity, with its wry grimaces, which Grace has failed to get a purchase on—in favour of whom or of what does it testify? There is the Christian objection.

He has to admit that this Christian objection is powerful. In response he now says, more modestly than in earlier days, that the artist does not in fact know what he is doing as he writes. And therefore in the last resort

10. *La Table Ronde,* Dec. 1951, p. 77 (reprinted as Pref. to *Galigaï*).

he has to 'resign himself to having no other excuse than that of his vocation'. Is this an arrogant claim, to have such a vocation? And are there no vocations to evil too?

> Exactly! Perhaps I have been created and placed in this little canton of the universe, at a time when Rebellion is the theme on which our best minds most readily exercise themselves, only to bear witness to the guilt of man before the infinite innocence of God; and, as R. M. Albérès wrote à propos *The Little Misery*, 'to set in opposition to metaphysical literature, where man complains of everything, a psychological literature where he complains only of himself'.

This is a claim and a defence which must be acknowledged to have some validity, at least in theory. But only if they can be made good in the flesh and blood of the novels themselves. Can they?

(ii) But before we try to answer that question a little more specifically, we must remember Mauriac's apologetic directed outwards: for he has also to defend himself on the other flank. In 1928 Gide wrote Mauriac a letter, à propos the latter's *Life of Jean Racine*:

> You rejoice in the fact that God, before seizing hold of Racine again, left him time to write his plays, to write them *despite* his conversion. In short, what you seek is . . . permission to be a Christian without having to burn your books; and this is what makes you write them in such a way that, though a Christian, you will not have to disavow them. All this (this reassuring compromise that allows one to love God without losing sight of Mammon) . . . gives one that anguished conscience which lends such charm to your face, such savour

> to your writings . . . You are not sufficiently Christian to cease being a writer.[11]

It was this crude, indeed monstrous over-statement of the dilemma that prompted Mauriac to write *God and Mammon* in reply. And the controversy did not stop there. Mauriac wrote in 1931: 'Even in the state of grace my creatures are born of the murkiest part of myself'.[12] And Gide comments triumphantly in his diary, 'What a confession! This amounts to saying that if he were a perfect Christian, he would cease to have any material from which to make his novels. Is not this precisely what I told him?' [13] But once again, the matter is not so simple as Gide likes to make out. The inability of the artist to paint paradise and carry conviction is no condemnation either of paradise or of art. Mauriac observes wisely later on:

> It happens that in the presence of beings who have progressed far towards God (I think of certain little Sisters, certain novices) we are reminded of those diaphanous cocoons abandoned by the chrysalis—they seem, as it were, so emptied of themselves. The devil loses his rights (and here the devil is the novelist 'who sees everything in sable black', or an author of pitiless 'maxims' [sc. La Rochefoucauld]), the devil loses his rights over the creature who is stripped before his Creator. And that is why the novel about sanctity will never be written.[14]

(iii) This brings us nearer at last to the real issue. 'The novel about sanctity will never be written'; but will even

11. Cit., Gide, *Journal* (E.T., J. O'Brien, III, 162–3n.)
12. *Nouvelle Revue Française,* June 1931.
13. Gide, op. cit., p. 162.
14. Mauriac, *Journal,* p. 54.

the novel about damnation be a good novel if it is too consciously and deliberately about damnation? That is the question that literary criticism will ask. And the corresponding question that theology will ask: is anyone but God qualified to write a novel about either sanctity or damnation? If anyone is in fact damned, He alone can know about it.

This is the context in which to look at the well-known accusation by M. Jean-Paul Sartre. In the *Nouvelle Revue Française* for February 1939, M. Sartre wrote on 'M. François Mauriac et la liberté'.[15] He discusses *The End of the Night* in particular, and quotes the passage about Thérèse:

> She heard nine o'clock strike. She must still find some way of killing time, for it was too early as yet to swallow the cachet which would assure her a few hours of sleep. As a rule, *though hope was dead in her, she was too proud to have recourse to drugs.* But to-night she could not resist the promise of their help.[16]

But here the translator has been kind to Mauriac, and softened the sentence to which M. Sartre takes exception. Mauriac wrote, for the sentence italicised above, 'non que ce fut dans les habitudes de cette désespérée prudente';[17] and Sartre asks: 'who judges that Thérèse is a "désespérée prudente"? It can't be Thérèse herself. No, it is M. Mauriac, it is I myself: we have the Desquey-roux dossier in our hands, and we file our accusation'. Here, says M. Sartre, is the novelist's ambiguity in the use of the third person. Sometimes it is 'she-subject', as when the passage opens with 'She heard nine o'clock

15. Reprinted in *Situations*.
16. *Night*, p. 172 (italics mine).
17. *La Fin de la Nuit*, p. 17.

strike. She must . . .' Sometimes, however, it is 'she-object', when the novelist stands outside and judges her. And the trouble, M. Sartre continues, is that Mauriac before writing 'forges the essence' of his characters, decrees that they shall be this or that. Sometimes he even takes us by the hand and tips us the wink that he has done well. For instance when Mauriac says of Thérèse: 'She interrupted herself then in the middle of a sentence (for she was acting in entire good faith) . . .' [18] M. Sartre comments: 'I know of no cruder artifice than this admonishing between parentheses'. And he concludes that Mauriac's great weakness is that he wishes to be God: but the novelist is not God. He describes *The End of the Night* as:

> This angular and frozen work, with bits from the theatre, bits of analysis, poetic meditations . . . this motionless narrative, which exhibits its intellectual mechanism at the first glance, where the dumb figures of the heroes are inscribed like angles in a circle.

And having discussed the relation between his own existentialist conception of freedom and the freedom which a novel, and the characters within a novel, must have, he concludes that Mauriac, through the sin of pride, is not a novelist:

> He has wanted to ignore the fact—as have indeed most of our authors—that the theory of relativity applies entirely to the universe of the novel; that in a true novel there is no more room than there is in the world of Einstein for a privileged observer, and that in the system of a novel, as in a physicist's system, there exists no experience which enables

18. Ibid., p. 162 (*Thérèse*, p. 246).

one to discover whether this system is in movement or in repose. M. Mauriac has preferred himself. He has chosen the divine omniscience and omnipotence. But a novel is written by a man for men. In the sight of God, who penetrates through appearances without coming to a halt in them, there is no novel, there is no art, since art lives by appearances. God is not an artist; neither is M. Mauriac.

Critics have come to Mauriac's aid. M. Joseph Majault[19] quotes against M. Sartre some words used by Mauriac himself which show that Mauriac is not at all ignorant of the kind of issue M. Sartre is discussing. Mauriac has been saying that the novelist's difficulties in relation to his characters are like those of God in relation to man:

> In each case it is a question of reconciling the freedom of the creature and the freedom of the creator. The heroes of our novels must be free in the sense in which a theologian says that man is free; the novelist must not intervene arbitrarily in their destiny . . . But on the other hand, God also must be free, infinitely free to act on His creature.[20]

And elsewhere Mauriac has also observed that authors are not

> emulators of God—they are apes of God . . . The characters which they invent are by no means created, if creation consists in making something out of nothing.[21]

This shows us, we must agree, that M. Sartre was not saying anything very new, and that Mauriac was well aware of the problem, at least in theory. We find it dif-

19. Majault, p. 270.
20. *Le Roman*, p. 60.
21. *Le Romancier et ses Personnages*, p. 95f. (Quoted Majault, p. 61).

ficult, though, to reconcile that awareness with Mauriac's treatment of some of his characters; for instance with his remarks about Landin, of whom he tells us, at the time of his death, that there is

> . . . a frontier beyond which no human aid could be of any avail to Landin, and where no salvation on earth or in heaven awaited him . . . The unquenchable fires of hell are *lit* in this world, and those whom theologians count as lost are marked for damnation at their birth and even before it.[22]

Double predestination is neither good Catholic doctrine nor a good basis for novel-writing.

Mlle Nelly Cormeau's defence of Mauriac is even more strenuous. Her main point is that a similar 'omniscience' of the author, similar intrusions by him into his novels, and a similar 'ambiguity of the third person' can be found in passages from the most distinguished writers. She quotes passages from Balzac and Stendhal, and refers to critical writings on Flaubert, Proust, etc.[23] I cannot say that I find her parallels convincing, given the total context, technique and tone of the works from which they are taken. It would be possible, admittedly, to select from a major English novelist such as George Eliot plenty of passages in which the canon against the intrusion of 'author's comment' was infringed. But George Eliot is a different sort of novelist from Mauriac, and so are Stendhal, Flaubert, and Proust. The real weakness in the passages which M. Sartre (rightly, I believe) attacks, is this: that the transposition from 'she-subject' to 'she-object', from participatory narrative to external comment, is sudden, unprepared-for, and therefore jolting—the author himself is clearly unaware of

22. *Sea*, p. 186f.
23. Cormeau, appendix, pp. 364–380.

what is happening, and the resulting jolt that he gives us betrays a loss of grip on his part.

M. Sartre's criticism depends in no wise upon his existential philosophy, but is evidence of a rather surprising acuity (surprising, when we remember the same author's curious valuation of Baudelaire and serious over-praise of William Faulkner). Let me endorse M. Sartre's point by giving some further examples of the sort of failure that he is indicating. We may divide them into two types: direct external intrusions by the author into the narrative; and internal evidence of a shift from genuine living speech and thought to a sort of ventriloquizing through his characters' mouths.

Of the first type there are many instances. Raymond Courrèges is lamenting the absence of Maria Cross, his beloved:

> He carried with him a tearing, frantic capability of passion, inherited from his father . . . There could be no hope for either of them, father or son, unless, before they died, He should reveal Himself Who, unknown to them, had drawn and summoned from the depths of their beings this burning, bitter tide.[24]

Here the author bursts frankly into the narrative, wagging an admonitory finger. Or here is an example where we see a character, first through the eyes of another character in the same novel, and then, without warning, through the author's own eyes. Fanny has appeared, and first Fabien, then gradually Mauriac, look at her:

> There she stood, her young body apparently untouched by the passing of the years, strong as steel, tempered and hardened and possessed. Sin, in its

24. *Desert*, p. 162f.

way, is a form of life. There is such a thing as *infernal* Grace, and it can galvanize, just for as long as may be necessary, that adorable shape which, according to St Catherine of Siena, stinks in all its parts.[25]

The citation itself, which is characteristic of Mauriac's taste, gives the case away, even if we have not suspected before that the description is becoming homiletic. Or again here one sentence betrays the shift: Hervé is setting off to spend the evening with his mistress; the passage starts off in his own mind, with his thoughts about how to deceive his mother, and then we can see his mind being faded away and Mauriac's mind being slipped in instead:

> He [Hervé] promised to do his best and she [his mother] understood quite clearly that he would not return home before evening. He sat with his face turned away from her. Nothing could prevent him from doing this afternoon what he intended to do, from savouring to the full his sorry delight, from plunging into surroundings which could not even be imagined by this elderly woman in front of him.[26]

At least these intrusions are not as crude as the unblushing remark in *Le Démon de Connaissance*. Maryan, the hero, has been day-dreaming how to create his soul a model of Francis, Dominic, Ignatius; and the text continues: 'Ainsi délire cet orgueilleux: comme il est loin du Maître humble de coeur! Mais il ne le sait pas'.[27]

25. *Enemy,* p. 198.
26. *Lost,* p. 49.
27. *Récits,* p. 214. ('Thus did this swollen-head deliriously dream: what a long way he was from the humble-hearted Master! But he did not know it.')

But there is a parenthesis in a later and maturer novel which is almost as disconcerting. The priest, Alain Forcas, wakes one morning at a later hour than he had meant to:

> The Angelus. And he had meant to get up at dawn! It was already full day . . . He ran to the window and pushed open the shutters . . . He would leave off shaving till after Mass (though he was not one of those priests who have the effrontery to approach the altar uncleansed). He must hurry. . . . [etc.] [28]

Can we not, in that parenthesis, see M. Mauriac getting ready to write a letter of complaint to the bishop? Occasionally he reads a lesson from the Catechism to his characters—sometimes even literally:

> The child [Marie de Lados' little boy] sat with his elbows propped upon it [the table], busy with his Catechism . . . He was still muttering to himself: '*Are there then three Gods?*'—as though he did not know that there is but one—one sole and single Love.[29]

This time we can hear the Sunday-School master prodding the boy, and saying: 'Come now, you do know, don't you, that there is but one . . . ?'

Even more abrupt is the spiritual counsel delivered to Brigitte Pian, ill-concealed beneath a negative. It starts from her own thoughts, and then the announcer's voice breaks in to the script:

> Was she a saint? She was making great efforts to be one, and, at each step forward, fought hard to hold the ground she had gained. No one had ever

28. *Angels*, p. 215f.
29. *Genetrix*, p. 180.

told her that the closer a man gets to sanctity the more conscious does he become of his own worthlessness, his own nothingness, and gives to God . . . all credit for the few good activities with which Grace has endowed him.[30]

But these blemishes are so obvious as to stare one in the face; and in most of these passages Mauriac has given us some slight warning that he is moving out of the congregation to preach a retreat from the pulpit. What is more disturbing, because less easily detectable, is the second type of intrusion, where he ventriloquizes from within the characters, so to speak. Let us start with an early example of what might be called the author's internal (as opposed to external) intrusion. Jérome and Vincent, the young Catholic Social leaders, are discussing whether to exploit the enthusiasm of Jean-Paul (the hero of the novel):

> 'We'll have to be careful', said Vincent: 'Jean-Paul will resist: he's got some character.'
> The Leader seemed anxious. 'So much the worse', said he [sc. Jérome]: 'I want to have round me people with docile temperaments, not personalities who stand up to me'.[31]

What has happened here? Clearly Mauriac has mentally composed this about Jérome in the third person ('he is the sort who wants to have round him people with docile temperaments . . .', etc.) and has then carelessly written it direct into the first person. The result is unconvincing—for who in fact would say this of himself, even to one of his own henchmen? And this defect is not confined to the early novels; two examples must suffice, both

30. *Pharisees*, p. 133.
31. *L'Enfant*, p. 61. ('Je veux autour de moi des tempéraments qui me servant, non des personnalités qui me résistent.')

from one of his most successful. Both occur in the diary of the protagonist, Louis. The first, addressed to his wife Isa, reminds her of their time of courting. She had always said to Louis:

> 'I fell in love with you from the moment we met. We had said many, many prayers at Lourdes . . . and as soon as I set my eye on you, I knew that they had been answered.'
>
> You were far from guessing [Louis comments] how those words grated on my nerves. Those who oppose you in religion have, really, a very much nobler idea of it than you realize, *or than they realize themselves* . . .[32]

Those last words, italicised, give the case away: the old man has ceased to speak, or rather to write in his diary, and Mauriac is whispering behind him. Much later in the novel the old grandfather Louis again is talking to Janine, whom he has taken in after the collapse of her marriage with Phili. He, the professed agnostic, suddenly mentions her faith: surely, he asks, that will help her in her trouble? Janine is puzzled by this, and finally rejects the suggestion. She says that

> she didn't like mixing up religion with matters of this kind, that she was a practising Christian and regularly performed her religious duties, but that she had a horror of morbidity. She might have been saying that she always paid her taxes. It is precisely the attitude that, all my life, I have loathed and detested, the caricature and mean interpretation of the Christian life which I had deliberately chosen to regard as the essence of the religious mind, in order that I might feel free to hate it.[33]

32. *Knot,* p. 48 (italics mine).
33. Ibid., p. 198.

It is true that here the translator has made Mauriac sound rather cruder than he is. The sentence 'I had deliberately chosen to regard . . .' actually runs in the original 'j'avais feint d'y voir . . .', which is much less objectionable. Yet even with that slight qualification, do we not feel a subtle slide of the ground towards the end of the paragraph? Even granted the awkward technique, the confession-journal, which Mauriac has elected to employ in this novel, can we really believe that it is still Louis speaking, writing himself: 'I pretended to consider this the acme of religious thought so that I could hate it with justification'? Or do we not rather sense at this point that it is again Mauriac who has stepped in to dot the i's and cross the t's of self-analysis? 'Pour avoir le droit de la haïr'—is that what a man, even a Louis, writes of himself? I shall not go so far as to say with M. Sartre that this is not novel-writing; but there is something seriously wrong with a work that pulls us up to ask these questions.

(iv) There is a second kind of disquiet which we feel also when Mauriac intrudes, especially when he intrudes with a *Gratia ex machina,* and the source of this disquiet is worth examining. Let us take some examples. When old Félicité Cazenave is dying, her only consolation is the sight of her son Fernand when he comes to visit her in the evenings:

> For her the whole long day was but preliminary to these evening hours. Her eyes were taking their last fill of him before darkness should overwhelm them . . .
>
> Only when it was hard upon the third hour was the sponge offered to the victim. How much more bitter than gall was the sight, upon that taut and suffering face, of so much love offered to another!

Yet Félicité Cazenave felt dimly that it was a good thing she should suffer for her son. What she did not know was that she had been crucified.[34]

This rather nauseating importation of echoes from Good Friday is not only in bad taste, but is quite gratuitous. But something like it, though less crude, occurs in a much maturer novel, *That Which Was Lost*. When Alain is beginning to shake himself free from Tota, he begins also to have a premonition of his future priestly vocation.

> In future . . . many others would clutch on to him and he would have to bear the weight not of one but of many . . . A vocation. It is not for nothing that a man is set apart from his fellows and marked, even before he reaches manhood. Alain had in good faith been retracing the delectable reaches of his life back through the years and now here was the well-spring at last; a little hill, crowned with a malefactor's cross glimpsed through the everlasting clouds of contumely, hatred and love that cling to it, and surrounded by the terrifying indifference of the world (the ancient and oft repeated act, the heedless arm thrusting the same lance home).[35]

When we find these sudden invocations of the act of Redemption why is it that we feel embarrassed? Why, again, do we feel restive when we read this, for instance, of the death of Irène:

> Sinking, drowning, she could not regain the surface and the air; her strength was gone. She clutched frenziedly, until her nails were broken,

34. *Genetrix*, p. 187.
35. *Lost*, p. 143f.

her elbows torn and bleeding. The great discovery was not for her; not hers to fall upon her knees, to weep for joy . . . She must pass through this darkness into which she had so madly plunged now to the bitter end. But as she slipped into the very abyss she knew, she saw, she cried aloud at last unto that love by the name which is above all other names.[36]

The restiveness which this induces in us is by no means allayed when we learn that the unknown priest who hears Mme de Blénauge's confession has the sudden intuition that Irène died in the presence of Christ.[37] For though the scene is beautifully portrayed, it strikes us as having something arbitrary, something willed *ab extra*, at its core. The same is even true of the much more modest, more tentative ending of *Galigaï* to which Mauriac, as we have seen above,[38] himself refers. Nicolas Plassac walks away from his home, his love having foundered.

He walked alone, a prey to this sad hunger which all the kingdoms of the earth could not have appeased, alone with this tenderness, which had withdrawn from all human faces and remained spread out like the sea under the mindless stars. At the place where a clearing among the trees revealed a wide patch of sky, he stopped, turned his head, and saw, all mixed with the roof-tops, the black abandoned cathedral. Yet the human termites had built this enormous nave to the measure of the love which smothers some of them. Nicolas Plassac walked on to the spot where the road crosses the Leyrot. A

36. Ibid., p. 98.
37. Ibid., p. 110.
38. Vide sup., p. 37.

> stranger to himself, detached from all creatures, he
> sat on the parapet, and he stayed there as if he had
> arranged to meet someone.[39]

It is effective in its way; yet even here there is a moment's disquiet as we read it, which can be defined perhaps by the sudden and uncalled-for occurrence of the words 'les insectes humains'. Can it be that the sense of artificiality, of the *voulu*, which we feel in all these however distant invocations of Rescue, lies in this: that the pictures of the Wreck itself, which the rescue-squad is called in to deal with, are artificial and in the last resort arbitrary?

This requires further clarification. No one should object to Mauriac for his realistic desire to depict a fallen world. Those who do so object, have surely allowed their dislike of theology to cloud the clarity of their vision. And more, from a picture of the Fall a genuine and valid apologetic for the Faith can be constructed. But it must in that case be a *genuine* picture of the Fall. And a genuine picture of the Fall requires two conditions: a realisation, first, of the primal innocence; and, second, a real compassion for the fallen *qua* fallen. It is precisely these two requirements, I think, that we find so often missing in Mauriac's work. Whenever Mauriac discusses Port-Royal or Pascal, as he does in many of his works, he almost tumbles over backwards in his eagerness to dissociate himself from the Jansenist heresy. But the influence always remained. In an address, already cited, to the students of his old college, Grand-Lebrun, in 1951, he paid tribute to his old teacher who, among other things, taught him to love Pascal and Racine:

> You didn't only introduce them into my memory
> as an examinee, but into the most secret places of

39. *Galigaï*, p. 168.

my mind and flesh—which perhaps you have had
to expiate by an extra spell of Purgatory, for it is
you indeed who in no small part have made me the
novelist I have become.[40]

But it is the two requirements above-mentioned whose
absence marks the Jansenist: and we cannot but feel that
Mauriac never really got Port-Royal out of his system.[41]
 This is most clearly seen in some of his pictures of
sexual relations. It is true that Mauriac tries to dissociate himself from the view of old Mme Dézaymeries. She
wrote to her Director:

> I remember reading in Pascal that marriage is
> the lowest of all Christian states, vile and unpleas-
> ing to God. How strongly I feel the truth of that!
> How convinced I am that the traffic of the flesh is
> a grim and filthy business.[42]

And the priest has to reply that it is 'very reprehensible
on her part to espouse the derogatory views of a heretic
on that great Sacrament'. But consider the searing pictures the author gives us, and even sometimes seems to
delight in giving us, of the sexual relations between,
e.g., Noémie and Jean Péloueyre:

> Long was the battle waged by Jean Péloueyre, at
> first with his own ice-bound senses, and then with
> the woman who was as one dead. As day was dawn-
> ing a stifled groan marked the end of a struggle
> that had lasted six long hours. Soaked with sweat,
> Jean Péloueyre dared not make a movement. He

40. *La Table Ronde*, l.c., p. 43.
41. Cf. the passage cited above, implying a rigorous form of predestination, p. 41, sup.
42. *Enemy*, p. 194.

lay there, looking more hideous than a worm beside the corpse it has at last abandoned.[43]

or between Thérèse and Bernard Desqueyroux:

> Nothing is so severing as the frenzy that seizes upon our partner in the act. I always saw Bernard as a man who charged head-down at pleasure, while I lay like a corpse, motionless, as though fearing that, at the slightest gesture on my part, this madman, this epileptic, might strangle me. As often as not, balanced on the very edge of ultimate excruciation, he would discover suddenly that he was alone. The gloomy battle would be broken off, and Bernard, retracing his steps, would, as it were, stand back and see me there, like a dead body thrown up on the shore, my teeth clenched, my body cold to the touch.[44]

These pictures, though they have an appearance of justification in their contexts, are given with a little too much relish; and they do not encourage us to think that Mauriac's dissociation from Mme Dézaymeries's view is so radical after all. Young Louis in the *Woman of the Pharisees* comes to conclusions which he may, of course, owe to some extent to his step-mother Brigitte, but which Mauriac at least does not do anything ostensibly to correct:

> My views on this matter have not greatly changed. I believe that all the miseries of our human state come from our inability to remain chaste, and that men vowed to chastity would be spared most of the evils that weigh them down . . .

43. *Leper*, p. 43.
44. *Thérèse*, p. 30 (and cf. p. 38).

> Wherever I have found it [happiness based on gen-
> erosity and love], the movements of the heart and
> the promptings of the flesh have been kept under
> strict discipline.[45]

No doubt this is meant to convey the thoughts of a prig-
gish young man—though we must remember that he is
supposed to be writing years after the event. But we cannot feel that Mauriac is so far away. And this is perhaps
confirmed by a much more casual, and therefore a more
revealing, remark the author throws out in another
novel. Fabien is returning to Paris after the Easter holidays.

> The old stones of palaces and bridges lay basking
> in the soft radiance of a misty sun. The city was full
> of young bodies responsive to the call of spring,
> meeting at every corner, sitting on the terrace of
> every café. The air was full of stale romance. It was
> the time of year when *the enemy within us* finds a
> ready ally in the outward scene . . . A thousand
> posters called temptingly from the sun-baked walls.
> It was that season when the streets are full of faces
> that no longer try to hide their secret yearning,
> when parted lips and seeking eyes take no account
> of the dangerous abyss.[46]

We have no wish to deny that there is an 'enemy within';
but that he should so immediately spring to mind at the
mention of spring is surely suggestive of Mauriac's
preoccupations.

It is, indeed, the casual phrase, the imagery that comes
spontaneously to the pen, that best reveals an author's
deepest convictions. And here we have plenty of evi-

45. *Pharisees,* p. 119.
46. *Enemy,* p. 181 (italics mine).

dence to hand. Jérome, the writer in *Un Homme de Lettres*, exclaims:

> Besides, happy love, now: does it exist? Oh yes, it does! It exists in a land we do not know. I believe in the existence of satisfied lovers in the same way that I believe in the existence of angels. Somewhere or other there is harp-music, the beating of wings—But where? [47]

Hardly once in the novels do we come across a happy marriage—except the vaguely delineated but moving relationship between old Brigitte Pian and the doctor, and one delicate and just passage on fidelity, which, however, does not occur in a novel but in the *Journal*.

> How few love-affairs find enough strength within themselves to remain sedentary! Perhaps that is why married love which persists through countless vicissitudes seems to me the loveliest of miracles, though it is the commonest. After many years, still to have so many things to say to each other, from the most trivial to the most serious, without the intention or the desire to astonish or to be admired —what a wonderful thing! No need to tell lies to each other: lying is no use from now on, husband and wife have become so transparent to each other. That is the only love which loves immobility, which feeds on habit and the daily event. [48]

But do we ever in the novels see a hint of this? The normal attitude there is this, from the introduction to *Trois Récits*: 'How can lovers escape their métier of executioner? They are not gods: they are not God'. [49]

47. *Récits*, p. 97.
48. *Journal*, p. 38.
49. *Récits*, p. xix.

Or this, describing Paula's loathing for her mother-in-law, the Baronne de Galéas: 'We speak of "making love": we should be able, too, to speak of "making hate". To make hate is comforting. It rests the mind and relaxes the nerves'.[50] Or, for the imagery that accompanies this frame of mind, there is this, when Alain Forcas comes across Thérèse in the park: 'There on an iron chair, with her back against the shaft of a lamp, was a woman seated upright with her head thrown back as if in the act of offering her throat to the knife'.[51] Or, more cruelly, this picture of the old Baronne:

> Hatred had quickened the senile jerking of the aged head which was bare and bald and prepared already for the nothingness of death . . . The Baronne kept turning and twisting her bald vulture's head among the pillows.[52]

What in fact we feel from all this kind of imagery is not so much that Mauriac is mistaken in thinking of the world as fallen and needing Grace—the Christian believes this, and the non-Christian frequently agrees: but rather that what Mauriac is picturing as fallen is in fact only diseased. Because he has a clinical, almost a purely physiological, conception of the fallen state, so he naturally tends to have a chemist's conception of redemption. Grace is injected or swallowed whole like a pill. It is simply the first conception that is wrong. Mauriac's sinners are frequently not sinners at all, or not sinners in the particular aspects that he underlines, but unreal creatures seen through a sombre lens. And at his best moments Mauriac himself is aware of this. It is with a

50. *Misery*, p. 42.
51. *Lost*, p. 59f.
52. *Misery*, pp. 101, 109 ('the nothingness of death' translates 'le néant'; and 'her bald . . . etc.' translates 'sa vieille tête de rapace').

remarkably lucid self-knowledge that he said once of his own writing:

> I had hoped that Mozart, who had opened me the gates of his paradise, would suddenly release a flight of angels in my work—angels who would not be 'dark angels'. But as soon as I set to work, everything takes on a colour according to my eternal colours; even my most beautiful characters enter into a kind of sulphurous light which is natural to me and which I do not defend—for it is simply mine.[53]

53. *Journal,* p. 220.

4

ACHIEVEMENT

The divergent estimates of Mauriac's place as a novelist
are most striking. We have had M. Sartre's severe judgement that he is not a novelist at all. Elsewhere, on the
other hand, he has been described variously as: 'un-
rivalled by any living novelist in any country' (Mr Raymond Mortimer): 'perhaps the greatest living European
novelist' (Mr A. Calder-Marshall): and so on. Mr Graham Greene[1] and M. Mauriac himself [2] have exchanged
mutual eulogies. But Miss Helen Gardner[3] has tried to
define Mauriac's success precisely by a contrast with Mr
Graham Greene and the English Catholic novels:

> They [the latter] are constructions which can be
> used to express their author's views on good and
> evil, the natural and the supernatural; [whereas]
> the solid bourgeois and peasant world of M. Mau-
> riac has an existence of its own apart from its
> author's beliefs.

Moreover, the confidence of the English writers about
the destiny of their characters compares unfavourably,
she says,

1. Essay 'François Mauriac' in *The Lost Childhood,* 1951.
2. Essay 'Graham Greene' in *Great Men.*
3. Article 'François Mauriac: A Woman of the Pharisees', in *Penguin
New Writing,* No. 31, 1947.

with M. Mauriac's reticence and religious agnosticism about the ultimate fate of his main characters. Though no living writer excels him in suggesting, in some of his minor figures, the grace of holiness, he shows towards the creatures of his imagination the humility and respect that is owing to persons.

We can only sigh, *Utinam semper sit!* Miss Gardner is a fine critic; but the evidence presented in the previous chapter must surely qualify so totally favourable a judgement. What, on balance, are we then to conclude?

(i) Mauriac's most widely acknowledged achievement consists in his style. And we do not mean by that, of course, that he merely has certain purple passages to his credit, but that his writing does normally do its work so well. It may be an exaggeration to say, as M. Gaéton Bernoville does, that he is, 'along with Montherlant, the greatest living prose-writer in the French language,' [4] but the distinction of his style cannot be denied. Even in novels that as a whole are failures we find the characteristic and effective Mauriac periods occurring. Denis Revolou, for instance, has been talking to his sister Rose in the paddock; she leaves him, and the sounds of hidden life, disturbed by their conversation, now begin again:

> Sounds of summer evenings that rise in us from the depths of our unhappy childhood. He seemed in his misery to have taken root. For the insects he might have been a tree. A butterfly, of the kind known as 'aiguillons', perched on his shoulders,

4. 'Réflections sur l'état présent de la Littérature Catholique', as Pref. to R. North, p. xxxii. The best study of Mauriac's style occurs in the chapter 'l'Expression' in Mlle Nelly Cormeau's otherwise over-enthusiastic book (Cormeau, Chap. VI).

opening and shutting its wings. Ants clung to this strange trunk of woven stuff. Beetles and cock-chafers boomed in the lower leaves of the oaks which the sun had turned to flame. This was how one ought to die—growing into death by sheer virtue of immobility, feeling the blood turn to sap, slipping without effort into the vegetable world, passing from one place to another, from love and wretchedness to sleep, which is but another form of life.[5]

Or, if we want something more directly human, here are Raymond Courrèges's memories of the early-morning tram journeys on which he first got to know Maria Cross:

Nothing in his life had ever meant so much to him as those moments when they had sat facing one another in a crowd of poor work-people with coal-blackened faces and heads drooping with sleep. He could see the scene in imagination—a newspaper slipping to the floor from a hand gone numb; a bare-headed woman holding up her novelette to catch the light of the lamps, her lips moving as though in prayer. He could hear again the great raindrops splashing in the dust of the lane behind the church at Talence, could watch the passing figure of a workman crouched over the handlebar of his bicycle, a canvas sack, with a bottle protruding from it, slung over his shoulder. The trees behind the railings were stretching out their dusty leaves like hands begging for water.[6]

In the original the slightly pathetic, and perhaps also patronising, tone that attends the words 'poor work-

5. *Sea*, p. 107.
6. *Desert*, p. 147f.

people . . .', etc., is less marked. The picture is hazy, perhaps; but that is what a reminiscence should be, and within its limits it is very successful.

What Mauriac so powerfully conveys in both these passages is the sense of and the significance of a situation —the place, the people, the particularity of the moment. One last example must suffice; and this time, since to discuss style without reference to the original is absurd, I shall quote both the French and the English. Louis is describing in his diary how, after his wife Isa's death, he goes back to visit Calèse.

> Les ormes des routes et les peupliers des prairies dessinent de larges plans superposés, et entre leur lignes sombres la brume s'accumule,—la brume et la fumée des feux d'herbes, et cette haleine immense de la terre qui a bu. Car nous nous réveillons en plein automne et les grappes, où un peu de pluie demeure prise et brille, ne retrouveront plus ce dont les a frustrées l'août pluvieux. Mais pour nous, peutêtre n'est il jamais trop tard. J'ai besoin de me répéter qu'il n'est jamais trop tard.
>
> [He goes into his wife's old room.]
>
> Le désœuvrement, cette disponibilité totale dont je ne sais si je jouis ou si je souffre à la campagne, cela seul m'incita à pousser la porte entrebaîllée . . . Les domestiques avaient fait place nette, et le soleil dévorait, jusque dans les moindres encoignures, les restes impalpables d'une destinée finie. L'après-midi de septembre bourdonnait de mouches réveillées. Les tilleuls épais et ronds ressemblaient à des fruits touchés. L'azur, foncé au zenith, palissait contre les collines endormies. Un éclat de rire jaillisait d'une fille que je ne voyais pas; des chapeaux de soleil bougeaient au ras des vignes: les vendanges étaient commencées.

> Mais la vie merveilleuse s'était retirée de la cham-
> bre d'Isa; et au bas de l'armoire, une paire de gants,
> une ombrelle avaient l'air mort . . .[7]

It is extremely effective, because simple and economical.
The rhythm is sometimes a little too close to poetry ('et
cette haleine immense de la terre qui a bu') but it carries
us on without drawing attention to itself. And the situation is vividly conveyed by the natural and unforced
contrasts: the contrast between the heavy weight of the
rain upon the vine crop and the hope that man must
cling to, and the opposite contrast that follows between
the vigour and joy of harvesting and the dead room
from which 'la vie merveilleuse s'était retirée' and which
is marked now only by the flotsam of life—gloves and
an umbrella. There are not many writers left who can
so convey 'the spirit of place'.

(ii) Moreover, since Mauriac is usually thought of as the
author of long, weighted and atmospheric periods, it is

7. *Le Noeud de Vipères*, pp. 126–8, *Knot*, pp. 178–9: 'The elms along
the roads and the poplars in the meadows stand massed together. Between their dark-hued trunks the mist accumulates, and the smoke of
bonfires, and the breath of the huge earth when it has drunk deep. For
we have waked to find the autumn all about us. The grapes still glit-
tering from the recent storm will never recover what this rainy August
stole. But for us, perhaps, it is never too late. I must never stop telling
myself that it is never too late.

What led me there was idleness, that complete lack of occupation
which seizes me in the country. I never know whether I most enjoy or
dislike it. I was tempted to push the half-open door . . . The servants
had swept the place clean, and the sun, even in the farthest corners, had
eaten up the last impalpable remains of a completed destiny. The
September afternoon was buzzing with sleepy flies. The thick round
tops of the lime trees looked like bruised fruit. The blue, deep at the
zenith, showed pale behind the dozing hills. A burst of laughter came
up to me from some girl I could not see. Sun-bonnets were moving
among the vines. The grape-harvest had begun.

But the wonder of life had withdrawn from Isa's room. A pair of
gloves and an umbrella lying on the floor of the wardrobe looked
dead . . .'

worth remembering that he also can achieve the pregnant phrase. For a writer who as a whole is so humourless, the occasional flashes of epigrammatic wit are striking. On All Souls' Eve 1939 he suddenly observes in his diary: 'This night of November 1st the dead from the Great War have grown twenty years younger'.[8] Old Louis takes the hand of Marinette 'as I might have taken the hand of an unhappy child, and like a child she leaned her head upon my shoulder. I received the gift of it merely because I happened to be there. The earth receives the fallen peach'.[9] Brigitte Pian 'buried her grievances and dug them up weeks later when no one remembered what had caused them.'[10] Gilles in the middle of a conversation with Mme Agathe suddenly forgets her and thinks only of his friend Nicolas, whom she wants to marry, but whom Gilles will not release: 'He forgot this woman in the corner of the room, a bat clinging to the curtains'.[11] A friend is 'someone who helps you to throw a corpse into the water without asking any questions'.[12] (How characteristic of Mauriac, this metaphor!) And, a last example, Gabriel Gradère has been arguing with Mathilde Desbats about her plan to marry her daughter, Catharine, to Andrès. She considers it only a *marriage de convenance,* but Gabriel insists on what it involves: 'Nothing will be changed', she says; but Gabriel points out that they'll be sleeping in the same room—indeed, in the same bed. 'All right, then—in the same bed', she exclaims, pretending to laugh it off. But 'Gabriel detected a note of suffering in

8. *Journal*, p. 420.
9. *Knot*, p. 93. (The original is even more concise: 'je la reçevais parce que j'étais là; l'argile reçoit une pêche qui se détache,' p. 108.)
10. *Pharisees*, p. 67.
11. *Galigaï*, p. 57.
12. Ibid., p. 68.

her voice. It was as though he were holding a pigeon in his hands and pressing it rather too tightly'.[13]

(iii) This last is also a good instance of the way in which Mauriac handles the relationships *between* his characters. Indeed, these relationships are usually more delicately presented than the characters seen full-face—which reveals the direct relationship between them and the author. Put in another way, Mauriac's characters are better commentators on each other than he is on them. There is, for instance, a beautiful tact in the relationship between old Dr. Courrèges and his beloved Maria Cross, especially in the well-known scene where he gives her a medical examination.[14] Earlier in the same novel there is a dramatic scene when Mme Courrèges declares that the death of Maria Cross's illegitimate boy is God's judgement, and the doctor stamps out of the room.[15] Some of the overheard conversations of the rapacious and plotting sons and daughters-in-law, recorded by the old man Louis in *The Knot of Vipers* are effective;[16] and so too is the embarrassed conversation between him and his natural son Robert, the ne'er-do-well.[17] The growing understanding between the wild, suspicious, ungovernable Jean Mirbel and the Abbé Calou[18] could hardly be bettered. The scene, too, when Brigitte travels to Octave's death-bed—the first time that cracks begin to show in her marmoreal self-conceit—the train journey, with Brigitte's step-children silent, and she imploring, and shrinking in size as they

13. *Angels*, p. 207.
14. *Desert*, p. 129f.
15. Ibid., p. 17.
16. *Knot*, e.g., pp. 122–5.
17. Ibid., pp. 142–4.
18. *Pharisees*, e.g., pp. 107–9.

look at her: this is superb.[19] And finally there is the close of the same novel, too hurried and sketchy perhaps, as we have admitted above,[20] but wonderfully restrained, and without any forced attempt to make out Brigitte as a saint.

Even in the novel which M. Sartre has criticized so severely, *The End of the Night,* we must acknowledge the gentleness with which Thérèse treats her daughter and shakes off the would-be lover, George—the gentleness with which, in fact, she expiates her crime. And in one of Mauriac's most successful novels, *The Knot of Vipers,* it is remarkable how the characters, especially the wife, Isa, gradually emerge in their true light through and in spite of the distorting narration by Louis, the protagonist. Even the oppressive *Genetrix* succeeds brilliantly in suggesting first the tyranny of the mother over the son, and then the 'counter-attack' by the dead wife from beyond the grave. The psychological understanding in these cases, and many others, is acquired by letting the characters *be,* without *arrières-pensées* about their eternal destiny. The paradox is that it is precisely then that their salvation or damnation becomes most significant and most believable. Mauriac has the misfortune (in one sense) to be a believing writer in an unbelieving age. A novelist like Manzoni can move freely, largely, within his total Catholic world. Mauriac has the advantage which the Faith gives him of realism, honesty and spiritual penetration. But he cannot all the time exclude from his attention the heretic, the sceptic or the atheist who exist in the same world; they peep over the window-sill as he writes, and whenever he lets their presence distract him, his writing falters. When, as in the above instances, he gives his

19. Ibid., p. 171.
20. Vide sup., p. 32.

characters freedom to be the persons they are, they then become truly damnable or redeemable—and this is the real, the only real, task of the Catholic novelist in this or any age.

(iv) All this must be set on the credit side of what we have presented so far as a heavily debit account. And, to show that it is not a question of singling out chance passages and accidental successes for commendation, but of a genuine, if seriously qualified, achievement, let us end with some reference to the (in my view) most totally successful of the novels: *Le Mystère Frontenac*.[21] What probably gives it its consistency is that the thread running through it—family loyalty and the grip of 'place'—is nearest to Mauriac's own heart:

> 'They leave nothing to chance' [cries Yves Fron-tenac], 'they organize everybody's happiness; they don't understand that we want to be happy in a different way.'
>
> 'It isn't a question, for them, of happiness' [re-plies Jean-Louis, his brother], 'but of acting for the common good and in the interest of the family. No, it isn't a question of happiness. Have you noticed? It's a word that never appears on their lips—happiness.'[22]

Sheltered and linked together by the family—Blanche, the mother, and the gruff, affectionate Uncle Xavier,—the children prolong their infancy as long as possible.

21. As critics have been divided about the merits of Mauriac himself, so too they have been divided about the relative merits of the novels. Emile Rideau considers *Knot* the *chef d'oeuvre* of Catholic novels (Rideau, p. 67). Nelly Cormeau, surprisingly, singles out the short story, *Coups de Couteau*, as the summit of his art (Cormeau, p. 119). I think it sufficient to say that the novels which will endure are *Fron-tenac, Knot, Pharisees, Angels, Thérèse, Night*, and perhaps *Destins*.
22. *Frontenac*, p. 122.

But Yves is set apart, the boy poet, the quiet one who ponders the mystery of suffering as he watches an ant struggling in the sand.[23] He resists the divine vocation that comes to him, dismissing it as his own voice. For a time he runs wild in Paris, but the call comes again when he is at the end of his tether. In the thick of the traffic and bustling humanity of Paris he suddenly sees his old home, the Landes:

> Around him human beings and cars twisted, mingled, separated at the cross-roads, and he felt himself as solitary as long ago, in the middle of the narrow space where, surrounded with ferns and bushes, he used to lie hid, a little boy run wild. The uniform din of the road was like the soft noises of nature, and the passers-by were more strangers to him than the pines of Bourideys whose tops once watched over this little Frontenac nestling at their feet in the thickest part of the undergrowth. To-day these men and women buzzed like the flies in the Landes, hesitated like dragon-flies, and one of them sometimes landed down beside Yves, against his sleeve, without even seeing him, and then flew off. But how muffled and distant the voice had become which pursued the Frontenac child, at the bottom of his lair, and which he sensed again at this moment.[24]

This use of the 'flash-back' is a familiar technique, but it is just right in its place. The death of old Uncle Xavier, who pathetically had wanted till the last to conceal from the children the fact (which they knew all along) that he had a mistress, is an emotional turning-point both in the novel and in Yves's experience;

23. Ibid., p. 140ff.
24. Ibid., pp. 272-4.

and the elderly mistress herself, Joséfa, common and unattractive, small-minded but intensely loyal, is presented (for once in Mauriac's novels) with real compassion. In the end Yves is reconciled to family and place through a severe illness, during which his elder brother visits him; the superbly quiet, tactful visit of the dull, prosy, affectionate Jean-Louis is beautifully handled.

It will be seen that the range of this novel is limited. There are none of the violent passions, the tremendous collapses and sudden deliverances, that some of Mauriac's other novels attempt—and so rarely achieve. But perhaps for that very reason it is on the whole consistently effective. The bitterness has been absorbed into the moss, the marsh, the resin of the Landes; and here at last in one of his novels we find what Mauriac says that the poets give him.

> All of them, whether they believed in eternal life, or like Anna de Noailles denied it, bear witness to the grandeur of the human soul, its divine vocation. The poets have always protected me against doubt. Even though they may be covered in mud, like Rimbaud and Verlaine, they awaken in us the sentiment of a paradisal purity, of a lost purity which we must recover in self-abasement and in tears.[25]

25. *Journal,* p. 63f.

SELECT BIBLIOGRAPHY

The following are listed in order of publication; titles of English translations (where available) are followed, in square brackets, by the abbreviated titles used in the footnotes.

NOVELS

L'Enfant Chargé de Chaînes, 1913 [*L'Enfant*].
La Robe Prétexte, 1914 [*Robe*].
La Chair et le Sang, 1920 [*Chair*].
Préséances, 1921.
Le Baiser au Lépreux (*A Kiss for the Leper*), 1922 [*Leper*].
Genitrix (*Genetrix*), 1923 [*Genetrix*].
Le Fleuve de Feu, 1923 [*Fleuve*].
Le mal (*The Enemy*), 1924 [*Enemy*].
Le Désert de l'Amour (*The Desert of Love*), 1925 [*Desert*].
Coups de Couteau, 1926 [*Coups*].
Un Homme de Lettres, 1926 [*Lettres*].
Thérèse Desqueyroux (*Thérèse*), 1927 [*Therese*].
Le Démon de Connaissance, 1928 [*Démon*].
Destins, 1928.
Ce Qui était Perdu (*That Which Was Lost*), 1930 [*Lost*].
Le Noeud de Vipères (*The Knot of Vipers*), 1932 [*Knot*].
Le Mystère Frontenac (*The Frontenac Mystery*), 1933 [*Frontenac*].
La Fin de la Nuit (*The End of the Night*), 1935 [*Night*].
Les Anges Noirs (*The Dark Angels*), 1936 [*Angels*].
Plongées (*Studies*), 1938.
Les Chemins de la Mer (*The Unknown Sea*), 1939 [*Sea*].
La Pharisienne (*Woman of the Pharisees*), 1941 [*Pharisees*].
Le Sagouin (*The Little Misery*), 1951 [*Misery*].
Galigaï (*The Loved and the Unloved*), 1952 [*Galigaï*].

PLAYS

Asmodée (*Asmodée, or The Intruder*), 1938 [*Asmodée*].
Les Mal-Aimés, 1945 [*Aimés*].
Le Passage du Malin, 1948 [*Malin*].

GENERAL

Commencements d'une Vie, 1932 [*Commencements*].
Dieu et Mammon (*God and Mammon*), 1929 [*Mammon*].
Mes Grands Hommes (*Great Men*), 1950 [*Great Men*].
La Pierre d'Achoppement, 1951 [*Pierre*].

STUDIES

Charles du Bos: *François Mauriac et le problème du romancier catholique,* 1933 [du Bos].
Georges Hourdin: *Mauriac, Romancier Chrétien,* 1945 [Hourdin].
Joseph Majault: *Mauriac et l'art du roman,* 1946 [Majault].
Emile Rideau: *François Mauriac,* 1947 [Rideau].
Nelly Cormeau: *L'Art de François Mauriac,* 1951 [Cormeau].
Robert J. North: *Le Catholicisme dans l'oeuvre de François Mauriac,* 1950 [North].